'People with disabilities have, too often, been denied sexual happiness and expression. Although attitudes are slowly changing, there is a long way to go. Tuppy's helpful anecdotes and lack of jargon make for an inspiring read which will give practitioners the confidence to discuss sex with their disabled clients.'

— *Helen Dunman, PSHE SEN Teacher and SHADA Member*

'Tuppy deserves national recognition for decades of challenging our collective neglect of the emotional, social and sexual needs of people with impairments. In the face of media, fashion and beauty industry promotion of perfect bodies, which cruelly makes disabled people "outsiders", Tuppy has tirelessly campaigned and developed resources for the hundreds of thousands of UK people whose needs for friendship, affection and sex we marginalize and ignore.'

— *Andy Beckingham, FFPH, Consultant in Public Health*

'Our sex lives have been censored, ignored and unsupported, and Tuppy suggests many simple, respectful and clever ways in which this can be turned around. I hope her insightful book can contribute to improve the sex lives of many previously isolated or sexually frustrated disabled people.'

— *Mat Fraser*

'This book is relevant to a broad range of professionals coming into contact with a broad range of disabled people. Whether physically, visually or hearing impaired, or with learning difficulties, deafblind or those with ME, social anxiety or Asperger's syndrome, this remarkable book will support all.'

— *Maria Oshodi, VI Artistic Director and CEO of Extant*

D0171206

of related interest

**Sexuality and Relationships in the Lives of People
with Intellectual Disabilities**
Standing in My Shoes
Edited by Rohhss Chapman, Sue Ledger and Louise Townson with Daniel Docherty
ISBN 978 1 84905 250 4
eISBN 978 0 85700 530 4

The Autism Spectrum, Sexuality and the Law
What every parent and professional needs to know
Tony Attwood, Isabelle Hénault and Nick Dubin
ISBN 978 1 84905 919 0
eISBN 978 0 85700 679 0

Active Support
Enabling and Empowering People with Intellectual Disabilities
Jim Mansell and Julie Beadle-Brown
ISBN 978 1 84905 111 8
eISBN 978 0 85700 300 3

Sexuality and Severe Autism
A Practical Guide for Parents, Caregivers and Health Educators
Kate E. Reynolds
ISBN 978 1 84905 327 3
eISBN 978 0 85700 666 0

Learning Difficulties and Sexual Vulnerability
A Social Approach
Andrea Hollomotz
ISBN 978 1 84905 167 5
eISBN 978 0 85700 381 2

**Preventing the Emotional Abuse and Neglect of
People with Intellectual Disability**
Stopping Insult and Injury
Sally Robinson
ISBN 978 1 84905 230 6
eISBN 978 0 85700 472 7

Understanding Cerebral Palsy
A Guide for Parents and Professionals
Marion Stanton
Foreword by Joe Whittaker
ISBN 978 1 84905 060 9
eISBN 978 0 85700 256 3
JKP Essentials Series

SUPPORTING DISABLED PEOPLE WITH THEIR SEXUAL LIVES

A CLEAR GUIDE FOR HEALTH AND SOCIAL CARE PROFESSIONALS

Tuppy Owens with Claire de Than

Jessica Kingsley *Publishers*
London and Philadelphia

The four 'Good Communication' images on pages 126–8 are reproduced with kind permission of Widgit Symbols. The deafblind manual alphabet illustration on page 130 is reproduced with kind permission of Action on Hearing Loss (previously the RNID).

First published in 2015
by Jessica Kingsley Publishers
73 Collier Street
London N1 9BE, UK
and
400 Market Street, Suite 400
Philadelphia, PA 19106, USA

www.jkp.com

Library of Congress Cataloging in Publication Data
Owens, Tuppy, 1944-
 Supporting disabled people with their sexual lives : a clear guide
for health and social care professionals / Tuppy Owens.
   pages cm
 Includes bibliographical references and index.
 ISBN 978-1-84905-396-9 (alk. paper)
 1. People with disabilities--Sexual behavior. 2. Sex instruction for people
with disabilities. 3. People with disabilites--Services for. I. Title.
 HQ30.5.O94 2015
 362.4--dc23
                                                                    2014021854

British Library Cataloguing in Publication Data
A CIP catalogue record for this book is available from the British Library

ISBN 978 1 84905 396 9
eISBN 978 0 85700 762 9

Printed and bound in Great Britain

MIX
Paper from
responsible sources
FSC® C013056

CONTENTS

ACKNOWLEDGEMENTS

I would like to thank everyone for the support they have given me writing this book. In particular, my good friends Viv and Bruce Abrahams and colleagues Claire de Than, Victoria McKenzie, Helen Dunman, Sally Lee, Amy Parkin, Randy Ralston, Jamie Willmott, Master Dominic, Sue Newsome, Val Ruscoe, Zoe and Deborah, eirwen, Sarah Battan and Tess de Gange. Thanks too for the immaculate scrutiny of Ian Hudson, and all the stories which Outsiders members shared to make this book possible. Thanks to Jessica Kingsley Publishers for asking me to produce this book, and to Caroline Walton, Rachel Menzies and all the staff at Jessica Kingsley Publishers for looking after me so well. Thanks also go to David Steinberg for his lovely photograph which has been used for our front cover, featuring the sexual revolutionaries Frank Moore and Linda. Frank was a powerful poet and painter, respected shaman and teacher, controversial performance artist, rock'n'roll singer, publisher, author, director and award-winning video maker. He was a wheelchair user whose speech was impaired, with cerebral palsy. Lastly, thanks to my partner, Antony, and his pack, who felt the full impact of me giving birth to this book.

DISCLAIMER

PREFACE

Human sexuality has evolved to provide us with the unique capacity to enjoy pleasure on many levels – from long-term intimate relationships and erotic play with the person we love, to all kinds of other fun including self-pleasuring. Females even evolved to have larger breasts and males larger penises.[1] It would be great to think that we could all be making the most of our delightful opportunities.

That disabled people are so often left out is both sad and unnecessary. I have always believed that if a person cannot see, or cannot hear, or cannot walk – in fact, whatever their impairment – they can still enjoy sexual pleasure. All professionals agree that it is essential that disabled people be encouraged to enjoy whatever they can in life, and it is now becoming widely recognized that this includes their sexuality.

It is particularly inhumane to deny disabled people sexual pleasures in their lives, when other pleasures have been taken away from them, and I am shocked every time I hear such complaints from disabled people.

When I started to work with the disabled members of Outsiders,[2] they were delighted with my openness, encouraging them to find what they craved. This, sadly, gave me a 'bad reputation' which has taken decades to shake off. It is thus a gift from heaven that Jessica Kingsley Publishers have commissioned me to write this book in my own style of sexual candidness. I am also flattered that Claire de Than has agreed to write the chapter on law. I couldn't wish for a more informed and enthusiastic expert to see me straight on matters legal, which are so essential but beyond my capabilities.

First of all, you might like to know where I am coming from. I have never worked as a health or social care professional, don't have a disabled child, and don't pretend to be an expert on either. I myself am not physically disabled: the stroke I had in 2011 was very mild, and I have pretty much fully recovered. I have worked as a volunteer independently, a free spirit, running projects with and for disabled people to enable them to gain confidence, learn and enjoy.

For example, for a long time Outsiders has put on Tactile Fashion Shows so that disabled models can dress up, and everyone, including visually impaired people, can touch the garments. Much of what I say in this book comes from 35 years of experience, rather than being substantiated by academic research.

To go back to the beginning. After disappearing off to the Serengeti, aged 17, to join my boyfriend, I acquired a degree in Zoology from Exeter, and worked as a zoologist in Trinidad and elsewhere. In the late 1960s I made a career jump, and began writing and publishing my own style of books about sex, working from my subterranean Mayfair labyrinth. My success gave me spare time and, in 1978, I started to support two disabled people I'd met, helping them to find new relationships and the sexual outlets they wanted.

One of these was Nigel, who had just lost his sight, his girlfriend, and most of his friends. Losing my sight was my biggest fear, so I vowed to stick by him. The other, David, was a wheelchair user whose body shook and sweated constantly, with the result that he felt sexually undesirable. I set about introducing them to the kind of women they were looking for. It was really good fun: so much so that the three of us, together with psychologist Dr Patricia Gillan, decided to start a social club for disabled people. Outsiders was born in 1979, and still thrives. Membership swelled from the start, thanks to a small article by Katherine Whitehorn in the *Observer*, followed by a half page by Ann Hills in the *Guardian*. We held a party in London at the progressive residence for disabled people, 48 Boundary Road, and 150 people came from all over the country. Members paid fees which, combined with their generous donations, covered expenses, and we were happy to be independent and focus on our members' needs, rather than worrying what funders might think. I decided to take a two-year course in sex therapy, to ensure that I was qualified to answer our members' personal questions.

I took on my new role like a duck to water and, looking back, I remember hanging out with the school kids who were shunned because of their appearance, and acting as a 'go-between' for friends seeking partners in my early teens. I'd also experienced a lonely period with panic attacks, after a relationship break-up.

Outsiders has stayed much the same throughout our long history, with me at the helm, a membership secretary (usually disabled) plus a range of disabled volunteers who are mostly people who have succeeded in the club. They love their roles and I give them total freedom, for example, to work when they feel like it. We have enjoyed big anniversary celebrations in The Landmark, Marylebone, where one of our early speakers remarked on how all our events are held in splendid venues. I have attempted to repeat this in our online Clubhouse, with a picture on its banner of a glorious mansion. The transition to having a virtual club instead of an office where we could discuss application forms and phone calls has been both challenging and exciting. Outsiders no longer throws all-night parties but still holds monthly lunches and a big annual jamboree. The members who become proactive in Outsiders feel the mutual trust of belonging to a big family of people who support each other in crises. Many have helped me in my research for this book and give their blessing to me, describing themselves and their struggles for fulfillment, in these pages.

Our members have a huge range of physical and social impairments; many have visual impairment, cerebral palsy, spina bifida, spinal injury, spinal atrophy, MS, brittle bones (OI), arthritis, disfigurement, ME, acute shyness, phobias or Asperger's syndrome. We have had a management committee comprising a chair who could not speak, and members who could not hear, see or move, which still achieved many things.

My experience comes not only from Outsiders and our projects, but also from past research in my writing career, from being chair of the Sexual Freedom Coalition, and from meeting other pioneers selected in the Erotic Awards, one of Outsiders' fundraising projects.

People ask me how things have changed over the years and, I have to say, things have got worse. Back in the 1970s and 1980s people were more free-thinking and experimental, so disabled people were better accepted sexually. Nowadays people worry more what others will think, so they pick good-looking, fit partners with jobs. When some highly vocal feminists with sex-negative agendas came along, this seemed like the end of sexual freedom. You will see in this book that some of the best resources were written many years ago.

There was a parallel organization which started at the same time as Outsiders and was funded by the Department of Health. SPOD (Sexual Problems of the Disabled) was set up by Duncan Guthrie and Dr Wendy Greengross. They largely focused on supporting health professionals. When they closed down in 2003, I called the telephone company and asked for their helpline to be diverted to my phone, and named it 'The Sex and Disability Helpline'. I still have it. The number is listed on the Outsiders website and in many professional listings. I receive as many calls from disabled people as I do from professionals.

I soon realized that professionals now felt very much on their own with their work to support their disabled clients in sexual matters. Thus, I set up the Sexual Health and Disability Alliance (SHADA)[3] for health and social care professionals. SHADA meets twice a year in London, and we aim to tackle all the unresolved problems around sex and disability, with law specialist Claire de Than and other pioneers working in the field.

I then created the Sexual Respect Tool Kit,[4] which is an online resource for GPs and other health and social care professionals to use to feel more confident in initiating discussions with patients and clients around sex. It includes a training film, a hand-out, wall posters and a huge range of resources.

Finally, I have created a sexual advocacy service, Ask a Sexual Advocate Professional (ASAP),[5] with a team of advocates who support both disabled people and professionals in negotiations and problem-solving around sexuality.

Awards For All provide some funding for our projects, and we raise the rest of what we need ourselves, putting on erotic events using volunteers. Many of our volunteers give their time because they relate to what we are doing: our lorry driver spent many years of his life without a girlfriend because of his reluctance to ask a girl out while he had psoriasis.

I have been called a 'Saviour of Horny Disabled People' by an Outsiders member, and one of my volunteers refers to me as 'a National Treasure', and that feels nice. However, it's been a long struggle, and frustrating that the world just didn't want to know us and the press made us sound sleazy.

On 15 March 2012, I received a telephone call on the Sex and Disability Helpline about a young lady with cerebral palsy who was having sex with her boyfriend, but it was not working out. Apparently, she could not 'get it in' because of spasms, not helped by the anxiety brought about by continual failure felt by both her and her boyfriend. In her residential college for young disabled people, she'd been allowed to share a double bed with her boyfriend, but nobody had asked whether things were going well or not, so they were never supported to overcome their serious sexual problem.

It confirmed what I'd already found: that, however well-meaning, professionals don't go far enough in their support, and often miss out one important element: *discussion*. If the teachers are not allowed to engage in such discussions, the school or college needs to employ an expert who can.

Long before this call, I learned of a policy used in some residential homes where staff are allowed to place a physically disabled couple, who cannot move themselves, into position for sexual intercourse, but are *not* allowed to put the penis inside the vagina. Just imagine the two of them lying there, so close and yet so far, in perpetual frustration! Ludicrous! There was no suggestion of bringing help in.

My experience of people with mental health problems, brain injury and learning difficulties is limited to the helpline and SHADA, and although this book sometimes discusses such people, the main focus is on physically and socially impaired people. Much has been written on sex and learning difficulties, and not enough work has been done in the areas of brain injury and mental health. Although this book encourages you to focus on pleasure rather than safeguarding, Chapter 4 on the law does cover this aspect of the subject of sex.

Most people think fuzzily about sex. This book and its resources set out to help you, in a clear and straightforward manner, to support disabled people in their sexual lives. No more excuses. No more 'not going far enough'.

The law can always change, and we keep the law section up to date on the Sexual Respect Tool Kit website, so that you can double-check whenever you need to.

Supporting disabled people to find partners and enjoy sex brings me endless joy and satisfaction, The smiles on people's faces when they at last experience intimate human contact, feel sexually valued and satisfied, and perhaps find love are wider smiles, more gleeful and heart-felt, than any other kind of smile. It radiates out to the rest of us, and I feel that radiance in my life all the time. You can, I hope, enjoy that radiance too. Please don't look upon this work as a chore or something to be feared. It's going to be fun, challenging and exciting.

Here is a quote from a young man with progressive spinal atrophy, which came in response to me asking him what he thought of one of my ideas to solve frustration amongst disabled people who cannot masturbate themselves (which he cannot):

That's very interesting about your idea of finding someone local who is willing to assist disabled people with masturbation. It's been a few months since I was last able to have a release, and much longer since I had one completely free of any sense of guilt. The thought of having to pay a lot of money to rectify this is an emotionally difficult thing as well as a financial concern. From my own personal experience, I can only say that when done by someone with a generous heart who can make it feel normal and natural and even fun, the relief of ejaculation is very profound and physiologically changes me, 'brings me into balance', if you like. Not in quite the same way as sex would, but something like that. I am sure there must be people out there who could take a lot of personal satisfaction in helping disabled people to achieve this balance, and function better in society. When you think about it, it's a pretty straightforward thing to do with such a powerful outcome; it's almost rude not to! The challenge is persuading society that masturbation is not something that has to be done alone in secret or as part of a relationship. I don't know anything about that, but perhaps you do. Tuppy, I wish you luck with your work.

Humans took a great leap forward when we evolved to have a voice. Once able to speak, we became capable of discussing how to create things, and civilization commenced.[1]

I hope likewise, that this book will inspire you to use your voice to discuss sex with your disabled patients and clients, so they too can take a great leap forward in their sexual lives.

Resources

1. Diamond, J. (1991) *The Rise and Fall of the Third Chimpanzee.* London, UK: Random House.
2. Outsiders: www.Outsiders.org.uk.
3. The Sexual Health and Disability Alliance (SHADA): www.SHADA.org.uk.
4. The Sexual Respect Tool Kit: www.SexualRespect.com.
5. Ask a Sexual Advocate Professional (ASAP): www.AdvocacyProfessional.com.

CHAPTER 1

DISABLED PEOPLE'S SEXUAL NEEDS

Being part of a very safe and secure peer support group like Outsiders, as I have been since 1979, is really great for sharing personal problems and aspirations. Answering the Sex and Disability Helpline and being the convenor of the Sexual Health and Disability Alliance have also both given me access to, and awareness of, many people with various impairments and their moving stories and complaints, some repeated here.

From all these sources I have created a list of needs, which acts as a gentle introduction to the rest of my book. My list may inspire you to ask your clients questions, perhaps using something from my list as a prompt if they find it difficult to express what it is that they want.

My list is divided into four sections:

1. Feel sexually free.

2. Become educated about sex and their own sexuality.

3. Enjoy sexual activities.

4. Support in a crisis.

Remember, working with your clients on these can be a joy to experience, not a problem.

1. Feel sexually free

Freedom to express their sexuality

Sexuality is the second most important human drive, after survival, and an essential part of who we are. It cannot be suppressed. Accept your clients' sexuality as part of them. Accept that each client is different from the others, and that they are all on their own sexual journey. If this journey is stopped because of shame, inhibition, regulations, or by your care (or lack of it), this may lead to unacceptable behaviour or even illness (both mental and physical), so that the person cannot function properly.

Sexuality can be expressed through outwardly showing the sexual identity which the person feels inside. So you can encourage your client to find ways to express this, through clothing, hair styles, customizing their wheelchair, or expressing their passions through art or conversations – whichever way they want. They may feel no need, and prefer to keep things private. What's essential, though, if you are going to be supporting them in their sexuality, is that they feel free to express themselves to you. They may also want to communicate their feelings to others who matter in their lives, and certainly this will apply to lovers.

Sufficient sexual self-confidence to operate as a sexual being

Encourage disabled people to think enough of themselves to make that special effort to overcome their personal physical restrictions, so they can enjoy sexual pleasure. You can do this by treating their personal lives with respect, and knowing where to suggest they go to gain this confidence. There is more on this at the end of Chapter 7.

Feeling good in their own body

Having doctors, nurses and care staff looking at, washing, and performing procedures on their body can make a disabled person feel as if their body does not belong to them. People who have lived with their disability since birth or acquired it at an early age complain to me that they had only ever been poked, never touched nicely (except by their parents). People with cerebral palsy in particular complain that their bodies have only been treated in a functional way, with no attention paid to their feelings or desires.

Disabled people may experience their bodies differently from people without disabilities, and may have problems such as finding physical contact difficult.[1] They may need support in reclaiming their bodies. This can come in different ways, from lovers, massage therapists, sex workers, from having a tattoo, or from the wide range of artists and therapists who I call body image therapists, discussed in Chapter 7.

Ask your disabled clients what they think about their bodies, and how they feel about them; and perhaps make suggestions about moving towards accepting and liking, even loving, their bodies, because the body can give a human being so much pleasure. Mirrors can be helpful.

I have even experienced both disabled men and women telling me that they don't like their own genitals. Some may never have seen them or had the pleasure of touching them. There are workshops designed to help women learn to accept their genitals (see Chapter 7). A Tantric sex worker or escort could also help turn this around (see Chapter 8).

Being accepted as sexual

You can support people to feel accepted as sexual beings by having positive, constructive discussion about their sex lives. For example, don't be afraid to discuss masturbation, to see if they are enjoying themselves without guilt or worrying they may be discovered, or experiencing physical or other difficulties. Encourage them to go to social events where they might meet the kind of people who they would find attractive, and to pal up with buddies who might support and accompany them. Support them if they want to start dating – more about this in the next chapter. If the right opportunity for them can't be found, you could ask around, and put the word out and encourage one to be created.

Thinking clearly to move forward

Once you and your client have identified what they want, you could borrow from the Outsiders 'Beyond Impairment' project, where we list the positive things individuals can use to move forward to achieve their goals. Then we list the things which might make it difficult, and ways to overcome these hurdles. It doesn't always work, though, because some people believe that everything should happen naturally, and that is their choice.

Privacy

Disabled people who depend on personal care tell me they never feel totally uninhibited because of lack of privacy. This must be awful.

Ask them to list the things that bother them, and work together to overcome, or at least minimize, the impact. For example, if their door cannot be locked, it may need a 'Do Not Disturb' sign, or a system of knocking which offers them time to re-adjust their activity. People with hearing impairments can be given a flashing light. Those with speech impairments could have some kind of yes/no button installed, which they can trigger. Perhaps they don't feel able to enjoy sexual pleasure with everybody around them knowing about it, because everything about them is discussed by the team. The system they use in Denmark, and some establishments in the UK, is that they can choose a member of staff, confidante or sexual advocate to confide in, with the understanding that details will not be passed on to other members of staff, unless the information is dangerous.

Catching up

Many disabled people who have been deprived of sexual expression may simply want to have the chance to catch up, gain confidence, start having fun and dating, and living life to the full. You only need to think of the sexual journey of your own life and compare it with that of some of your clients to see how meagre their opportunities and chances to learn can be, especially in their teens. Some may find lovers to experiment with, while others struggle. A visit to a professional escort can offer non-judgemental experimentation, forgiveness of mistakes, and support to help them move forward.

Pleasing their parents

I have been told by disabled people that, even when they are well into middle age, they do not feel able join Outsiders, visit a sex worker, or be open about their sexual preferences, because their parents would be upset, ashamed or worried. They feel they owe this to their parents who have done so much for them. One disabled woman told me she was waiting till her father died before she could consider finding a partner.

If a client tells you this kind of thing, you could question whether they really believe their parents never had sex. Suggest that the parents may want the best for their son or daughter, and might actually welcome the big smile which would appear on their son or daughter's face if they enjoyed sexual pleasure and perhaps a loving relationship.

Being accepted as a sexual partner

Acceptance can come with confidence, which you can help them gain. It may be encouraging to know, for example, that ultimately it is our imperfections which make us beautiful, unique and loved.

There may be profound reasons why the disabled individual may crave a sexual partner. Having been cared for in life, they may wish for the opportunity to actually care for another, if not physically, then mentally. They may be facing an early death and determined to make the most of life, and so enjoying a relationship and sex now is doubly important to them.

It is good to tell a disabled client that it is not until they love themselves, including their impairments, that they can expect to be loved by someone else. When they accept their impairments, they can also accept other people's, and find commonality in realizing that it is the stigma that is much more disabling than the impairments.

2. Become educated about sex and their own sexuality

Positive communication and education on sex from the start

Age-appropriate sex education at home and sex and disability education in schools are often both sadly lacking, and this is discussed in Chapters 3 and 5. This situation may be leaving the disabled individual needing your support now. They may not think to ask you, as they may be assuming that, having had their sex-education needs ignored in the past, that's the way it's always going to be.

If disabled people are to have their sexual needs taken seriously, you need to know what they are, so ask, in a warm and reassuring way. Shyness, mistrust of confidentiality, feeling their sex life is private, or just not really knowing, can be overcome with a little reassurance and prompting. Tell them what others in their situation have said, but never push. They may not be ready to talk, or may be managing quite well without you.

If they are happy to tell you their needs, and you have listened respectfully, you could ask if they would like your support to meet those needs. With their agreement, you could start off by discussing with them all their assets, skills and qualities which might make it easy for each need to be met. Write the list out. This makes a positive start, and then you can discuss how doors could open for them – many of which are contained in this book. Confirm that they can ask whenever they need help.

Disabled females may need more education to understand their bodies, because their genitals are so hidden away, perhaps completely unknown to them. Their impairment may be affecting what and how they feel sensations. Telling a disabled woman simple facts such as how her orgasm need not be a goal in sex, and that she may be able to enjoy sexual pleasure in many different ways, in different places in her body, may inspire her to open her mind. Women have complained to me that because they are disabled, their husband is almost afraid to touch them. They should be supported to gain confidence and skills, speak out about what they want, and show their partner, with enthusiasm. Outsiders sometimes runs a 'V Group' for disabled women to discuss their sex lives (so named because some disabled women have difficulty parting their legs) and this has proved that peer support can really work.

Some disabled people have very little contact with health professionals, so it is really important that the one opportunity to find out if they are struggling with their socio-sexual lives must be grabbed. It should not be omitted in consultations, hospital check-ups or assessments. Open questions on how they are getting on can be followed up with more specific ones about loneliness, sexual frustration, or intimate or personal problems which are often experienced by people with their condition.

So that clients know that sex is something they can discuss, we produced a range of posters for our Sexual Respect Tool Kit[2] which you can print. They have the message that 'Sex is Talked about Here' and can be the start of this positive message in your workplace.

Many disabled adults have experienced an abusive or sex-negative upbringing, lack of age-appropriate, specialist sex education, or bad sexual experiences. Ask about this, and offer support. If necessary, find out where to access further expertise.

Using sexual services for educational purposes

If your client failed to enjoy normal teenage sexual experimentation and has never experienced sexual contact or had a chance to try things out, escorts can provide such an opportunity. This physical education can be invaluable, helping them discover sexual pleasure in various parts of their body, and learn how to enjoy sex without being able to feel sensations like others do, without an erection, or without orgasm.

Escorts can help disabled people expand their horizons so that what may be a narrow understanding of sex can open out. Instead of teenage experimentation, they can explore the options which appeal to them, within the safety of the escort's care, and discover their sexual selves. They can realize their own sexual identity, their sexual preferences and what kinds of sex they enjoy. Only then are they really ready to move forward to form lasting relationships.

3. Enjoy sexual activities

Being hugged (if and when appropriate)

Many single disabled people really like the idea of a hug, because physical contact can be so rare for them. Others, who are susceptible to infection, may have to decline being hugged 'hello', and they need to learn to explain this to people nicely. Encouraging playful hugging might be appreciated in your workplace amongst disabled clients, although heterosexual men may only want to hug women.

Sharing their bed

This might be quite complicated because their current bed may be specially designed to suit them, not big enough for two, or unsuitable for the partner. Few adults these days sleep in single beds, so why should disabled adults?

If sleeping together seems impossible because of their particular needs, one alternative is to place a large mattress on the floor, provide whatever might be necessary for sex beside it, and give the two disabled people time together, with the appropriate adaptations to their continence equipment, in their special sex nest.

Using pornography

Many people use porn to masturbate, and disabled people may also choose to do so. It is essential to make it clear that porn is mostly about fantasy, not reality, and must not be used as sex education. More about pornography and disabled people can be found in Chapter 8 on sexual services.

Using sex toys

Details about using sex toys are given in Chapter 2. I would like to mention here that, because of media promotion and marketing, many people assume a sex toy is needed to masturbate. In fact vibrations can numb the penis or clitoris, and masturbation can be a more intuitive, beautiful sensual experience, and more so, without the buzz of a vibrator – using fingers, perhaps with lubricant. A man can finger the highly sensitive parts of his foreskin (if he has one) and its journey over the shaft of his penis, the frenulum, his testicles, perineum, anal rim, prostate gland and nipples. A woman can finger her clitoris, vulva, G-spot, vagina, anus and nipples. Both can explore, touch and stimulate other erogenous zones. This should be made clear to disabled clients, to save them money. They may want to discuss what to do if these places cannot be reached or adequately stimulated, and this is also dealt with in Chapter 2.

Partnered sex

There is a whole section on this in Chapter 2, and more in Chapter 9 on same-sex partnered sex. Do give your clients encouragement to find partners. You can use this quote from a young lady who joined Outsiders as a virgin aged 40 and soon made up for lost time: 'Disabled people make the best lovers because we know how to ask for things nicely, and are ingenious in finding ways around obstacles in life.'

Using sexual services for reasons other than education

The whole of Chapter 8 is devoted to the topic of sexual services, but here I would like to stress that seeing a professional escort who specializes in disabled people has been an emotional tonic and a fulfilling journey for many disabled people I have known. It can change their lives around.

Finding financial support to pay for sex products and services

Your clients may need money to pay for sex toys, equipment, talking erotica, and sexual services. Even though an official in the personal budgets department at the Department of Health told me in 2012 that sex and relationships should be considered in working out care packages, I see no sign of it. Indeed, disabled people tell me they would never dare ask for expenses for this type of thing, for fear of being accused of unnecessary extravagance! Women say they won't even wear make-up when they expect visits, for fear of having their budgets reduced as a result of appearing to be spending their money on luxuries! Hopefully progress can be made on this front, and disabled people need your support to help make the necessary changes.

Specialist sex toys, sexual services, sexual support rails and hoists, if needed, should be included in budgets as necessary items of expenditure. Apparently, standard sex toys are given out by the NHS in some areas, so do ask!

4. Support in a crisis

Support with sex and relationships after being diagnosed with a condition

Professionals may assume that sex is the last thing on people's minds when their receive their diagnosis, but experience tells me, from listening to people, that sex is often the first thing they worry about. Men in spinal units all seem to agree that the *first* thing that pops into their minds when they come round from the accident is 'will my cock still work?'

Sometimes, when support is available, those in need never get to hear about it. For example, the Emotional Support Services at the Royal National Institute for the Blind tell me that they wait for people to get in touch, because they cannot be aware of everyone in the country who loses their sight, but many newly blind people may never be told that their service exists.

Support when they get depressed about not having a personal relationship in their lives

Disabled people say they watch other people of their age holding hands and having fun, but they may always go to bed alone, never experiencing sexual intimacy. They watch as their friends, one by one, get married and drift away. If they do have a partner, they may put up with being treated badly, and dare not leave, perhaps with a fear of having to go into a residential home and thinking they will never find another partner. Living with depression for a long time may end up with them having no friends at all.

Ask if it would help if you were to discuss their situation, with a view to you both recognizing what is holding them back. You can, together, work out some strategies to support them to make steps to remedy their situation, cheer up and move forward.

Support when they've been told they can't consent to sex

Even if the disabled adult has been considered unable to make reliable decisions, and cannot consent to sex, they are not banned from having sex with another person or being helped to pleasure themselves, if this is what they want and is in their best interest, as decided by the team who work with them. See Chapter 4 for discussion of the relevant law.

Support with making life-changing decisions

Support with moving out of the parental home is discussed in Chapter 5. There are many other important steps disabled people take which could put them in jeopardy of becoming extremely isolated and alone. Many Outsiders members have talked about missing out at university because of accessibility. One of the campuses most praised is Bradford, in Yorkshire, but the town is too hilly for a manual wheelchair user to wheel themselves around, so even though the accommodation is accessible, the city is not! Because many people tend to meet their partners at college or at work, disabled people prefer jobs where the staff get together and work together. Research needs to be done to facilitate all this so that you can point your disabled clients to a website resource offering the relevant advice.

This is a small taster of the things to come in this book, and to prepare you for the whole range of problems and some ideas which I use in my work.

Resources

1. Wiegerink, D., Roebroeck, M., Bender, J., Stam, H., Cohen-Kettenis, P. and Transition Research Group South West Netherlands (2011) 'Sexuality of young adults with cerebral palsy: Experienced limitations and needs.' *Sexuality and Disability 29*, 2, 119–128. Published online. Available at www.ncbi.nlm.nih.gov/pmc/articles/PMC3093545, accessed on 8 July 2014.
2. The Sexual Respect Tool Kit: www.SexualRespect.com.

CHAPTER 2

DIFFICULTIES THAT DISABLED PEOPLE EXPERIENCE

To list all the difficulties which disabled people experience with sex would fill an entire book. I thus decided to limit this chapter to my own personal expertise, gained from Outsiders, the Sex and Disability Helpline, and the Sexual Health and Disability Alliance (SHADA). I am focusing on three topics: masturbation, finding a partner and enjoying sex with a partner. Questions commonly asked on the Sex and Disability Helpline are listed in the FAQ section on the Outsiders website[1] but may be expanded on here.

Masturbation (also called self-pleasuring)

I would suggest that it needs to become standard practice to say to disabled people that it's OK to talk about masturbation if they wish, and to ask them whether they are able to masturbate successfully in an enjoyable way. Then you can reassure them that enjoying themselves in this way is healthy and good for them: orgasms are therapeutic they bring a person less pain and make them feel better in themselves. You can use whichever term feels right for the two of you: playing with yourself, wanking, tossing or jerking off; ask the person which term they prefer, so that they feel they can talk comfortably.

Many disabled people live in sexually repressive environments, which are known to make people feel sexually excited. They may seek out the most extreme pornography, and masturbate obsessively. This sexless environment may entice a disabled person to snuggle under the bedclothes, or sit at a computer, as a refuge, to play with themselves for hours (if they can physically manage it)!

So it is doubly tragic that some disabled people cannot manage to masturbate, either because of physical difficulties or because of their depression and sadness about being unloved. They may have been told it is wrong, or simply feel they have no privacy. Supporting such clients in this area is essential.

Being lonely, depressed and with a poor body image can make masturbation seem either compulsive or a waste of time. It can feel initially comforting but they may fail to reach orgasm and it ends up bringing on a huge sense of yearning and frustration. The person may have no memory, or only faded memories, of happy sexual experiences, and feel unable to fantasize. They may not be able to afford sexual services often enough to keep happy sexual memories alive.

Disabled women email the Sex and Disability Helpline with no idea how to reach orgasm, and it can take 50 or more emails for them to get there! I have found that I have to be totally explicit about how to locate the clitoris by explaining they reach round beyond the base of the pubic bone, then feel around to find a harder protuberance, the clitoral head, which may swell and harden when rubbed or vibrated. They have to play with or around the clitoral head, maybe moving the skin above it, the hood. At the same time, they need to relax and let go: orgasm is the triumph of stimulation over inhibition. They may have to be told to try bodily positions, for example not to sit up but lie flat with their hips on a pillow to arch their back. They can be told to try using lubricant and a vibrator. Instructional DVDs can be purchased from the Dodson and Ross website.[2] The women are very happy when they get there!

You might find it useful to look at the North American publication *Pleasure Able – Sexual Device Manual for Persons with Disabilities*[3] which discusses sex toys and disabled people, and offers good drawings of genitals and pictures of toys.

Disabled people often come up with their own ways of masturbating, which may come from being secretive and grabbing a moment of privacy. Such methods include using an electric toothbrush, an innocent-looking sex toy, and using a shower nozzle on parts they cannot reach or do not have the strength to otherwise stimulate.

Some paraplegics use a specially designed, high-intensity vibrator, the Ferticare,[4] to experience orgasm, including ejaculation; and this can bring feelings of relaxation, diminish spasms and help bladder dysfunction. Ferticare is manufactured in Denmark by Multicept. There are films featuring Dr Stacy Elliot on the website Broadened Horizons[5] to show you how the Ferticare works and how spinally injured men can be vibrated by health professionals to produce sperm. Interestingly, they apply the vibrator to the frenulum, the most sensitive part of the penis and which is where all that is left of the foreskin's sensitivity is located once it has been removed. You can find out more about this in *The Foreskin, Circumcision and Sexuality.*[6]

Broadened Horizons also provides guidance on quadriplegics' danger of autonomic dysreflexia. This can come from stimulation below the level of injury. Most quads have been taught to know how to monitor this safely.

Those with spina bifida may need to stimulate other parts of their body than the clitoris or penis, such as the prostate or nipples, or they may need to explore to find their own erogenous zone. Specialist vibrators for the prostate are easily available. The range of vibrators is wide, and includes a vibrator designed for the testicles and others for couples to use together. People who have difficulty clasping a toy might use gripping aids.

Most sex toy shops have staff who are accustomed to discussing the needs of disabled customers and helping them find the right toy, but few sex toy websites offer really useful descriptions or advice. However, you can usually find a vibrator review on YouTube.

Those who are physically unable to masturbate can sometimes reach orgasm with a vibrating snake wrapped around them, on their tummy, moving their hips against the bedding or a bean bag, or lying face down on a vibrating cushion. A few may be able to get there by fantasizing. Some use a breathing technique that will be mentioned shortly. Other disabled people may need assistance.

The latest gadgets, which have the potential to be started, stopped and turned up and down by the disabled person themselves using their computer, phone or music system, are electrostimulation gadgets, such as ElectraStim and MyStim. These sometimes have straps. Some can be used on a variety of erogenous zones, from different parts of the genitals to the nipples, the area just above the level of paralysis, nape of the neck or the ear lobe.

More traditional and usually cheaper masturbators use vibration and physical movement. They need to be put into position just before the masturbation is to start (usually not possible in the middle of the night!).

This may be done by fixing it to a flat surface using a suction cup, which a version of the Fleshlight has, or:

- holding it in place with a clamp above the bed, or clamping it to a Hold-It stand[7]

- tucking it inside a pair of tight-fitting pants

- strapping it to the client's body using a harness

- for women, wearing butterfly vibrator panties fitted with a vibrating gusset.

Men will need to have their erection placed inside the toy, perhaps after a couple of strokes with some lubricant to stiffen it. This is simply preparing the client for sex, not sexual touching. The assistant then leaves the room, maybe needing to turn the toy on first, if the client cannot, or using a remote switch from outside the room. The best situation is if the client can operate a remote control, so they can select the desired speed and intensity as they proceed.

Toys for men which are most suitable for this are:

- Rends A10 Cyclone (Rends is Japanese; it is an acronym and stands for Reality, Extravagant, Neat, Dream, Satisfaction)

- Fleshlight, some models having a suction cup for attaching to surfaces

- Copra Libre, which only vibrates the top of the penis.

These toys vibrate or provide a circular movement, not the up and down or subtle movements normally used by a man with his hand when masturbating.

Women can try:

- standard vibrators

- butterfly vibrators, which are strapped on to sit over the clitoral head

- vibrating panties, which may give more general stimulation to the whole of the vulva.

The Humpus is a sex toy for both men and women, which has straps to hold it in place. The Humpus website[8] shows it in action.

There are also some expensive American 'hands-free' sex toys:

- Sybian, a vibrating box for women to sit on and enjoy, which has a cheaper version, the Wand Essentials Comfort Love Seat

- Venus 2000 for men. You can see a film of the Venus 2000 online.[9]

The Spokz website[10] usually stocks suitable toys. For a huge range of sex toys which disabled people might like to use, see the MA Guide by Narelle Higson,[11] which can be found on the Multiple Sclerosis Society of Western Australia website, under Downloads.

I have been searching for years for someone to make bespoke harnesses to hold the required sex toy firmly in place for disabled people who cannot hold a toy. Following a quote by me in the sex toy trade journal saying that disabled people who cannot masturbate were better off with a hand job because sex toys were not designed for them, I was contacted by a British design company. They are now working on producing a toy which disabled people can use without help, or with as little assistance as possible. I am delighted, and am giving them all the contacts and encouragement I can. Such a toy would provide disabled people with the chance to be spontaneous, as currently, if they get a rampant hard-on or feel horny in the middle of the night, they can't just ring a bell for assistance to get pleasurable relief.

The Magic Wand is a vibrator on a long handle, good for people who otherwise cannot reach.

Some people with spina bifida are allergic to latex and need to use latex-free condoms and toys. Information about allergy to sex toy materials, and also information for people with fibromyalgia, chronic fatigue syndrome and multiple chemical sensitivities, is listed on Immune Web – Support and Information Network.[12]

People who have missing genitals, such as women who have been genitally mutilated (FGM) or war veterans, may or may not find genital nerve endings which are still capable of producing an orgasm, and may need to find other erogenous zones to stimulate for sexual satisfaction.

Those with genitals paralyzed by spinal injury can still enjoy orgasm by stimulating their bodies, and feeling the orgasm in their head or else in an erogenous zone which is above the level of paralysis. This can be brought about either from stimulating their genitals or directly on an erogenous zone, such as the nipples or ear lobe. Often the area just above the level of paralysis can become sensitive, especially if they use sensory amplification to 'coax' the pleasurable feelings out. Others find unexpected other places on their body where stimulation can bring orgasm. Rafe Biggs, who founded Sexability,[13] discovered he can orgasm through having his thumbs sucked and massaged.[14]

The vagus nerve is a large nerve which does not travel through the spinal column. It innervates the voicebox, throat, upper palate and heart, connecting many of our energy centres, or *chakras*, and goes to the uterus and cervix. Spinal-injured women have been able to enjoy powerful orgasms by making deep sounds and opening up their chests through deep breathing. This is described in *Orgasms and the Vagus Nerve*.[15]

Breath work, together with moving sexual energy around the body, can bring a hands-free full body orgasm to both genders. The technique comes from the ancient practice of Taoism, described by Mantac Chia.[16] A disabled person can re-focus sexual energy to where they feel sensation. The beauty of orgasm through breath work is that it uses energy and, unlike vibrators and ejaculatory orgasms, does not lead to autonomic dysreflexia in spinal-injured people. You can see films to observe breath orgasms. One of them, *How To Have a Breath and Energy Orgasm (aka Thinking Off)*[17] shows the practitioner, Barbara Carrellas, experiencing orgasm herself, as part of her workshop. More films by Mitch Tepper[18] can be found on his website and Broadened Horizons. Mitch, who is quadriplegic, says that he finds breath orgasms easier if he is being massaged at the same time. Tantric and other practitioners such as the people at Channelled Bliss[19] can teach this to disabled people. You will see a little more on breath orgasms in Chapter 8 in the Sexual Massage and Breath Work sections. These techniques might not work with those with reduced strength in breathing.

Most people prefer fingers to machines and gadgets, and the human touch adds warmth and subtlety to the experience of masturbation. I have been trying for several years to launch a special service by people who would like to 'lend a hand' for a small fee. I am being guided by a disabled lawyer who is advising me, for example, to publicize the need, rather than ask students to do the work, which would be soliciting. Another is to find an escort locally who will provide the service when their work is slack. They would not have to dress up or be newly showered, simply have clean hands. The disabled person would probably have to visit the escort, rather than the escort visit them, and should only stay as long as it takes.

People who have not orgasmed recently may need to have two orgasms, as the first one only provides release. They need another to bring them a feeling of satisfaction, bodily relaxation and a return to good mental health. I discovered this decades ago when I supported one such person physically myself. He had cerebral palsy and no speech, but after the second orgasm, his limbs relaxed and I learned he had a Liverpool accent, as he could speak fluently for a few minutes!

Those learning disabled people who cannot masturbate because they don't know how, or are experiencing difficulties, can be taught by an escort or a sexual advocate. Much care needs to be taken to ensure there is real understanding of the situation before consent can be granted, and then boundaries need to be drawn up to protect both parties. Always aim at the less intrusive methods to achieve your goals; for example, if discussions and demonstration using a dildo with a foreskin will lead to success, there may be no need for hand-on-hand teaching. Hand-on-hand teaching involves guiding the client's hand with the teacher's hand. The background to attempts to do this in the UK is described in the section on sex workers as teachers in Chapter 8.

After all this emphasis on masturbation to reach orgasm, I should stress that people can also enjoy positive self-pleasuring without focus on orgasm. This might appeal to your clients – they simply explore their bodies to leisurely feel lingering sensual, or even kinky, pleasures (see Chapter 9). This might bring them endorphin highs or simply allow them to learn and reclaim their bodies for themselves. Explain that, just as partnered sex is not all about intercourse and orgasm, so too can masturbation be much more than just making themselves come, by dwelling on the pleasure and feeling in charge of their body. Masturbation can allow exploration of sexual responses to ideas and sensations. Encourage them to enjoy their fantasies and not to be afraid of them. Some books to recommend are *More Joy – An Advanced Guide to Solo Sex*[20] and *The New Male Sexuality*[21] for men, plus *Sex for One*[22] and *The Ultimate Guide to Orgasm for Women*[23] for women.

I am glad that discussions on masturbation are now more acceptable in society, and I hope that support for disabled people to enjoy themselves in this way, including assisted masturbation, will become widely acceptable too.

Finding a partner

Finding a partner is the thing which is most often listed as the biggest difficulty which disabled people face. The prejudice and fear felt by those who identify as able-bodied impacts on them. They may themselves be self-loathing, and need support to change this around. Low self-confidence can stem from many different reasons, such as lack of love from parents, bullying, sexual and other abuse, being stared at, being made to feel undesirable, continual rejection, marital abuse and lack of experience. You can offer your support by asking someone what they feel makes them lack confidence, then listening as they talk, taking what they say seriously and reassuring them. To help boost confidence, you can suggest trying things to gain confidence in any way which appeals, perhaps by being photographed, painted, massaged or whatever makes them feel good and their body being given positive attention. This is described in more detail as Body Image Therapy at the end of Chapter 7.

One way of building confidence could be by presenting oneself in an erotic way, through dress, speech and behaviour. This doesn't have to mean dressing as a stripper or dandy, but some find that it can help them to come out of their shell by expressing themselves as more outwardly playful, open and relaxed. There is a useful book by Carol Queen called *Exhibitionism for the Shy*[24] which you could recommend.

Low self-esteem can sometimes make disabled people settle for second-best. One Outsiders member told me that, before she joined Outsiders, the only sex she could get was with drunken men coming out of the pub at closing time. Growing old can increase the severity of impairments, and adds new ones, which can increase the likelihood of putting up with bad situations.

Going out can be quite a challenge for an obviously impaired person, as the public do strange things like try to kiss them in the street, push their wheelchair without being asked or ask how they have sex. There is always the threat of being mugged and ways to avoid this are offered on the Outsiders website under Resources for Disabled People.

The reluctance of others to take them seriously as potential partners results from many people thinking a disabled person would be inconvenient, hard work and an embarrassment! Also, many non-disabled people fear becoming blind, deaf or unable to walk, thinking things like, 'There, but for the grace of God, go I', and may feel uneasy in the company of those with such impairments.

Disabled people living at home with their parents may feel hopeless because, when they want to start dating, they feel they will be embarrassed bringing a date home and trying to enjoy a sex life with their parents in the house. The parents may be the only care support they have, and they don't want to upset the apple-cart. My advice for them is to ask their parents to go out, and hire a Personal Assistant (PA) who can support their undressing, and whatever hospitality they wish to offer. Eventually the date can do the undressing and so on, so they can enjoy the luxury of being alone together.

Disabled people needing to employ PAs need to ensure that the PA will support them in their life as they want to live it, and not the PA's version of their life. The disabled person needs to list their intimate requirements, assuring the candidate that they may need to be prepared for sex, but that this does not include sexual touching. The two of them need to discover whether they are compatible, and that the PA won't stop the disabled person enjoying themselves. A job description needs to be created and agreed, and then discussed periodically as time passes and as things crop up. For example, PAs sometimes use wet wipes when they change continence pads, but this can make the disabled person smell and taste really unpleasant to a lover. An assertive disabled employer simply adds this to the job specification or care plan, after a discussion. Having to have full-time care when wanting to get intimate with someone is always tricky, but just using mobile phones can allow the PA to be nearby, out of sight, and ready to be called back when necessary.

There are reasons, real and imagined, why disabled people fear they will be rejected as partners, and that fear can make them too nervous to try. Outsiders body image workshops are good for helping them move forward. The group take it in turns to say why they think people might like them, and be attracted to them, and what they think puts people off. Other members then comment, often having very different views on both. This helps individuals realize how wrong their negative self-image has been, and learn how to improve their appearance and attractiveness.

Now I'd like to list reasons why people with disabilities can make great romantic/sexual partners, so that you can encourage your clients with some good news:

- Chemistry is not prejudiced against disability and impairment. Sometimes, people meet and are lucky enough to feel immediate attraction, knowing it could be the beginning of lifelong love.

- Living with so many social, physical and mental challenges, many disabled people feel that they have grown in wisdom, in depth and in other ways, and that these qualities have become more highly developed. Having to know more about how their body works makes them more intuitive lovers and, overall, they make more interesting partners.

- If people are searching for someone with similar special views, interests and tastes (maybe sexual tastes), then – after finding such a person, perhaps on a specialist website or Facebook group – it may seem of no consequence that the person happens to be disabled.

- Many disabled people find that being disabled makes them feel less masculine or feminine. Men may not be able to play sports, to swagger around looking cool, or to speak suavely. Women may not be able to walk with a sexy demeanour, wear high heels or glamorous shoes. But this may be no bad thing, because some women prefer gentle, sensitive men who they can relate to, and some men prefer women to be less girlie or glammy.

- Those who have lived very sheltered lives, or who have had really difficult life experiences – for example, someone who lost a parent when young, or survived a war zone – may feel they share common ground with a disabled person.

- Disabled people may want a disabled partner because only they can really understand the whole of them and their lives.

- There are people who have already been happy in one relationship with a disabled person. Or maybe the person is disabled, or has been disabled in the past, and feel they relate to disabled people more than others.

- Some people realize that it might be advantageous to have a partner with a certain impairment. For example, a person who has Asperger's or social anxiety and finds eye contact difficult may seek a visually impaired partner. I shall never forget being with a group of disabled Outsiders members on a walk across some rough land and suggesting to a young man with such extreme social phobia that he had never touched a female, that he guide a blind girl by offering her his arm. His life was changed around.

- Some people have a fetish for disabled people. I discuss fetishes further in Chapter 9, but will deal here with 'devotees', the term for disability fetishists. Devotees are mostly men, but there are female devotees too. The fetish may be very specific, many finding amputees sexually attractive but others seeking wheelchair users, or people with other impairments. Some disabled people welcome the idea of being really fancied but others fear that devotees are controlling and refer to them as 'droolers'. Teen online forums describe how young devotees discovered that they were 'different' from a young age, and often discuss the need to 'come out' to families and friends about their devoteeism. They see it as a sexual identity, like being gay. There may be a worry about what other people think – what would you and your colleagues think if a service user started dating a fetishist? Writer Ruth Madison is a devotee and writes about her experiences and those of others online.[25] Female and gay devotees can find disabled males on the international site Paradevo.[26]

Some disabled people have complained to me that people select them as a partner because they will be faithful(!). People may want a date with them for the kicks of having sex with a disabled person. Other people search out people who are feeling low, as easy pickings. Predators seek out disabled people online, and I've heard some horrific stories, and that is why Outsiders vets our applicants. We sometimes hear from men offering to have sex with disabled women because they fancy themselves as good lovers and want to be appreciated. We do not accept such offers.

Obviously, disabled people seeking a partner need to be aware of the dangers; they have the worry of never really knowing whether the date is genuinely liking them or wanting to use, abuse or exploit them. Some take a friend with them on the first date, for safety.

Now we look at some challenges which various disabled people face, when trying to date and find love, and things you might suggest to your clients.

Some challenges

Having Asperger's syndrome (Autism Spectrum Disorder)

Some people with Asperger's ('Aspies' for short) are very good at expressing themselves and their needs clearly and factually. However, many struggle both to find a partner and to make the relationship work. Difficulty socializing, understanding social cues and often wanting to talk about special interests can make first dates seem really hard.

If a relationship starts, the partner may also have difficulty accepting the Aspie person's special interests, lack of social skills and perceived lack of empathy. However, an Aspie can be supported to know how to prepare others for their behaviour. For example, if they find empathy difficult, the partner might be urged to seek another friend to provide such support, when needed. Using the Outsiders' Beyond Impairment model, listing all the things they are good at and ways to overcome those things they struggle with can be useful here.

The virtual world website Second Life has proved to be helpful to Aspies, because it allows them to form relationships without having the confusing distractions of social situations. Programmes are now being developed in the USA using Second Life as a model.[27] Drama can also be of use, because the Aspie learns from acting the part of a person who forms a relationship and enjoys it.

Many of the Aspies I know struggle so hard to cope with socializing, especially when going on dates and contemplating seduction, that they never get around to having sex. You could provide a listening ear, as they may not have anyone to talk to about this. Supporting them to find clarity may help them along.

Not having facial expressions so cannot smile

This can be very disconcerting to new people meeting the individual for the first time. I hope you can encourage them to find other ways to express themselves and their emotions, and support them to feel confident in using these skills when searching for a partner. Perhaps carrying amusing cards on them to explain, or perhaps having pictures of facial expressions which they can point to, might break the ice. Making an effort like this says to the other person that the expressionless person has thought about the potential bewilderment that they bring to people, and has reached out to make it easier for them – always a good idea.

Being an unusual size or shape

Most people in this situation seem to need to work on themselves to overcome their embarrassment, inferiority or low self-esteem. Using body image therapy, described in Chapter 7, can help them on their journey, and you can support them with discussion, perhaps mentioning similar people who have become successful or popular.

One thing which has long been known to help is to go to a naturist resort. Amazingly, many people with unusual body shapes and disabilities do join naturist clubs. Somehow, when all the clothes are off, people become far more accepting of difference. After the first day, when many feel excited as well as self-conscious, people just relax and everyone seems normal. People see past the body, and simply enjoy each other's company.

Other off-putting appearances

Certain conditions are generally regarded by many as off-putting. For example, psoriasis, trembling and sweating, uncontrollable saliva production and bad breath, or severe disfigurement. There may be two stages in which such people can move forward, and they might appreciate your support.

First, ensure that everything possible is being done to improve your client's appearance. Using lateral thinking, and being down-to-earth, you can discuss practical ways around the situation for the person to make themselves more acceptable. For example, a person with cerebral palsy who produces frothy saliva in heated conversations, could carry a flamboyant handkerchief to mop it up.

Second, if the person learns self-acceptance, they will feel more calm and relaxed in company; their bodily differences may be, or at least appear, lessened. Self-acceptance can be achieved by having positive attention paid to their body through body image therapy (see Chapter 8 on sexual services and the end of Chapter 7). Using massage, body work and sex work, the professionals will be non-judgemental and accepting. It is interesting for talking therapists to know that you can only go so far with talk, and that the physical power of touch can take the therapist much further with a client and help them feel more positive about themselves. Pride in the ownership of their body, and thus not caring about the negative side of their appearance, can inspire potential partners.

Imagining that certain aspects of their body will put lovers off

Some individuals are discouraged by imagining that some aspect or another of their body will put lovers off – for example, problems such as incontinence and stammering.

Many disabled people allow these false suppositions to stop them making sexual advances, or responding positively to advances, for fear of having their impairment discovered. This can be almost more socially crippling than having more noticeable off-putting features. Finding fault with their body distracts a person away from the good feelings that their body can give them, and can take the positive sexual essence out of their very existence.

I have met so many people who are sexually paralyzed because of their incontinence, stomas and catheters, and sometimes nothing I do or say can convince them that other people don't actually mind (except the squeamish). What I suggest to a person with such fears is that they start off by telling a potential partner how they personally feel about their body. Their shame and fears may be a revelation to the other person, and help them empathize. The second step is to describe the cause of their feelings. They could, if all is going well, show them and describe the precautions the incontinent person can take to minimize wetting or soiling the bed during sex. Then they can listen to questions and discuss feelings and emotions, in an unrushed, loving, even sexy, way.

It all sounds so simple, but might meet deaf ears. I have sat in a restaurant with a young man who has both a stoma and a catheter, who I could see was the local heart-throb, and yet he had not had a girlfriend since his incontinence began. I tried to give him the courage to contemplate asking a girl out. I have even volunteered to act as go-between to inform the potentially new girlfriend or boyfriend that the individual has a stoma or catheter, because they themselves were just too shy and afraid to do it themselves. The response is always, 'That's fine'! People with continence issues really need to be supported to have a more positive view of themselves, and to become braver and more assertive. An online resource which could help is Cory Silverberg's *Bowel and Bladder Control During Sex* on sexuality.about.com[28] and there is also the website *Managing Life with Incontinence.*[29]

Attractive pouch covers designed to cover the ostomy are for sale from several suppliers online. Some women make their own sexy covers to match their saucy underwear, and use a smaller pouch or stoma cap, which doesn't get in the way for love-making. Men may wear a comfortable towelling cover with a smaller pouch or stoma cap.

If accidents happen during sex, it's best to be jovial about venturing into the shower together, and bundling the soiled linen into the washing machine.

The Motor Neurone Disease Association leaflets[30] are really good on this topic, discussing sex with a PEG and RIB tube.

Stammering can certainly be a very great problem when socializing, and speaking to someone they find attractive is one of the most stammer-inducing situations of all. If your client stammers and is nervous about how they will cope, again, having a card in their pocket which explains that they normally don't stammer except in certain circumstances such as meeting new people can help to see them through. Suggesting a dance, a walk or some activity which doesn't require speech is also a good idea.

Basically, you can support clients to rid themselves of imaginary barriers by rising above them, and being honest and open about their differences.

Off-putting behaviour

Sometimes a disabled person's behaviour can put other people off getting to know them. If this is the result of brain damage, mental health problems, autism, Asperger's syndrome or other neuro-diverse behavioural traits, they need be taught how to minimize the impact of their condition on finding potential partners.

Headway East London started an initiative to offer their clients social opportunities, and to guide them through. Those with hypersexuality and disinhibition will need specialist training to learn how to value their bodies and look after themselves, which could come from the Brook Advisory Service. Rea Danielle in North London has pioneered groups for the neuro-diverse on preparing themselves for dating. This work has been, sadly, discontinued due to lack of funding.

Neuro-diversity covers those with autism, attention deficit hyperactivity disorder (ADHD), bipolar disorder, dyslexia, Tourette's syndrome and other mental, intellectual and emotional differences. Some people with these conditions say that eye contact is difficult for them, which means they may not realize when someone likes them. Explaining their difficulty might sound strange and off-putting. Other behaviours, like rocking, are calming but may be off-putting to others. Again, people with visual impairment may be ideal partners for them, and the neuro-diverse person would probably prefer this kind of suggestion to anything which advises them to adapt their behaviour to fit the norm!

Social phobia and anxiety

The article *10 Tips for Finding Love and Dating With Social Anxiety* on Calm Clinic's website[31] might be very useful for your clients, but it doesn't cover people who cannot make friends. One of the biggest problems for people with this anxiety is acquiring the art of making casual conversation to make friends first. Things like making eye contact can be a huge problem, and if eye contact isn't made, or the person with social anxiety does not get their words out in time, the potential friend or date can often assume either that the interest is not there, or that the social anxiety sufferer has a learning difficulty. These are all things where discussion with you could support them to tell people they meet what their difficulties are.

Being dumped or feeling unrequited love

Getting dumped happens to most of us, and my advice to everyone is to go on holiday to somewhere very different and/or far away, where there's lots of socializing and fun, to help them forget and perhaps to see things in perspective. There is no point in pining for someone when there is no chance of a future with them. Warn your client that it is counterproductive to keep pestering someone, and that the best plan is to walk away in a dignified manner.

Dating

Many disabled people think others judge them as 'damaged goods'. Plus, they may have been rejected all through their teens, and have an abiding fear of rejection. There's an old saying that the sure way to success is to ask 100 people out, expecting rejection and laughing it off, perhaps with a pal, because one person in 100 will say yes, and one is all you need! A colleague with very severe physical impairment, who has the knack and a partner, confirms this. He says finding somebody for sex, an affair or a relationship is a matter of a numbers game plus confidence. You may have to work hard to build up the confidence to be brave enough to ask in a relaxed, good humoured way. Tinder (a smartphone app) could be of use, although many people use it for local hook-ups, most search for good looks, and it often requires speed and spontaneity.

It must feel difficult going on a date when you are feeling highly frustrated sexually, as many disabled people sometimes are, and I sometimes suggest a visit to an escort to help them feel more relaxed.

Visually impaired people have little or no eye contact and no chance of reading facial expressions. This is limiting when looking for, or building, new sexual relationships. Most blind and partially sighted people do care about looks. Knowing they have a good-looking partner contributes to their self-esteem. You could remind them that how people come across is very much more about how they present themselves than their basic facial and bodily features.

Individuals with brain injury or neuro-diversity have particular problems which crop up with dating that can lead them to stumble and fail. An example is memory loss, and even getting lost trying to find the meeting place for the date. This could perhaps be solved by having a map app on a smartphone.

Online dating is relatively new, and most people really struggle with it. The website Online Dating Experts[32] gives plenty of down-to-earth advice which you can advise your clients to study before venturing out and becoming frustrated. Sites for special interests tend to work better than general sites, but I advise disabled people not to use special sites for disabled people, except Outsiders, as we are the only site to vet our applicants in order to stop predators from entering. Another exception is 2date4love,[33] a dating site for people who cannot engage in sexual intercourse to meet and experience love, companionship and intimacy.

You could encourage your female clients by telling them that one of the great things about online dating is that women can be proactive, providing equality.

Disabled people not wanting disabled partners

Many disabled people who mix socially in society adopt the able-bodied prejudice against dating other disabled people. However, if they mixed more with disabled people, they might drop this prejudice. In Chapter 5 on supporting young people, I stress the importance of instilling self-acceptance and the eradication of shame. I discuss the value of keeping in touch with people with the same condition, if only for peer support and swapping notes.

Some disability organizations promote such thinking. Scope runs the Trendsetters Project for youngsters with cerebral palsy. The Brittle Bone Society holds annual conferences for its members with Osteogenesis Imperfecta (OI), where Outsiders' Patron, Caroline Bowditch, speaks about relationships and sex. Many people join Outsiders when they get fed up with seeing all their friends get married, and seek acceptance with us. We try to support them to accept themselves and their impairments before starting to date. Many who fall in love with another disabled person say how wonderful it is to find somebody, at last, who totally understands how they feel as a disabled person.

It is sad to know that some able-bodied people will desert their disabled lover because they don't want to handle a relationship with them, even though both knew the chemistry was there.

No friends and/or feeling lonely

Disabled people may have seen all their school friends drift away when they get married and have children and, as they became more isolated and lonely, may even lose their single friends too. Having no friends at all makes it difficult to meet new people. They may become insular and communicate with people online, but that is not like real company. As we learned in 2014, social isolation is as damaging to health as smoking and twice as damaging as obesity, impairing the immune system. It can also bring mental illness, greater risk of cardiovascular disease and stroke, a more rapid progression of Alzheimer's disease, and premature ageing.

One idea is to try talking to a stranger every time you go out, in a café, in the surgery, on a train, or in other places where people are not all in a rush. However, this is not easy for the shy or those lacking confidence. Of course, Outsiders offers friendship opportunities. A member with Asperger's, Eric, wrote:

When I joined Outsiders, I was happy living an isolated existence as an artist, but I thought it would be better if I made some friends. It was a boost to my life to actually make friends. Outsiders opened so many doors for me – I even found my job through another member. I had a girlfriend for a while, and the social events all hold their own kind of magic.

As mentioned earlier, some Headways are discussing the planning of social groups. To find social clubs for learning disabled people, type the name of your town and 'learning disability club' into a search engine. Stars in the Sky[34] support their learning disabled clients by accompanying them on the first date. Lots of clubs such as Beautiful Octopus,[35] which are run for and by learning disabled people and are good fun, have sprung up all over the country.

People who are hearing impaired from birth and who use signing, or who suddenly lose their hearing and use lip-reading, have difficulty conversing with others, and tend to be very isolated. Deaf people tend to socialize together and that is why you may see groups of deaf people in a bar, for example.

Loneliness can be felt even when surrounded by friends, if nobody is interested in your sexual happiness. Married people whose partners don't take a sexual interest feel lonely. I hope that this book helps to lift the stigma which is attached to loneliness, and encourages you to support your disabled clients to find friends. Loneliness is on the increase.[36]

Feeling that dating is impossible

Some individuals are convinced that nobody will accept them as lovers, because they imagine that even minor physical differences make dating impossible. I had an email from a 20-year-old virgin male in Turkey, who said his scoliosis meant that he could never have a sexy loving relationship with a girl. My advice: 'When you stop feeling you are not good enough, get brave and ask girls out with confidence and intelligence, you will find a girl you will be able to enjoy sex with. May I suggest you have an ordinary massage to make your whole body feel nice, including your back?' He seemed to go away happy. I do tell people about how cosmetic surgery can lead individuals into becoming eternally dissatisfied with their bodies, and how some people hate good-looking people because they seem to have everything.

Fear of rejection

Rejection feels especially bad when it is because of the way someone looks or moves, ignoring the beautiful person inside. Really, dating is only a sorting process to find that person with whom they have chemistry. Getting to know more people may increase their chances, as long as they don't all just become solely platonic friends.

Always a friend, never a partner

This is something I have heard from many disabled men, and it's probably true for disabled women too. They provide a shoulder to cry on, listening to complaints about failed dates and difficult partners, while they themselves fail to get taken seriously as a lover. If they are true friends, they can explain to them that they are looking for love, and maybe their friends can introduce them to other single people. Some people get on in a platonic way, but, if the disabled person feels a sexual attraction, taking an interest in the friend's deep sexual longings, and offering to take them there, might just turn the tables round!

Asking someone out

If your client is unsure of themselves and not wanting to bungle this, it is best to advise them to make a casual suggestion that they accompany the other person on something which they really want to do, or which they have to do, but which they may prefer to do accompanied by someone else. One disabled couple I know came together as a result of her accompanying him to the estate agents to find a more accessible flat. The agent assumed they were a couple, and that triggered it all off!

In Outsiders, we've had famous Pick-Up Artists (PUAs) come to speak about their techniques for attracting partners. The best one for me was when a man asks the woman to describe the best day she can ever remember having, and then offers to help re-create that day, for example having a lovely stroll beside the sea front. She would, they say, associate the nice memory with him, thus like him, and be flattered he wants to please her. However, some of our members found this a bit contrived.

Conducting a first date

This can be very nerve-wracking, but all the two people are doing is testing to see if there is chemistry between them, so it's not a matter of being judged. Explaining this to your client may help them to calm down and take it in their stride. Here are some guidelines to use to support them:

- Meet on neutral territory, a public place which you both agree would be suitable, checking for accessibility if this is needed. Ensure you both know how to get there.

- It's best if the place is easy to find, perhaps with parking nearby, not too crowded or noisy, and priced within your budget/s. You can always move on to somewhere else if things are going well.

- Swap mobile phone numbers and agree to let each other know if problems arise and one of you is going to be late, gets lost, or can no longer make it. You can also describe what you're both wearing so you'll recognize one another.

- Look immaculate, clean and in your own style. Set out in good time.

- If you think you might look nervous and anxious waiting for them, read a book.

- Welcome them warmly and ask about their journey. Take an interest in them. Only talk about yourself when asked. Tell them if you are feeling nervous or worried about stammering, for example, and ask them if they are feeling OK.

- Don't make assumptions that they will like you. If you find them attractive in any way, say so in an unthreatening and genuine style.

- Be yourself. Everyone is looking for somebody 'genuine' so covering up, or pretending to be something you are not, will be off-putting.

- Don't talk about past relationships.

- However you feel it's going, have fun and make the most of the situation. The person may not become the love of your life, but they might become a cherished friend.

- If they say that you are not for them, try to be gracious: smile, and wish them luck. If they warm to you, you could say you'd like to hold hands. Most people are looking for a physical relationship and will find you backward if you don't show interest, but never push.

Using a wheelchair and having impaired arms makes people feel restricted because they cannot reach out to touch their date. I tell them that the best way around this is to be brave enough to tell their date their sadness about this, and invite the date to take their hand, or otherwise guide it. As the relationship proceeds, the wheelchair user might be delighted to find their hand ends up in warmer places! In order to enjoy a kiss, it's a simple matter of asking the date if they'd like to kiss – if they think the other person is ready for this. They will probably be able to judge by the way, and by how much, the date looks your client in the eyes. But if they are visually impaired as well, they may be able to find out by saying that it's nice for a visually impaired person to have their hand held while someone is with them, to reassure them of the other person's presence. The way they hold hands (enthusiastically or coldly) communicates the message.

Yet, many disabled people, in my experience, are much too shy and nervous and lacking in confidence to manage all this soon enough for the date to stay around. Not only is finding someone to date difficult, but precious opportunities are continually missed. Confidence comes with practice.

If the date leads to sex, and performance anxiety kills any chance of an erection, the man can spend time listening to the new partner's dreams, while they play with each other using their fingers, tongue and mouth.

I hope that these examples show you that things I say to people with disabilities are not rocket science, not something health professionals need training for, just plain common sense. All you need to do is listen, put yourself in their shoes, and tell them how you'd think of getting around the problem. Disabled people are normally highly skilled at getting around problems, but for so many, anything to do with dating and sex sends them into confusion that stops them thinking logically.

Difficulties in communication on dates

The whole of Chapter 6 is about the difficulties disabled people have with communication: having a speech impairment, being deaf or deafblind, or not using words. With regard to dating, one man I know always took a married couple with him on the first date, because his speech was impaired, and they knew how to communicate fluently with him.

I hope I have given you a strong message that this is rewarding work, and inspired you to offer to support your clients in finding a partner, perhaps their most difficult challenge.

Difficulties enjoying partnered sex

This is a very basic guide on the difficulties which couples experience, where one has, or both have, an impairment or a condition, and simple ways to overcome any problems this may pose.

One of the things that many people, especially those with disabilities, fail to understand is that giving and receiving are equally important – it is important that individuals do both, as there is pleasure to be had in both. Even if a person cannot move, they can still create sexual pleasure by saying and suggesting sexy things. There is also pleasure to be enjoyed in watching somebody else enjoying themselves. People talk about a sympathetic orgasm (when someone gets pleasure from watching their partner have an orgasm). Polyamorous people – people who love more than one partner – have a word for this feeling of pleasure by observing it in others: 'compersion'.

Another important thing for a couple to realize is that romance may need to be kept alive or rekindled. If they want their partner to treat them better, they could do worse than start wooing them again.

As gay and other sexually diverse people know only too well, sex can be much more than sexual intercourse. It can include anything which feels beautiful, erotic and satisfying. Many people also like it to feel naughty, vulgar or obscene, and even enjoy frightening, depraved or outrageous things.

It's fun being inventive. People with bodily spasms sometimes use them to vibrate their partner's genitals. Other couples who know erections won't happen use a dildo in a thigh harness to enjoy intercourse with their partner who sits on the dildo while playing with their partner's genitalia with their fingers. If one person is physically more capable of being active, they can do all the more exhausting things and the other can do the more intricate things, and use their voice to conduct the sexual music, as it were. It doesn't matter which gender does what, who does what, so long as both are happy with what's going on, and are not bored or 'putting up' with it.

People with disabilities are sometimes forced to know their bodies more intimately than other people, through dealing with incontinence, for example, and have become accustomed to talking about their genitals. They use this knowledge to become more interesting lovers.

Yet disabled people can feel shy and inexperienced, and can be locked inside a sexually deprived, inhibited mindset. You can support such people by saying that we can all find other sides of ourselves, if we try. The shy person can use their shyness by being coy, which can look and feel sexy, or dress up to find the confidence to show off and become provocative. The section on exhibitionism and voyeurism in Chapter 9 goes into this in more detail.

Positions

I think disabled couples should be encouraged to explore, so that they find sex positions which work for them. This will involve discussions on what they want, maybe urging them to become more experienced in talking to each other about intimate matters. If they insist that they are stuck, there are plenty of positions pictured in *The New Joy of Sex*,[37] but I'll mention a few tips here:

- A person with cerebral palsy who finds it very difficult to part their legs might try the spoons position (both lying on their side facing the same way, man behind), or being massaged gently to ease the legs apart.

- If a person cannot take any pressure or weight on their torso, they may prefer being upright, or lying on their side. A hoist might also be used.

- If the couple find sex on a bed difficult because they are not getting enough support, they could use a large hammock with plenty of cushions and mats on it. The hammock can be set up with the two ends hung *together* from one hook inserted in a strong support bar in the ceiling. This provides freedom of movement while being very well supported from all sides.

- The use of rails beside the bed can facilitate lovers by supporting and steadying them.

- When a woman squats on top of a man, her vagina becomes really tight, and this can be good for women with loss of Kegel muscle tone.

- Hospital beds can be excellent, because they go up and down, and offer various heights for penetration by the standing person.

- The Intimate Rider is a gadget for disabled people to use for enjoying sexual intercourse if they cannot manage the movements themselves. It consists of a chair and couch which move in and out against each other. It is available from Spokz.[10]

- Chairs, slings and firm support cushions can be found online from companies such as Liberator. Silver Sex[38] make beautiful furniture for people who have arthritis, like their creator, and difficulty lying down.

More on this can be found on the Streetsie website in an article called *Wheelchair Sex, Love and Intimacy After Spinal Cord Injury.*[39]

Visual impairment

Visually impaired (VI) people are excluded from visual stimulation, which is difficult when they once enjoyed it in order to become turned on. Some use audio stimulation, and this can be sourced online from websites such as Literotica[40] or For Your Ears Only.[41] Nowhere is there a website, except Outsiders, where VI people can discuss where to buy erotic stories on CD, and swap notes on non-visual sex. People with visual impairment could be encouraged to try other sensory stimuli such as the taste and aroma of their partner, and the sounds they make when making love.

Spasms and spasticity

It may help to take antispasticity medication beforehand. Having an orgasm first from manual or oral stimulation, or by using a vibrator, can reduce spasms which women with cerebral palsy find impede intercourse.

Sensitivity

Disabled people who are unable to feel any sensation in their clitoris or penis can try stimulation of other parts of their body and erogenous zones.

Men can enjoy orgasm from stimulation of the prostate gland, using fingers or a prostate vibrator. Women may able to feel pleasure from the G-spot, which is rich in nerve endings and situated at the back of the vaginal entrance. Once a man knows this, he can stimulate the G-spot before and during intercourse, instead of plunging straight inside. The G-spot is an extension of the clitoral system where the sponge surrounding the urethra fills up with blood and becomes erect. Men who cannot actually penetrate their partner could stroke this area with their flaccid penis. It could lead to female ejaculation, which is not an orgasm but provides a beautiful release.

Both genders can orgasm and gain erotic pleasure from their nipples, and other parts of the body can learn to become more sensitive and sexual through sensory amplification. This means stroking and stimulating the area, perhaps using lubricant and concentrating on the feelings, so that the brain learns to feel the potential pleasure more and more.

MS can bring reduced or painfully heightened sensitivity of the clitoris and penis, and all kinds of changes in sensation of the body. People with these problems are advised to use body mapping, which is finding out exactly where and how their body is feeling at any one time, so that they can advise their partners accordingly.

Pain

A couple may decide to plan to have sex when the pain is normally less, as well as just grabbing the moment when there is no pain. They may need to discuss which parts of the body to avoid, or which activities. Although the pleasure and pain centres of the brain are side-by-side, few disabled people manage to experience their pain as pleasurable, although some do. You can read more about this in Chapter 9 on sexual diversity.

Lubrication

A woman who doesn't lubricate naturally, perhaps because of a spinal injury, needs to use a lubricant for vaginal penetration in order to ensure that the activity doesn't tear the delicate tissues. She also needs to take care, after penetration in the anus, that the partner's penis or finger is washed before inserting it into the vagina, because otherwise the dry vagina could allow germs into her body and cause an infection. Always use a water-based lubricant when using a condom.

Erections

An erection is very important to most men, and some feel that sex is impossible without one, but such fixed attitudes stop a couple exploring all the possibilities open to them.

If a client seeks your advice, the first step is for them to see their GP, if that is not you, because they need to check whether the lack of erection is because of physical change in their body, or their medication. The patient's GP can prescribe Viagra or similar pills if he or she considers it a safe option, and this route is far more advisable than buying from the internet. They can also prescribe gadgets such as a suction pump, or injections which cause the penis to become erect; or they can even discuss an operation for an implant. If the problem is not caused by illness, a physical condition or medication, it will be psychological, most often caused by performance anxiety. In this case, a sex therapist can usually support them back to enjoying erections in just a few hour-long sessions.

The sensation of entering the vagina is a sexual highlight, poetically described decades ago by Henry Miller as 'A dark, subterranean labyrinth fitted up with divans and cosy corners and rubber teeth and syringes and soft nettles and eiderdown and mulberry leaves.'[42] Men who cannot feel inside with their penis can use their fingers – or, if they are quadriplegic, their nose.

Some couples who miss erections decide to have sex with another man together so that they can enjoy *his* erection. There are plenty of men on offer – to find one, they just need to join a swinging website. The couple should, however, be sure that their relationship feels really bonded enough before going down this route.

Orgasm

Orgasms in men happen in distinct phases, and a man needs to recognize the approach of the 'point of no return' to delay his orgasm until he is ready. The sperm leave the testicles, gather fluid from the prostate, and are carried along by contractions and out through the end of the penis, usually with an explosion of orgasm which can totally take over the whole body with pleasurable waves. Both men and women usually experience regular contractions, and both can have multiple orgasms. Women tend to take longer to reach orgasm, and many complain that the man is too quick for her to reach her orgasm during intercourse. But intercourse alone rarely gives women orgasms anyway, because the clitoris might not become stimulated. The couple can be advised to discuss bringing the woman to orgasm with clitoral stimulation before, during and/or after intercourse, to ensure her satisfaction, and to see what works for them.

If a man orgasms too quickly, he should not use numbing sprays or ointments (he needs to become more aware of the feelings in his penis, not less), but seek medical advice and maybe a sex therapist. Premature ejaculation is often (but not always) caused by boys coming as fast as possible when they started masturbating, for fear of being discovered, and that is probably more common with boys who are disabled because of their having less privacy.

Many women never orgasm, which can make some very frustrated, but not all. Female orgasm was discussed earlier in this chapter in the section on masturbation. Those who feel frustration, and those who feel left out, need to learn how to give themselves an orgasm, and teach their partners by showing them.

People whose impairments affect their sexuality can be encouraged to explore all their options for enjoying their own versions of sexual pleasure. You could advise clients to stop seeking goals, like orgasm, instead focusing on intimacies which they otherwise find exciting. In their journeys, they may be pleasantly surprised that orgasm suddenly comes from attention being paid to unexpected places in their bodies and minds.

Asperger's syndrome

When it comes to sex, it may be the small clues which accompany seduction and making love that are too baffling for an Aspie. If they simply asked their partner to be more direct in stating what they want, the confusion could be untangled. Even better, the couple take it in turns to say what they want, being specific, and the Aspie can speak about any unusual sensitivities.

What Aspies need is guidance with sexuality that is full of facts and lists, nothing touchy-feely or emotional. I have done this with my Beyond Impairment document for Aspie members. Maxine Aston created a couples workbook for the couples she sees in sex therapy, containing things such as a wooing list.[43]

Lack of desire, fatigue, depression

If lack of desire might be due to medication, it's worth advising your client to check with their doctor (if that is not you) for whether an alternative may not have this side-effect. If it is due to fatigue or depression, then discussions can take place as to whether there are some moments of the day or night when they feel better. Deep discussions may lead to better understanding of what the fatigued or depressed person would enjoy to help them feel like making love; and talk during sex can allow the fatigued person a chance to relax and provide sexy feedback. Certainly they don't want to feel guilty about not always feeling like it, and they may need advising to keep reassuring their partner that their refusal is no reflection on their love or sexual attraction to them.

I am told by those with ME that one of the difficulties they have with relationships is never really getting the ideal support from doctors and healthcare professionals, so that they are never feeling as well as they might. They feel they have to overstate their condition, or else they are assumed to be OK. Professionals just don't always 'get' something that is so hidden. One woman told me, 'I sometimes purposefully wear no make-up just to look less healthy!' This can ultimately be quite depressing because, instead of focusing on how well they are doing, they have to overplay how ill they feel. Some professionals equate hidden disabilities with mental health issues, or add mental health issues to the list of ME symptoms. There are a huge range of different symptoms and experiences of ME, but the professionals who stand out are the ones who take an individualized approach, and who don't make assumptions but just *ask*. Ask what the symptoms are, how they are affecting activities (including social life, sex and relationships), and how they have changed their lives. Like everyone with a hidden impairment, people welcome an individualized approach. ME is hard to understand, but those with the condition really notice the difference when they speak to a professional who has experience of other people with it, or have read up on it, and know what the symptoms are, and what the lasting impacts can be. There is a very good leaflet about disability, sex and fatigue on the SHADA website: www.shada.org.uk.

When one person in a couple wants sex more than the other, it's important that the one with lower desire is not made to feel constantly pressurized or guilty. This requires honest and open discussion, and giving the partner permission to masturbate in agreed places (separately or in the same room/bed) or even to find satisfaction elsewhere. The couple can decide to share intimate sessions of non-sexual pleasure, like listening to music, telling each other jokes, even massage or rocking in a hammock, cuddling, and so on. These sessions might include masturbation, if that is agreed.

Lack of movement which inhibits the disabled person from touching their partner

Some impairments cause a lack of movement which inhibits the disabled person from touching their partner. The partner with more mobility can assist the impaired person to put their fingers, hand or arms where the person wants them – they can help guide them to the places which feel the nicest! If they want to be more adventurous, they can try putting their hand on the handle of a sex toy such as a vibrator or electrostim toy.

Lack of movement is what the person in bondage enjoys, becoming totally dependent on the partner who bound them up, and surrendering. It is worth the disabled person without movement learning more about this pleasure. The couple could work out a system where they can become dependent on each other for totally different things during sexual fun.

An enabler, perhaps a PA, care support worker, friend or professional advocate hired in, can help prepare a person with limited movement for sex, undressing and perhaps dressing them up so they look and feel lovely. During the sex, the enabler listens to instructions, or watches and helps out when they see the couple struggling, to position and manage their bodies, inserting the penis or moving a hand or face to where required. It's good if they can leave the room when not needed, to offer a degree of privacy, staying close by on the alert for when they are next needed.

Continence

Do advise your client to make the most of their health professionals, which could include consultants, colorectal staff, urologists or continence nurses, to assist them in their bowel or bladder problems, so that they have the best possible opportunities to enjoy sex. This may include, for example, discussion with the surgeon of where a supra-pubic catheter is placed, so that it doesn't get in the way of whatever sexual practice the couple enjoys. During the consultation, discussions can inspire the couple to learn how to talk openly about urine and faeces, so that they become normalized to the concept of these bodily products simply being just part of their partners, or their own bodily functions, and not something unspeakable. Once this normalization process takes place, any accident will no longer be considered an embarrassing disaster.

Mood changes, lack of concentration

Unless there is understanding of their partner's condition, a person might easily jump to the conclusion that they are no longer loved or valued. The couple could decide on a strategy such as making efforts to bring their focus in towards each other. They could be together in a candle-lit room where romance and love are heightened, whispering sweet things to each other, staying mentally in touch and enchanted.

Breathing

Difficulties with breathing can make sex tricky. One of our Outsiders members complained that having to take her breathing machine round to a potential lover's house when she was hoping to spend the night with them, and then having to sleep with a breathing mask on, was quite a big deal. People on a ventilator need to be reassured that it's OK to have sex. If they take their face mask off, it should be kept at hand. The British Lung Foundation published a good leaflet called *Sex and Breathlessness*,[44] downloadable from their website, and my colleague Marion Maz Mason has written two books, *CPAP and Ventilator Secrets*,[45] which deals with dating and relationships, and *A Monkey, a Mouse and a CPAP Machine*[46] for children.

Amputation or destruction of the penis

Men who have had their penis removed (because of cancer or injury) usually experience their first orgasm in a wet dream, and then manage to stimulate the testicles, scrotum and the skin covering the place where the penis was removed, to enjoy pleasure and even orgasm. A sex therapist can assist by guiding the couple to come to terms with the lack of penis, and to explore ways for them to enjoy each other's bodies and orgasms. You can ensure that all this runs smoothly.

Recovering from the trauma of war and regaining intimacy

It is not just physical wounds which cause relationship difficulties. Relationships are known to be under enormous stress, because being sexual with a partner means being vulnerable, and people who have fought in wars can find that extremely difficult. Dr Mitchell Tepper has written on this subject and you can find his various resources online. *Hidden Battles on Unseen Fronts*[47] by Patricia Driscoll and Celia Straus is a book focusing on this topic.

Sharing

A couple's sex life, and their self-esteem, are boosted through talking. Talk can provide feedback for the partner to respond to, making both feel better. Communication is said to be the best lubricant. Encourage couples to find ways of communicating, perhaps using agreed signals, and see the end of Chapter 6, which deals with communication. Sharing can include saying what they like and want, describing what is happening and what they are feeling, showing off their bodies, swapping fantasies and playing games to enact them, or reading or listening to erotic stories.

It may be good to remind a couple who have not explored or shared their fantasy life that having a fantasy about doing something doesn't mean they want it to happen in reality. You could suggest that they look upon sex as play, allowing themselves to laugh, maybe wear clothes they find exciting, and generally let their childish inner selves out. This can bring a new kind of honesty and closeness.

Some disabled people with a progressive condition are afraid of telling their partner about new symptoms, fearing it might be the last straw for them in the relationship. But it is essential for a good relationship to share thoughts, fears, feelings and fantasies with one's partner.

If one person in a couple wants to talk about sex, and their partner does not, this is likely to send them into a shell of gloom, especially if the person who wants to communicate has a speech impairment. You or a sex therapist may be able to support them to move forward.

The book, mentioned before, *Exhibitionism for the Shy*[24] by Carol Queen, offers plenty of ideas for sharing in sex. The content is much wider than exhibitionism.

Relationships can be enhanced by open and honest chats, fun and laughter, time taken to work things out and leaving prudery and limited thinking about sex behind.

Resources

1. Sex and Disability Helpline FAQ: www.outsiders.org.uk/helpline.html
2. Dodson and Ross: www.dodsonandross.com.
3. Naphtali, K., MacHattie, E. and Elliot, S.L. (2009) *Pleasure Able – Sexual Device Manual for Persons with Disabilities.* Disabilities Health Research Network. Available at www.dhrn.ca/files/sexualhealthmanual_lowres_2010_0208.pdf, accessed on 8 July 2014.
4. Ferticare: www.medicalvibrator.com/id69.html.
5. Dr Stacy Elliot, Broadened Horizons: www.broadenedhorizons.com/independent-living/sexuality.
6. The Foreskin, Circumcision and Sexuality: www.circumstitions.com/Sexuality.html#sorrells.
7. NRS The Hold-It® Book Holder & Writing/Laptop Stand: www.thinkinggifts.com/mall/productpage.cfm/ThinkingGifts/_THI1/%2D/the%20Hold%2Dit.
8. Humpus: www.humpus.com.
9. Venus 2000: www.venusformen.com.
10. Spokz: info@spokz.co.uk, www.spokz.co.uk.
11. MA Guide: http://ilc.com.au/resources/2/0000/0030/the_ma_guide.pdf.
12. Immune Web – Support and Information Network: www.immuneweb.org.
13. Sexability: www.Sexability.org.
14. Nelson, S.C. (2013, 22 April) 'Rafe Biggs, quadriplegic learns to orgasm through his thumb.' *Huffington Post.* Available at www.huffingtonpost.co.uk/2013/04/22/rafe-biggs-quadriplegic-orgasm-thumb-pictures_n_3130545.html, accessed on 8 July 2014.
15. Examiner.com (2011, 17 August) *Orgasms and the Vagus Nerve.* Available at www.examiner.com/article/orgasm-and-the-vagus-nerve, accessed on 8 July 2014.
16. Chia, M. (2014) *Inner Alchemy Formula – Primordial Force.* Available at http://mantakchia.com/inner-alchemy-formula-1-primordial-force, accessed on 8 July 2014.
17. Carrellas, B. (2013) *How To Have a Breath and Energy Orgasm (aka Thinking Off).* Available at www.youtube.com/watch?v=OEznv88LfbY, accessed on 8 July 2014.
18. Mitchell Tepper: www.mitchelltepper.com.
19. Channelled Bliss: www.channelledbliss.com.
20. Litten, H. and Shows, R.J. (1996) *More Joy – An Advanced Guide to Solo Sex.* Mobile, AL: Factor Press.
21. Zilbergeld, B. (1992) *The New Male Sexuality.* London, UK: Bantam Books
22. Dodson, B. (1987) *Sex for One.* New York, NY: Harmony Books.
23. Heart, M. (2004) *The Ultimate Guide to Orgasm for Women.* San Francisco, CA: Cleis Press.
24. Queen, C. (2009) *Exhibitionism for the Shy.* San Francisco, CA: Down There Press.

25. Ruth Madison: www.ruthmadison.com.

26. Paradevo: www.Paradevo.net.

27. Phillips, A. (2008, 15 January) 'Asperger's therapy hits second life.' *abc News.* Available at abcnews.go.com/Technology/OnCall/story?id=4133184, accessed on 8 July 2014.

28. Silverberg, C. (2010) *Bowel and Bladder Control During Sex.* Available at http://sexuality.about.com/od/sex_and_disability/a/Bowel-And-Bladder-Control-During-Sex.htm, accessed on 8 July 2014.

29. Norton, C., Saltmarche, A., Klein, M.R. and Gartley, C. (eds) (2012) *Managing Life with Incontinence.* Chicago, IL: Simon Foundation. Available at www.managinglifewithincontinence.org, accessed on 8 July 2014.

30. Motor Neurone Disease Association (2014) *Sex and Relationships: For people living with MND.* Information Sheet 20A. Available at www.mndassociation.org/Resources/MNDA/Life%20with%20MND/Information%20sheet%2020A%20-%20Sex%20and%20relationships%20for%20people%20living%20with%20MND.pdf, accessed on 8 July 2014.

31. CalmClinic (n.d.) *10 Tips for Finding Love and Dating With Social Anxiety.* Available at http://www.calmclinic.com/social-anxiety/dating, accessed on 8 July 2014.

32. Online Dating Experts: www.onlinedatingexperts.co.uk.

33. 2date4love: www.2date4love.com.

34. Stars in the Sky: www.starsinthesky.co.uk.

35. Beautiful Octopus: www.heartnsoul.co.uk/category/taking_part/details/beautiful octopusclub.

36. Griffin, J. (2011) *The Lonely Society?* London, UK: Mental Health Foundation. Available at www.mentalhealth.org.uk/publications/the-lonely-society, accessed on 8 July 2014.

37. Quilliam, S. (2008) *The New Joy of Sex.* London, UK: Octopus.

38. Silver Sex: www.silversex.net.

39. Streets, G. (2012) *Wheelchair Sex, Love and Intimacy After Spinal Cord Injury.* Available at www.streetsie.com/spinal-injury-wheelchair-sex, accessed on 8 July 2014.

40. Literotica: www.literotica.com.

41. For Your Ears Only: www.foryourearsonly.nl.

42. Miller, H. (1939) *Tropic of Capricorn.* London, UK: Caulder and Boyars; New York, NY: Grove Press.

43. Aston, M. (2012) 'Asperger's syndrome in the bedroom.' *Sexual and Relationship Therapy: International Perspectives on Theory, Research and Practice 27,* 1, 73–79. Available at www.maxineaston.co.uk/published/AS_in_the_Bedroom.shtml, accessed on 8 July 2014.

44. British Lung Foundation (n.d.) *Sex and Breathlessness.* Available at www.blf.org.uk/Page/Sex-and-breathlessness, accessed on 8 July 2014.

45. Mason, M.M. and Mason, S. (2011) *CPAP and Ventilator Secrets.* Available at www.asIliveandbreathe.co.uk, accessed on 8 July 2014.

46. Mason, M.M. and Mason, S. (2011) *A Monkey, a Mouse and a CPAP Machine.* Available at asIliveandbreathe.co.uk, accessed on 8 July 2014.

47. Driscoll, P. and Straus, C. (2009) *Hidden Battles on Unseen Fronts.* Drexel Hill, PA: Casemate.

CHAPTER 3

DIFFICULTIES THAT HEALTH AND SOCIAL CARE PROFESSIONALS EXPERIENCE

'One healthcare professional told me I was one of the unfortunates who would never be able to experience sex because of my disability, and to forget my feelings. I'm feeling like I'm the only one. Is there anybody who can advise me? Please help.'

This email came in 2013 on the Sex and Disability Helpline from Martin, a 55-year-old man with cerebral palsy who cannot masturbate, and had never had an orgasm. I would like to think that this chapter will ensure that I never receive such a message again, as it's too shocking for words. I hope I bring fresh light and inspiration, to you and to those who work with you, so that disabled people will never again suffer such indignity.

As Claire de Than points out in her chapter on the law (Chapter 4), it is illegal in Britain NOT to provide support for disabled adults to enjoy sexual expression.

Professionals working with some specific impairments may already be including support with disabled people's sexuality. People with spinal injury, MS, motor neurone disease and stroke are more likely to be supported. However, those with congenital and hidden impairments are often not so lucky.

There is a strong tradition of training all those who support learning disabled people to include sexuality in their care which resulted, I suspect, from the fact that learning disabled people may display sexual behaviour in socially unacceptable ways. However, people with physical, sensory and social impairments and neuro-diversity are not so well catered for, and can be left to their own devices.

As practitioners, you may feel unsupported because there is no policy and guidance document drawn up by your governing bodies, and you may have received no special training. You need to challenge this.

When your professional training includes disability and sexuality, you feel empowered by having been given permission to ask patients and clients about their sex lives, and to discuss how, for example, an imminent operation or procedure may affect them sexually. You won't feel alone in this work, and you'll know you can legitimately discuss it with colleagues.

If you work in an environment where sex, especially in relation to disability, is never mentioned except in a negative way (in terms of abuse and danger), you may well be made to feel that the subject does not belong in the remit of your work. Deep down, though, you may know this is wrong. Those who feel it most may decide to include sex in their work, but feel isolated and probably very cautious. That is why the Sexual Respect Tool Kit,[1] the Sexual Health and Disability Alliance (SHADA)[2] and this book are so important.

Where different professions work together as a multidisciplinary team under one roof, you can work out a system together whereby disabled clients have the opportunity to discuss sex and enjoy ongoing support. But when your colleagues work in different places and not as a team, it is not so easy, and sometimes everybody assumes someone else is taking responsibility for the sexual side of clients' lives.

In this chapter, I outline the professional difficulties which I have become aware of, which I hope coincide with your experiences. I then offer suggestions on how you might be able to overcome them. This is followed by a look at some of the ways in which some disabled people themselves may make it difficult for you, and how to cope with that.

I then mention impairments and problems which I have found my own unique ways for disabled people to deal with. These include those impairments which are often ignored in texts on sex and disability, and those which seem to be particularly challenging. Finally I offer some examples of good and poor practice.

Professional difficulties which you may be experiencing
Academic professionalism
There has been a tendency for professionals, academics and officials in charge of governmental bodies to promote a complicated web of problems and difficulties to confuse and delay actually supporting disabled people to enjoy what they want sexually. Whenever I hear someone say, 'It's complicated', I sometimes suspect they are trying to keep themselves in work rather than trying to untangle this web and find a way forward.

Such professionals tend to talk in a language which makes it inaccessible to most people who work on a practical level with disabled people, whilst giving out the impression that they know what they are talking about much better than anyone else (when they don't). I still go to conferences on sex and disability where highly paid academics tell the delegates that prostitution is illegal in Britain (whereas it never has been). I've been told on the helpline that they are not allowed to recommend their NHS clients to see sex workers, which is nonsense.

It's time to get down to earth. I hope this book and its resources are accessible to you, and will help you.

State, regulatory bodies and institutional control
Care homes where staff really want to focus on person-centred care are being blighted by inspections from both the Care Quality Commission (CQC) and social services, who are working to different criteria. The result has been that nobody wants to take responsibility for person-centred care, within which sexuality is a key part.

I have had first-hand experience of the CQC. SHADA received an email from them to tell us that it is not responsible for the sexual aspects of care! At a residential establishment for young people, the CQC recommended that all residents should have single rooms and so the home converted *most* of the rooms, but thankfully had the wisdom to leave some larger rooms intact, which means that they still have some available for couples or mates who want to share.

At another specialist college in the West Midlands, both the local inspector and the regional standards inspector at the CQC looked at their policy, and at the agreement they had with a particular student that he would have a willing member of staff place a vibrating sex toy on his penis to enable him to enjoy an orgasm. Both the CQC officials were happy with what the college were doing and how they were doing it. However, the college never received this in writing from them, despite trying on a number of occasions!

Compulsory training is now in place, which is pushing care homes into a liability and blame culture. Much good work has been lost due to the negative effect of the widely publicized abuse at the Winterbourne View Hospital. This negativity in the health industry is having a profound effect on the people who use its services and those that work in it. A new strategy is urgently needed where all forms of person-centred care can blossom. Strategies are discussed in the paper *Sexuality in the nursing home.*[3]

In 2010 Outsiders,[4] together with the TLC Trust,[5] sent out a Freedom of Information Request to 206 local authorities responsible for adult social services. Of these, 121 submitted a return, 47 per cent of which said they did not explicitly empower disabled men and women to make informed choices and to be at liberty to pursue their sexual aspirations. However, 72 per cent were on record as supporting the rights of disabled people to develop and maintain social, personal and/or sexual relationships, based on the recognition of their human rights. Only 4 per cent condoned the use of sex workers by disabled men and women. Nearly 80 per cent – four out of five – were totally against such use, with 17.5 per cent expressing themselves as neutral on the subject. In their answers, many of those who were against it said that they would not condone the hiring of sex workers because they believed it to be unsavoury and/or illegal. Again, this belief about illegality is totally mistaken about the law in the UK.

Only 3.3 per cent of authorities said they would permit disabled men and women to use funds channelled through local authorities to purchase sexual services; and the same proportion had policies dealing with the matter. We intend to send out a similar survey in 2015 to see if things have improved. The TLC Trust has had experiences of social services forcing the cancellation of appointments with sex workers made by disabled people in their area, often at the last minute, and forbidding staff to open the door to them. Some disabled people have got around this by hiring an independent advocate to open the door!

At SHADA, we work together to challenge negativity. Our multidisciplinary team, including lawyers, discuss issues and create strategy. Then we aim to present the strategy to those who need to hear it.

Giving both men and women the attention and support they deserve

Disabled men are generally more forthcoming and vocal than women about stating their sexual needs, and this probably explains why more research and attention has been paid to them. Men do have a penis (usually) which itself commands their attention, whereas women's genitals are more hidden away. Certainly, I get more calls on the helpline from men. Men are also usually easier to support, as they tend to be eager to learn and solve their problems.

Some disabled women say they feel they are not as attractive as other women in the conventional sense, so they abandon convention. As a result, they do seem to be more likely than men to want to enjoy sex in less conventional ways, while men can remain obsessed with having an erection and being able to enjoy intercourse. Women might welcome less focus on intercourse, and more on their clitoris, breasts and entire selves. Some men on our helpline say their female partners complain that the man cannot reach orgasm inside the vagina – men who masturbate with a tight fist may have this problem. The woman may find this an insult, or miss the mini-high they get from the mood-elevating compounds in semen. I suggest the man tries to masturbate then quickly enter.

All of us need to be certain that we don't shy away from asking both genders the same or similar questions. I guess most people feel women might be more likely to be offended, and men are less likely to be too shy to talk about themselves. In reality, both genders can be aggressively sexually demanding, or timid and compliant.

We should never make any assumption that one gender or the other can sort themselves out, or that they don't deserve support. In one Outsiders workshop, two men described how care staff had warned the disabled women in their residential home against mixing with the men! Radical feminists have accused me of encouraging disabled men to behave as badly as non-disabled men! Always double-check with yourself that you are not making assumptions about gender, orientation or sexual preferences.

Personally, I feel that disabled men – both heterosexual and gay – have a much rougher deal than women when it comes to finding a partner, but others say it's the other way round. Both men and women may struggle.

Balancing the rights of disabled clients and your own rights

Let us begin by establishing two important points:

1. You do not have the right to inflict your own moral beliefs on your clients by attempting to censor their sexual self-expression. All such values and beliefs must be left at home and not brought into the workplace.

2. If you say to your colleagues, employer, or consultant that you simply cannot deal with supporting your disabled clients in their sexual expression, this gives them the chance to make other arrangements for this aspect of their care or (if you are employed) to dismiss you. British law has changed recently to rule that dismissal needs no compensation if it is easy for the individual to get another job in the area, and employers must ensure that the rights of disabled clients are upheld.[a] As long as an employer has a clear policy based on human rights and has weighed up the rights of everyone involved, an employee who disagrees with it only has the right to resign. A religious or personal belief also cannot be used to justify discrimination.

Too many disabled people are denied their sexual expression. In 2013, one helpline caller complained that her staff didn't want one of the female residents with no bodily movement to own a vibrator because the staff would have to clean up afterwards! It is true that a small proportion of women ejaculate, but this ejaculate does not contain anything like the germs in excreta, and the staff can use rubber gloves. I urge managers to be more assertive.

I have listened to a healthcare professional working within a council disability unit telling me that the objection made to his proposal to start social opportunities for disabled people to meet up with each other to find partners is that 'we need to be inclusive'. This is taking the idea of inclusivity to a level of ridiculous political correctness, and I'm sure they don't apply the same argument to social groups for older people and children.

---

a.   *Eweida and others v UK*, European Court of Human Rights, 15/1/2013. The Court rejected three cases of discrimination brought by people claiming that their religious beliefs prevented them from complying with their employer's policies. The Court stated that they rejected the claims because the employers' policies '*aimed to secure the rights of others which are also protected under the Convention*'.

Balancing rights and safety

It is important to balance the safety and protection of your disabled clients with their rights to enjoy sex.

Claire de Than, criminal rights and human rights lawyer at City University (who has helped me with this book, and written the chapter on the law), has adopted a 'Rights not Safety' approach. For too long, disabled people have been protected against perceived exploitation and the dangers of dating and sexual abuse rather than being encouraged to go out and take risks, enjoy their bodies, explore sex and find love. In order to allow such freedoms, you need a good working relationship with your service users, because they do indeed need to feel safe. You need a safe way of dealing with the intimate aspects of personal care. Boundaries need to be clear, and both parties need to feel comfortable sharing intimate information before you can proceed.

In preparation for their first meeting with a client, a care support worker or PA can introduce themselves to the client by sharing their basic personal information with the client. This includes facts such as their sexual orientation, and whether they are partnered or not, and that can be followed up with an invitation for them to swap notes. This way, both can relax and feel there is an honesty and openness between them. Neither will be suspicious or make false assumptions which can make the client feel inhibited or unsafe. Everyone knows where they are. Then the care support worker or PA can reassure the client that they can be supported in their sexual expression, whatever their needs, whenever they ask. This must not, of course, include sexual touching. See the Canadian research on this in *Sexuality and Access Project.*[6]

If clients have difficulty expressing their intimate needs to a particular member of staff, they should, if possible, be given the choice of selecting another member of staff, and of not discussing at all any things which they do not want to share. Your aim is to work side-by-side in harmony, so that you go home satisfied, knowing you have done your best to ensure that your client lives as full a life as they wish; and that they feel well supported without their privacy having been invaded more than necessary.

In practice, there will always be some care staff and PAs who are the obvious person for the disabled person to choose, because they are relaxed about discussing sex openly and are easy to confide in. Often, a client will select one of their PAs, maybe the same one who takes them out to places where they have fun, just like they may select best cooks to cook their food, for example.

I have learned much from Asger Persson, who started Handisex in Denmark providing a masturbation service, using vibrators, for disabled people unable to masturbate. Basically, he fixes the vibration machine in place, leaves the room, and comes back to clear and tidy up. He also teaches learning disabled people how to masturbate, using his hands on their hands. Asger says that it doesn't matter if either party in the work finds the other attractive, or doesn't fancy them, or feels a special bond with them, or doesn't, because the boundaries set out are clear and are adhered to, and nobody need feel worried about exploitation, abuse or malpractice.

Asger makes it doubly clear about stating his intentions and boundaries; he always asks for each client's boundaries to be made clear to them, and makes sure that they have consented. The more hands-on his work, the more consent he needs; he may get his client's PA to also sign the consent document, which outlines what will happen during the session.

I am bringing this up here to prove to you that you can operate without any troubles if you take simple precautions: ensuring that there is total consent, with the boundaries worked out, written down and clearly in place.

Writing policies and guidelines, and putting them into practice

Basic policy templates on sexuality and disability have been written and are available on the SHADA website.[2] However, it is important that you write your own policy, so that it suits your needs and the needs of your client group. Both the clients and the staff involved will feel empowered that they have been consulted, and feel ownership, thus wanting to work within that policy. First, you need to speak to your client group to be certain of their needs. Then you need to take this to the staff and work out how they can best support those needs. Research and work may have to be done before you can everything drafted out, before a final document is being passed and put into practice. Regular checks should be made to ensure that the current service users are having their needs addressed.

Within the policy, you need guidelines for staff dealing with each aspect of personal care, such as dealing with erections, requests for private time in their rooms for masturbation or just to be naked and explore their bodies, and support with masturbation when necessary.

Guidelines need to give clear advice on maintaining professional boundaries, dealing sensitively with the client and treating sexuality as normal and natural. You can advise staff to call on someone more experienced to help and advise, if ever they are unsure of anything. Of course, it is important for them to know who those experienced staff are. Care workers need specialist training on the right way to carry out intimate care, in the most positive, respectful way, which empowers clients as much as possible.

Health professionals who go into the homes of disabled individuals need to have their behavioural (including sexual) boundaries written into their employment policy (this is in the codes of practice and professional standards as well as criminal law). They may need to explain to their clients that, however much they may enjoy the professional's visits, they must refrain from showing too much affection or be sexually demanding. When the client is sexually frustrated, the professional could discuss and support the client to use a sexual service.

Approval of policies may take a long time, and governing bodies should be advised that modern-day care needs to include sexuality to comply with the law. Serious objections must be met with strong legal and humanitarian responses. It is just not fair on disabled people coming to a hospice, for example, to be denied their rights. They may be accustomed to waiting, but not really eager about waiting to experience sexual pleasure until after they are dead! Providing a 'private' or 'privacy' room for sexual encounters, set away from the residential area, should be standard practice. Romantic or erotic décor, candles or low lights, for example, can be kept in a cupboard and put in place as and when required.

The most difficult thing of all, it seems, even when the policy has been passed by the board, is watching all the good work you have done being side-stepped, with excuses and other priorities getting in the way. You may have to continue to put your case forward for the rights of your clients. Policies must be kept alive, put into practice, and discussed at intervals. Put this on the agenda for every meeting!

Including sexuality in assessments

Indeed, it should be in all policies that sexuality be written into assessments. Some disabled people just never get asked about their personal happiness, I am told. They feel let down when they have to trudge through a boring list of questions on topics which have much less impact on their lives. Obviously, it would take a brave soul to interrupt, and ask, 'Hang on, what about my failing sex life?' Even if their sex lives are going well and you are short of time, sex belongs on the list and should not be left out. Asking the question won't 'open a can of worms' but simply provides a chance for the patient or client to mention difficulties and worries, and they will feel that the whole of them is at last being listened to.

You, yourself, may not be in the right 'head-space'

None of us always feels sexually confident or open. You may be going through a difficult marriage or divorce, may be experiencing sexual problems of your own, and feel quite fragile in this area. It's important to admit to colleagues if you just don't feel up to dealing with clients' sexual needs right now. Only start again when you are ready.

Various problems met when supporting disabled people with their sexual needs

Providing better sex and relationship education

I have discussed this with many different disabled people and they all feel their sex and relationship education was worse than useless. One 20-year-old recently expressed the view that a sex worker who sees disabled clients would make the best teacher, for only they know. I can see that this would never be accepted, but what is worth considering is opening up to provide the kind of sex education which the pupils say they want, and find the best people to provide it. You can then create a team around you, consisting perhaps of a qualified teacher, a sex therapist, a sex worker experienced in seeing disabled clients, and a parent who feels comfortable talking about the subject. The team could look at the student's needs and decide how to work together.

Respecting cultural and religious differences

Sometimes staff are selected to reflect the cultural and religious diversity of the clients. This may be advantageous so long as they, like other staff, agree to leave their sexual beliefs and views at home, so that they can provide the same appropriate support for their clients in relation to sexuality. Sexuality is universal, and does not vary across different cultures or religions (apart from levels of guilt and acceptance). Yet religion can have an enormous influence on views and morality, and can have a devastatingly negative effect on disabled people's ability feel positive about all their desires. Things like discussing sex, masturbation, sex education, sex out of marriage, open relationships and gay sex may be demonized and this is neither tolerant nor helpful.

Unless you treat all disabled people the same, you can face disaster. Suppose, for example, that a young disabled person from a culture where sex is not allowed before marriage is banned from having sex education, and is then discovered having unprotected intercourse with another disabled student. This could lead to pregnancy, or to sexually transmitted infection. The difficulty can sometimes be calmed by talking to the students and the parents in a positive, supportive way, so that sensible contraceptive advice and safe sex education can take place, but such a situation could have been avoided with safer sex education being given as part of health education.

I'd like to quote my colleague, a Canadian healthcare ethicist, Kevin Reel, who says:

> For me as a healthcare ethicist, sexuality offers an ever wonderful teaching tool – it is so mixed up with personal mores that it illustrates client-centred professionalism really well – how do you set aside your own morals and work with the values and beliefs of your client, even if they might cause some level of affront to your own sensibilities? If people actually grapple with that, they get some deep-seated ethical reflection going on.

Clients with mild and hidden disabilities

Some people with mild disabilities may live their lives feeling that they 'pass' as able-bodied, and so may pretend that everything is all right. You may, therefore, not know that their impairments are actually causing serious problems, including sexual ones. Ask everyone, listen, and take everyone seriously.

Somebody with ME, for example, may look able-bodied but their life may be more impaired than that of a wheelchair user, who may be able to enjoy sex at any time, for as long as they like, as energetically as they want. The person with ME may need to pace themselves and take it easy, or may even feel too fatigued to enjoy any sexual activity at all, for a while. I have listened to such people saying how difficult it is for them to start sexual relationships, and to find the right person to have a relationship with. Be sure to listen, consider and apply your particular wisdom carefully with all the clients you see, without making any assumptions from the way they look.

Supporting newly disabled people to adapt

Spinal injuries units are realizing that sexual function is one of the things many people worry about when they first come round from their accident or operation. Conversations about sexuality need to start whenever the client is ready, which may be from the very beginning. Units are now ensuring that patients are supported in adapting their sex lives accordingly.

War-injured personnel are supported by Ministry of Defence casualty key workers. As well as having their genitals blown off along with their legs, some military personnel return from conflicts with visual, auditory and other sensory impairments, disfigurement, stomas, and many emotional problems. Many are young, and perhaps with young children and a wife who is proud of them, but still many may struggle to keep a sex life going. *The Ultimate Guide to Sex and Disability*[7] provides inspiration for changing attitudes to sex.

The other thing that can happen to suddenly change a person's sexual life is a stroke. Fortunately, couples are, I hear, being allowed to spend the night together if they wish before the patient leaves hospital. The patient needs to be asked if they have sexual worries or questions. Those who are single, or left on their own, perhaps unable to speak, may feel stranded; I have always thought how great it would be to bring a professional masseur, escort or surrogate to communicate with them physically.

Other disabled people may not be hospitalized when they become impaired, so they may be out on their own. For example, people who lose their sight, hearing or mobility may feel terribly stressed and depressed, and the loss will more than likely totally change the balance of their sexual and whole relationship with a partner. It may scare off friends. There needs to be good local support from social services to refer newly disabled people to specialist support agencies such as the RNIB, who can listen to what is happening in their private lives, and offer support. The partner having to become a carer, even for a short while, can find that this blurs their role as lover; and when there is no partner, and friends desert them, the patient needs clubs such as Outsiders for peer support and friendship.

Supporting clients to be in touch with their own bodies

Pioneers agree that all physically and learning disabled people need good quality mirrors in bathrooms and bedrooms, so that they get to see their own bodies. Once mirrors are installed, staff can empower clients to ask about their bodies, and to welcome dialogue. This can happen during washing and changing clothes, and be very constructive. Providing a water bed for disabled people to enjoy together can help them learn. There are professionals called body workers who help people discover pleasure in their bodies, and their role is discussed in Chapter 8 on sexual services.

Supporting people who cannot masturbate themselves for physical reasons

Methods for doing this were outlined in the previous chapter but here I want to talk about other practicalities. A willing member of staff might need to place a sex toy on a penis or clitoris, turn it on, then leave the room, return after the orgasms have finished and tidy up. Some residences may feel that this is beyond the remit of their staff, but it would be more inconvenient and expensive to bring someone in from elsewhere to support the individual just for this activity. So long as confidentiality, consent and boundaries are discussed, and agreements are written up, using willing staff is really the best way forward. If you purchase a Hold-It,[8] the sex toy could be clamped on and held in position, rather than being more precariously stuffed inside the client's pants.

Care workers are allowed to do this within some policies, and forbidden in others. Staff who don't want to do it should not, as others won't mind. It is not 'touching in a sexual way', and is probably less intimate than washing the genitals. If you need to put a client's erect penis inside the sex toy, and it is too flaccid, putting lubricant on with a firm hand may make it sufficiently tumescent. Don't worry if you find the process slightly arousing yourself – this is normal and doesn't mean you are gay (if you are male), or fancy your client, or anything untoward. It may also bring up other strange emotions, and you can discuss these in confidence with a colleague, if it helps.

Sometimes, vibrations can numb rather than stimulate the clitoris or penis. If this happens, either the toy needs to be on a lower setting, or you need to place padding around the vibrator. Remote controls which the client can operate are ideal.

Teaching people how to masturbate

With people with learning difficulties, you may need first of all to teach them about what a *private* place is, and that they must only masturbate in such a place, not in public. A one-off chat isn't usually enough, and you may have to use a variety of methods to ensure that they remember. These could include role play, and anatomically correct models. The DVD called *You, Your Body and Sex*[9] deals with masturbation and privacy; it is animated, and usefully explicit. But if the service user cannot concentrate on films, a sex worker could be brought in to teach. This is discussed in Chapters 2 and 8.

Models and pictures of genitals can show them how and where fingering and vibrators can be used. Clear drawings to help learning disabled people to learn about masturbation and sexual anatomy can be found in the pack *Sex and the 3 Rs: Rights, Responsibilities and Risks*.[10] You can encourage erotic fantasy by discussing what kind of erotic images (stills and moving) of men, women, couples and various diversities appeal to them and might turn them on. Tell them, at all times, that they must say if they don't feel good about discussion, if it's not working for them, or if they have any other problems or worries about it. Those who work at Brook[11] are trained in educating disabled people under 25 on sexual matters, so do use them if you need to. The Family Planning Association, fpa,[12] also runs educational training.

Washing

Men with foreskins need to have them retracted in order to clean behind them, and the same goes for clitoral hoods. If a disabled person becomes erect or sexually excited whilst being washed, it is best if the care worker tells them that they will be left alone for a while, so they can have some quiet time to masturbate and/or calm down. If it is unsafe to leave them, the carer can stand just outside the door so the disabled person is not obviously being watched. There will be some members of staff who are not comfortable with this – another member of staff who is comfortable with it can take over. If you are a care worker in your client's home, you may have little choice, but it's obviously better to be able to joke about it than to suffer in silence or berate the client for getting excited.

Disabled clients fancying care staff or getting a crush on them

When a client's sexual desire is focused on a member of staff (who is not interested), just being around each other can feel very uncomfortable. The client may not understand why love can't happen, and get confused and upset. The way to try and overcome this problem is to keep talking and explaining to the client the reasons why. If feelings become overwhelming (or mutual), there should be a change in care staff.

Fear of scandal

The fear of creating a scandal over disabled people having sex, especially with sex workers, in your place of work is sometimes a big deterrent, especially for trustees who are responsible for funding. However, please believe me, as someone who was caught up in the 'sex workers working in a care home' scandal of 2012, both the press and the public, even in Northern Ireland, were on the side of disabled people being allowed to enjoy themselves as they choose. Indeed, now two years later, I am supporting Channel 4 News on a feature exposing care homes for *not* allowing their disabled residents to enjoy sexual expression, including with sex workers!

Supporting clients with dating

You may feel ill-equipped supporting disabled clients with online dating, in that everybody is struggling with understanding how best to use it. People still don't understand the etiquette required to make it work happily. For example, individuals might send intimate messages to many potential lovers and then suddenly cut out all of them except their chosen one, leaving the others feeling deserted and let down. If you want to learn more, look at Online Dating Experts[13] to feel better empowered. One very useful tip on this website is that everybody should find a buddy to support them through the process. I have always advised Outsiders members to do this. Perhaps you could support your clients to find a buddy, or become the buddy yourself.

Juggling relatives, trustees, and everyone!

As you may know, relatives of people can take objection to their son or daughter, no matter how old, having sex with a sex worker in their care home. Legal advice is to have 'freedom of sexual expression' written into the contract which the relative signs before the individual is admitted into the home. This can be explained so that relatives cannot object.

The board of trustees, other residents and everyone else involved in your residence or place of work need to understand the importance of the legal duty of care to support disabled residents in enjoying the same pleasures as other people enjoy in the privacy of their own homes.

Supporting disabled clients to make big decisions

Disabled people may wish to discuss all kinds of options to improve their sexual lives. For example, they may want to move out of their parents' house, but be afraid of becoming lonely. Some settle for moving out to a house or flat that is close by to their parents, and some do a house or flat-share. Some join clubs, to surround themselves with new friends, before leaving home. You can support your client to list the pros and cons for each of these options, and act as a sounding board.

Another more sex-focused example is where a client has insufficient knowledge and confidence to decide whether to listen to a doctor who is willing to prescribe pills or surgical procedures to fix sexual *function*, or else listen to the therapist who advocates simply adapting sexual *practices* to enjoy themselves. My view, as a therapist, is this. A man who cannot feel his penis or get an erection is better off seeing a therapist than having to take a pill every time he wants to have an erection. A couple is better off enjoying non-penetrative sex and the stimulation of the parts of their bodies which can enjoy sensation, rather than the man having a prosthesis or taking medication for the rest of his life. Of course, it might not be an either/or situation, and has to be the client's own choice.

Disabled people making it difficult for you
Lethargy
I have heard many complaints about an increasing lethargy amongst disabled people. It is difficult when you prepare to support them in their sexual expression, and they don't show much interest or want to make any effort. Not having a sex life at all, maybe not even being able to self-pleasure, can make a person very depressed – sometimes

too depressed to masturbate. If the disabled person sees no hope of improvement, they may live with this depression as the norm, and turn in on themselves. No wonder some seem lethargic! They may have found ways to shut down their sexual urges so as not to get frantically frustrated. It is not healthy to live like this.

One of the best ways of lifting them out of the gloom is to find someone who has been in that position but managed to climb out of it, and ask them to have a chat.

When I spoke at the AGM of the charity ASBAH (the Association for Spina Bifida and Hydrocephalus), now called Shine, I was told that, for many of their clients, joining Outsiders was too big a step. Some people with spina bifida can lead really sheltered lives at home with their parents, where they have been kept child-like and perhaps made to feel bad about their continence issues, with zero sexual confidence.

I hope that the internet will eventually bring even the most impaired disabled people towards enjoying friendship, peer support and opportunities to find sexual pleasure, and love. Now that Outsiders functions online, I hope we will seem less of a challenge to shy and inexperienced disabled people.

What can you do? Slowly, slowly, find ways to introduce the idea of sexual pleasure to your clients – perhaps offer to put striptease on the agenda of possible entertainment. Both men and women can enjoy watching a female striptease artist – it is aspirational, rather like ballet. Striptease works like magic for waking people up to erotic pleasure! More about this is written in Chapter 8 on sexual services.

Other ideas are workshops around sexuality, dressing up sessions, and sexual education film nights; you could offer some options while empowering service users to make their own suggestions and decisions.

Passivity

People living with complex support needs may tend to be passive, as they may live in a world where things have been brought to them rather than the other way round. When they become adult, many health professionals feel they must wait for such people to ask for sexual experiences. Why is sexuality so different from other activities? There are gentle ways to bring a sexual and sensual awareness into their lives. You can spark things off by asking questions such as what kind of person they find attractive, or how they enjoy various erotic sensations such as the touch of various materials or the aromas around them. Discussing experiences and feelings in their own bodies could also help to open them up. From the expressions on their faces, pleasure can be measured. If you make it fun for you both, they will feel encouraged and happy, perhaps stepping out of their passivity.

Passivity also comes from being treated as powerless. Just by taking this individual seriously, empowering them by offering choices and opportunities, and by treating them as sexual beings, you can help to dig them out of this hole. It may start with a wink to say that you can imagine what they are thinking, and lead on to being jovial while asking questions, coaxing answers out of them, and supporting them in their dreams.

In order to get disabled people to open up, they need to trust you and your claims of confidentiality, so spend time just listening. Ask them if they would like to discuss sex with other similarly disabled people in the same age group.

I have found that some disabled people enjoy the chance to articulate their sexual situation in interviews for research, because it gives them a sense of being useful. So, when a disabled person clams up, you can say how useful it would be for you to learn more, so as to understand what is going on inside their head. Explain that the more people tell their story, the more the world can obtain a total picture of the joys and sorrows of how it feels for a disabled person to be alive.

If you can teach disabled people to enjoy their differences, instead of always feeling second-class and no good, then this positivity may change the way they interact with the world.

Role models are few and far between, but there are some. Mat Fraser must be at the top of the list. Impaired by the effects of thalidomide, he has at last begun to love his short arms. This has all come about by becoming a drummer, learning martial arts, being photographed by Ashley Savage (see Chapter 7) in sexy pictures, presenting shows, developing his own hilarious striptease which includes stripping off a pair of false arms, and marrying New York's top striptease artist! What a journey, portrayed in a theatre production called *Beauty and the Beast!* Mat also flies around the world to train aspiring disabled actors and presenters.

Loree Erickson is a young wheelchair-using lesbian in Canada, who made a film, *Want,* about her disability and sex life. She has a niche following. Role models could be a topic which young disabled people may benefit from discussing.

Disabled people who have no idea, or are unable to articulate, what their sexual needs are

When I talked to staff working in a hospice, they complained about this. They said that some residents were totally unable to state what they wanted sexually. You could ask them to describe their yearnings for a partner, their ambitions and dreams.

If they haven't already done so, perhaps you could encourage them to explore sites and blogs on the internet, including those written by disabled people, to read about their sexual realities (rather than look at porn, which is about fantasy). They could look at the work of Mitchell Tepper[14] and Kirsty Liddiard, and websites such as Accessible Sexuality,[15] Andrew Morrison-Gurza (disabled gay men),[16] Marius Sucan (Romanian campaigner for sexual freedom for disabled people),[17] *Sexuality and Disability* (written by disabled women in India)[18] and Disability Horizons,[19] which has articles about sex and sexuality and disability by disabled writers. I've also always liked the Mad Spaz Club.[20]

Angry and aggressive disabled people

Clients and patients may be angry because they feel let down by never being taken seriously on adult matters, and don't expect you to take them seriously either. They may be very independent individuals who may be in disability rights movements or radical political groups. You may need to earn their trust and respect, by being warm, showing interest in their happiness, without being patronizing, and asking questions in an unhurried fashion. You can say that you understand their anger and hostility and say you would feel the same if your feelings had been ignored.

They may welcome alternatives such as peer support, which they might like to organize themselves, and you could offer to support them to do this. You can also tell them that they can ask you any time in the future for support they feel they need from you.

Disabled people being obsessed with porn

The best way I have found with supporting disabled people who have such a problem is suggesting that they take some control over it by writing their own sexy stories, and perhaps publishing them in a blog, initiating discussions with other disabled enthusiasts. There is more about porn in Chapter 8.

Various impairments
Acquired brain injury

In their 2013 paper *Talking about sex after traumatic brain injury: perceptions and experiences of multidisciplinary rehabilitation professionals,*[21] Kerry Dyer and Roshan das Nair say that although 50–60 per cent of traumatic brain injured (TBI) people report disruption to sexual function, no more than 11 per cent of TBI patients or their family report that professionals have made enquiries about sexual problems. Their conclusions found that much more training is required to educate practitioners and change the reactive approach, which is generally taken, to become a proactive one.

Problems I have observed with people who become brain injured can result from having huge compensation payments. The first problem arises with such people who spend much of their money on sex workers. If just one sex worker is being hired, they will probably be worrying too. It is always possible to have a word with them, to suggest that they tailor their services more towards supporting the client to gain the confidence to start a relationship. The sex worker could educate the client in becoming a skilled and considerate lover, to give them the best possible preparation. The problem I have found with men seeing sex workers on a regular basis is that they may lose both their capacity and the will to form sexual relationships, because sex becomes one-way. However, this may suit them and be what they want, so long as they can afford to carry on.

The second problem is that they may get ripped off by someone who is only after their money. Interestingly, one sex worker was paid by a brain injured man's mother to try to help him regain faith in women again after he had been ripped off by his wife!

As you probably know, frontal brain injury can bring a condition whereby the client has less inhibition and cannot help but reach out to touch others in a sexual way with a view to having sex with them. Extraordinarily, this is often accompanied by a low sex drive. These days, with zero tolerance of touching without consent, supporting sexually uninhibited people really requires being strict with them to keep them out of trouble. Headway seems to be dealing with these problems nowadays, as I no longer get frantic phone calls on the helpline from mothers.

Autism, including Asperger's

Many autistic people don't go along with convention and authority, so may enjoy sexual pleasure and diversity. They may need discussions around sex to be in very straightforward, matter-of-fact language. Once mutually understandable communication is established, you should be able to get a long way in supporting them in what they need, by listening, taking what they say seriously, and speaking plainly back to them. Be prepared for them to complain that finding a partner can be very difficult. Invite them to describe what they are doing, step-by-step, and share ideas with common sense. You could support them to try social skills training for gaining confidence with things like asking a person out on a date.

Cerebral palsy

Some women with spastic quadriplegia cerebral palsy cannot spread their legs easily to enjoy intercourse, because the part of their brain which deals with motor function is damaged and the limbs remain stiff and tight. A gentle, patient lover, perhaps using massage, can help them relax. See the interview towards the end of Chapter 8 on sexual services. Women with cerebral palsy may also experience spasms which prevent entry to the vagina, similar to vaginismus. In my attempts to find ways for such women to enjoy sexual intercourse, I gathered a group together so they could swap notes by relating tips to each other. The best piece of advice I can offer, which is usually successful, is that the woman has an orgasm – using oral sex, a vibrator or fingering – before attempting intercourse. This relaxes her, and stops her spasms for a while.

People with athetoid cerebral palsy can initiate movement but have no fine control (spastic diplegia) and this means that enjoying sexual play with a partner can be very hit-and-miss! A rail by the bed could help to steady them. As mentioned in the previous chapter, some people ask for an enabler to help them achieve what they want to do, and perhaps teach them how to cope better in the future. Staff members, sexual advocates and sex workers might do such enabling.

Incontinence

I don't know why more can't be done to support people with urinary and bowel incontinence to feel more comfortable forming relationships and enjoying sex. I discussed this problem for disabled people in the previous chapter. There is a culture of shame and over-sensitivity which needs to be demolished. Those who specialize in incontinence in colorectal clinics tend to be down-to-earth practitioners who will discuss the sexual consequences of leakage, but the trouble is that many people are afraid to seek help, even though they are seriously impaired by their condition. With any interaction you can make, please try to help your clients along.

Learning difficulties

Sexuality issues around consent are discussed in Chapter 4 on the law. Learning disabled people who received negative messages during their upbringing, or experienced sexual abuse (or both), may need extra support. Running an optional sexuality event would, I imagine, be extremely popular, and could involve all kinds of fun that non-disabled adults enjoy, such as dressing up with photography, amateur pole dancing and workshops. One powerful workshop developed by Outsiders volunteer Victoria McKenzie divides the women from the men. (If you have lesbian or gay participants you may need to adapt.) The women discuss what they think men really want from them, and vice versa. Then each group tells the other group its findings. What each gender thinks the other wants is always way off mark from what they really want. For example, women may think that all men want is sex, and men think women are only interested in money. In fact, both genders usually want similar things. Hopefully everyone learns a lot from this, and many of their social (and even love) lives may become easier as a result.

Sensory impairments

Note: I am giving substantial space here to sensory impairments, because they are so often left out of texts on disability.

Visual impairment (VI)

I talk about supporting visually impaired children and teenagers in Chapter 5. Many newly blind people experience relationship break-ups which could be avoided, or support offered, if only more local provision were forthcoming. It is no good having a team of trained people in the RNIB HQ in London, however amazing their telephone and counselling skills for supporting newly blind people might be, if social workers and local care staff fail to put the newly blind person in touch with the RNIB and support the people themselves. You yourself could perhaps learn from the RNIB experts how to offer better support locally.

It's great that nowadays visually impaired people can use the internet and emails with voice activation, because talking books and newspapers rarely included sexual topics or information. This means that many older blind people who have never learned to use a computer can be quite ignorant on sexual matters.

Most visually impaired people can see a little, but they are usually unable to recognize people or see their expressions, so socializing is difficult. Single blind adults have difficulties socializing at parties and in crowded clubs, because they cannot tell if somebody is talking to them or to someone else. Others might not realize that they are blind, because they can't see a stick or guide dog in the crowd. It's much easier for blind people if they have a friend beside them to facilitate socializing.

Not being able to see during sexual activities means that talking can become essential. Not being seen can make their partner feel isolated, so blind people need to make efforts to voice appreciation of other sensations such as aroma and touch. Your support and encouragement would be highly appreciated.

Visually impaired people may enjoy and benefit from flirting and intimacy workshops so that they share notes and experiences, and swap ways to enjoy sex more. Maria Oshodi, the visually impaired woman who runs a performance group, Extant,[22] agrees. She and her cast of VI performers create performances to educate blind people on sexual matters and present the blind performers as sexy.

Hearing impairment

In case you don't know, there are basically three types of hearing impairment:

- those who are born deaf and don't use words, but use sign language

- those who lose all hearing after learning to talk, so have a vocabulary, and use lip-reading

- those who gradually lose hearing and use hearing aids and loop systems, so can actually hear (except when they take their aids out, such as in bed at night). They may not be able to cope with telephone conversations.

Many of these individuals may also have tinnitus, which they find very annoying, as you can imagine, with crashing and grinding sounds distracting their thoughts. Some also have balance problems.

Supporting deaf people with their sexuality can be challenging, unless you are experienced. Consultations and informal chats may be kept to a minimum by the deaf person, because they are so often unsatisfactory. Indeed, deaf people are unlikely to ask for support at all, and many health professionals are equally unlikely to think it necessary to offer it. So deaf people suffer in silence, in all senses of the word. If you encounter hearing impaired people in your client group, please do let them know you are willing to support them with any social or sexual issues, using the communication method of their choice.

Hearing loss can make people feel unattractive and isolated; it can thus have unexpected effects on behaviour. In a crowded party, a deaf person may feel frightened, and maybe even paranoid, thinking that nobody likes them. Such fears can easily spread into their previously loving relationship and, unless good communication and discussions help the couple to stay in touch on an emotional level, the relationship can slide into disaster.

People who have been deaf from birth tend to mix in a closed community, and may not consider themselves disabled. Some of them get married to each other. Signers have special secret signs for sexual activities. Some tell me they won't attend Outsiders events because there are no signers (even though there were no deaf people coming) instead of asking for a signer to be there, or simply bringing their own.

One of my colleagues, who became deaf at the age of 21, wrote this:

I suppose people react to acquiring a disability in different ways. You can either let it get you completely down, or you can come out fighting. That may be a slight over-simplification; there are times when the communication problems are wearing and, despite my positivity, certain people's presumptions and/or ignorance can be hard to bear. But I've never let it rule my life, and I've made many friends (some deaf, more hearing) and a decent career since going deaf at 21. None of this was handed to me on a plate; I've had to work hard for it.

One thing, though, is that it is obviously more difficult to meet members of the opposite sex, so deafness can be very limiting in that respect. You can't usually just go up to someone at a club or wherever and attempt to chat them up, it just doesn't work! And naturally, there will always be able-bodied people who aren't interested in having a partner with a disability of any kind. So I've tended to get to know women who already have some 'deaf awareness', for example have previously met other deaf people, though this hasn't always been the case.

Thankfully, there are people who take others completely as they find them, though from my own experience this is admittedly rare. I'm sure there are deafened people who are isolated, both physically and sexually. Unfortunately, some deafened people I have met blame absolutely everything that goes wrong in their life on the disability, and I find it hard to sympathize completely. But as I say, there are obvious limitations. I've had periods of loneliness, and I'd most probably have had more success in love if I hadn't lost my hearing. But there you go.

Deafblind people

The difficulties faced by health professionals working with deafblind people to support them in their sexuality are gigantic, compared with all other impairments. They have the law against them, and that seems right now to be immovable. Lawmakers are discriminating against disabled people which is, in itself, illegal!

Some really good work, generated in Scotland, is still available from the proceedings of a Sex Education And Visual Impairment Conference in 1997 organized by the Scottish Sensory Centre. It culminated in the mammoth publication *Batteries Not Included*, produced by Susan Douglas-Scott and Paul Hart of Sense Scotland, which is currently being updated. Sense Scotland use the same name, 'Batteries Not Included', for their intensive ten-month training course for health professionals wishing to support deafblind people with their sexuality. The name was chosen because it indicates that not everything is possible, mainly due to issues of consent and the law which does not allow physical touch to be used in sex education, or for staff to assist or be involved whatsoever in sexual activity.

SHADA supporters working with deafblind people have told us at meetings that they have struggled hard with the Home Office, and actually had meetings with them, to get the 2003 Sexual Offences

Act amended to allow touch to be used in sex education for deafblind people. The lack of support from their employers led them to feel that the only way forward is to break the law and have the situation tested in court. That way, precedents can be set, and this would change the face of sex education for many disabled people with multiple disabilities. But who will take this risk with their career? Claire de Than is now taking up the challenge of the right to sex education for deafblind people and will be campaigning for the necessary legal change by using human rights and discrimination law.

As well as the communication difficulties deafblind people may have with sex, their social skills are often sadly lacking. If a deafblind person wants a relationship with someone, which many of them do, they may find it very difficult to understand that first they must get to know them before asking for sex. Socializing is very important for young people to learn about, but they spend much time alone or with care staff, and mixing can be a great challenge. Seeing a sex worker can cheer them up, but this may not help them learn how to start a relationship.

Paul Hart's excellent work at Sense Scotland, where non-deafblind communication partners are used to teach deafblind children, share experiences, discover who they are and move forward, is discussed in Chapter 5.

Outsiders welcomed a very beautiful Indian deafblind girl who came to our parties dressed in lovely silk dresses which looked as if they would be sensual to touch. She liked to dance but seemed unimpressed with all the men whom I knew to be good dancers and brought for her to dance with – which was not surprising, it turned out, because she was a lesbian. Shame on me, I should not have made assumptions, and should have asked first!

Another deafblind member made an unfortunate demand. Although he was a very intelligent man at university, he asked every woman he met to urinate on his hand. No amount of telling him to stop would make any difference. Somebody should have been training him better!

Examples of bad and good support

I've never ceased to be amazed by the stories told to me. This one had a very sad ending. An Outsiders member, Michael, was a wheelchair user with athetoid cerebral palsy, who always managed to kick my shins when I stood in front of his wheelchair table to talk to him. One day, he asked me to find two female sex workers, so he could have a threesome, which probably was for practical reasons, as two could deal with his flailing body better than one.

Then Michael fell in love with a fellow resident: a lady who also had cerebral palsy. She had no speech, and communicated by eye movement. This budding relationship lasted a year or more, but eventually stopped when a member of staff decided to take it upon herself to tell Michael's girlfriend that he had paid for sex. I was infuriated. Then Michael died. It was totally unacceptable that his girlfriend had been told that he had paid for sex, and precautions against such things need to be written into policy.

On the other hand, I have been impressed at Outsiders lunches to observe PAs and care staff who know exactly how to provide their care without being intrusive. They may assist in the feeding and toileting, but otherwise they sit discreetly to the side reading a book, or leave, with the understanding they will be on the alert for a text to ask them to return. Flirting and seduction can be difficult if support is needed to translate speech into clear words. A good PA learns the skill of reducing the impact of their presence, to kind of make them transparent. The encounter can be especially difficult if the PA is continually drawn into conversations and the disabled client is ignored, so good PAs discourage such interactions.

When Helen Dunman asked the adult residents at Futures in the Chailey Heritage Foundation for severely multiple disabled students, she found out they wanted to be supported to do four things:

- share a bed

- view pornography (having the firewall removed from their internet and perhaps with the CCTV in their rooms turned off)

- use sex toys

- use sex workers.

Through talking to the staff, and doing her research, Helen was able to write guidelines which everyone was happy with. These policies then went to the board to be passed.

During this period, because sex workers were one of the clients' requirements, Helen asked me to bring a sex worker to visit, so that everybody would know what to expect when sex workers visit their disabled students. This story is described fully in Chapter 8 on sexual services.

Another college asked which members of staff would feel comfortable placing a sex toy on a student who could not do this themselves, which may involve touching genitals in a non-sexual way. Once they were happy that boundaries were well defined so that these staff members would not be technically abusing the client, nor gossiping about what they were doing, an agreement was written down and signed. They take each case as it comes, because everyone is slightly different, and sometimes the staff members are needed to position couples and enable their movements.

A spinal injured man told me, 'It certainly makes a difference to get some sheer enjoyment out of a body that is more often the source of distress or discomfort.'

Resources

1. The Sexual Respect Tool Kit: www.SexualRespect.com.
2. The Sexual Health and Disability Alliance: www.SHADA.org.uk.
3. Hajjar R.R. and Kamel H.K. (2004) 'Sexuality in the nursing home, part 1: Attitudes and barriers to sexual expression.' *Journal of American Medical Directors Association 5*, 2 Suppl., S42–47.
4. Outsiders Trust: www.Outsiders.org.uk and http://sexologicalbodywork.co.uk.
5. TLC Trust: www.TLC-Trust.org.uk.
6. Sexuality and Access Project: http://sexuality-and-access.com.
7. Kaufman, M., Silverberg, C. and Odette, F. (2007) *The Ultimate Guide to Sex and Disability*. San Francisco, CA: Cleis Press.
8. NRS The Hold-It® Book Holder & Writing/Laptop Stand: www.thinkinggifts. com/mall/productpage.cfm/ThinkingGifts/_THI1/%2D/the%20Hold%2Dit.
9. Life Support Productions (n.d.) *You, Your Body and Sex*. DVD. Available at www. lifesupportproductions.co.uk/ysdvd.php, accessed on 8 July 2014.
10. McCarthy, M. and Thompson, D. (2008) *Sex and the 3 Rs: Rights, Responsibilities and Risks*. Brighton: Pavilion.
11. Brook Advisory Service: www.brook.org.uk.
12. fpa (Family Planning Association): www.fpa.org.uk.
13. Online Dating Experts: www.onlinedatingexperts.co.uk.
14. Mitchell Tepper: http://mitchelltepper.com.
15. Accessible Sexuality: www.accessiblesexuality.co.uk.
16. Andrew Morrison-Gurza: www.huffingtonpost.com/andrew-morrisongurza.
17. Marius Sucan: http://marius.sucan.ro.
18. Sexuality and Disability: www.sexualityanddisability.org.
19. Disability Horizons: www.disabilityhorizons.com.
20. Mad Spaz Club: www.streetsie.com.

21. Dyer, K. and das Nair, R. (2013) 'Talking about sex after traumatic brain injury: perceptions and experiences of multidisciplinary rehabilitation professionals.' *Disability and Rehabilitation.* Epub ahead of print available from http://informahealthcare.com/doi/abs/10.3109/09638288.2013.859747, accessed on 8 July 2014.

22. Extant: http://extant.org.uk.

CHAPTER 4

SEX, DISABILITY AND HUMAN RIGHTS

Current Legal and Practical Problems

CLAIRE DE THAN

After meeting SHADA members when I was speaking at a medical conference, I am proud to have worked with them for several years. During that time I have encountered many inspiring healthcare professionals who have open and positive attitudes towards the right to sexual expression, and who understand that people with disabilities have at least the same rights as everyone else. However, I have also repeatedly found myths about the right to sexual expression, and understandable fears that supporting people with disabilities to express themselves sexually might lead to civil or even criminal legal liability.

The government has shifted the focus of public services towards safeguarding of people perceived as vulnerable, and this has led to a heightened concentration on the prevention of risk rather than the enabling of rights. This chapter will explain why fears of breaking the law are largely based on misunderstandings, and argue that the rights of people with disabilities require the law to support and enable sexual expression. It will also point out where the law needs reform, so that campaigners have a focus. The key argument will be that everyone has a right to sexual expression, relationships and fun. These rights should be supported and enabled whenever no harm will be caused by doing so.

The human rights approach

> The fact is that all life involves risk…we must avoid the temptation always to put the physical health and safety of the elderly and the vulnerable before everything else… Physical health and safety can sometimes be bought at too high a price in happiness and emotional welfare. What good is it making someone safer if it merely makes them miserable? None at all![1]

The quote above is from a court case about a very vulnerable young woman who had mental health issues and learning disabilities but was found by judges to have capacity to consent to sex. The local authority had wrongly tried to stop her from having a sex life. Sir James Munby, now the President of the Family Court, has repeatedly urged those involved in supporting disabled people to avoid 'wrapping them up in cotton wool'. But as we shall see, not everyone with disabilities has been allowed by the courts or by professionals to have a sex life or even any sexual expression at all; it is arguable that some people are undergoing the equivalent of being bubble-wrapped and placed into storage. That is a human rights violation, and could lead to legal liability for those whose decisions restrict the rights of people with disabilities.

The evidence heard by the House of Lords Select Committee on the Mental Capacity Act[2] contains worrying examples of miscalculations by well-meaning carers and professionals who thought that they were complying with the law and with 'safeguarding policies' when they restricted the rights of people with disabilities to express themselves sexually; for example a woman with learning disabilities who was told that she was no longer allowed to be alone with her boyfriend, without any explanation and without her capacity being assessed. As we shall see, although some people with disabilities are vulnerable and may require protection from some risks, safeguarding does not trump fundamental human rights such as sexual expression.

The most relevant human rights guarantee for English law is the European Convention on Human Rights (ECHR), although as we shall see that is changing. Under Article 8 of the Convention, as incorporated by the Human Rights Act 1998, everyone has the right to respect for their private life, family life, home and correspondence. The European Court of Human Rights has held that Article 8 protects sexual autonomy, confidentiality, dignity, forming and maintaining personal relationships and allowing them to develop normally; in *Pretty v UK*[3] the Court stated that 'Elements such as sexual life fall within the personal sphere protected by Article 8... Article 8 also protects a right to personal development and the right to establish and develop relationships with other human beings and the outside world.'

The rights protected go beyond sex lives, and include, essentially, a right for a person to have fun in their preferred ways, with others or alone, as long as they are not hurting others. These rights may only be limited by the State if the State has a legitimate aim such as preventing crime or upholding the rights of others, and if the measures taken are a proportionate response to a pressing social need.

In *ADT v UK* and *Dudgeon v UK*[4] the Court stated that there would need to be very strong reasons to justify regulating consensual sexual acts (and other intimate acts) carried out in private. Further, the State must take action to enable people to exercise their sexual autonomy rights, for example by passing laws or providing resources.

Where existing legislation prevents a person from expressing themselves sexually, there may well be a violation of Article 8, as in *X v UK*.[5] So, it can now be said that there is an equal right for all adults to consensual sexual activity in private, including the right to choose what relationship their conduct has to reproduction, and whether it is linked to any relationship or intimacy.

But the helpful requirements of human rights law do not end there. Article 10 of the ECHR protects freedom of expression rights and the public right to know; the latter includes the right to receive information about sex, contraception and so on. The right to share extreme views and receive explicit information may be protected by Article 10. In *Handyside v UK*[6] the Court emphasized that the right to freedom of expression is one of the essential foundations of a democratic society and protects the right to receive ideas and information which may 'offend, shock or disturb the State or any sector of the population. Such are the demands of that pluralism, tolerance and broadmindedness without which there is no democratic society.' There is a duty on the State to provide education and support so that people can make their own decisions about their private lives. One clear way in which Article 10 could be used strategically is to press the government and educators to provide better and more tailored sex education for people with disabilities, including people with mental capacity issues.

Article 14 of the ECHR also bans discrimination on any unjustified ground in the enjoyment of the other Convention rights, but is not a particularly useful or well-used right yet. However, further developments are underway; advocacy for the sexual expression rights of disabled people has increased greatly in recent years. Another aspect of international law which is much more promising for disability rights in the future is the United Nations Convention on the Rights of Persons with Disabilities[7] (the Disability Convention), which was ratified by the UK in June 2009. Under that Convention disabled people must be able to enjoy, on the same basis as others, the same rights as others. The Convention aims to ensure, protect and enable the human rights, dignity and freedom of disabled people. But it is not yet enforceable in the UK courts and has caused disagreement as to its impact on English law. However, the government has to report to the UN regularly, guaranteeing that it is complying with the Convention's requirements, and so at the very least it gives ammunition for pressing politicians to improve the law.

Article 12 of the Disability Convention states 'that persons with disabilities enjoy legal capacity on an equal basis with others in all aspects of life' and that States 'shall take appropriate measures to provide access by persons with disabilities to the support they may require in exercising their legal capacity.' In other words, even when a person lacks mental capacity under the definitions used in the UK, they still have the same rights as everyone else, and are entitled to support to make decisions about their lives. Article 23 of the Disability Convention requires States to 'take effective and appropriate measures to eliminate discrimination against persons with disabilities in all matters relating to marriage, family, parenthood and relationships, on an equal basis with others' and Article 24 protects health-related rights.

But there is still work to be done by disability rights advocates: unfortunately, some States involved in the drafting process for the Disability Convention objected to the planned inclusion of a requirement that 'persons with disabilities are not denied the equal opportunity to experience their sexuality, have sexual and other intimate relationships, and experience parenthood', and so there is no explicit reference to the right to sexual expression in the Disability Convention.

Other UN statements have recognized the sexual rights of disabled people with some powerful language: the United Nations

Standard Rules on the Equalization of Opportunities for Persons with Disabilities from 1993[8] are not legally binding and cannot be enforced in the UK but, again, could be used effectively in disability rights advocacy. Rule 9 of the Standard Rules goes further than the Disability Convention, stating that:

> States should promote [persons with disabilities'] right to personal integrity and ensure that laws do not discriminate against persons with disabilities with respect to sexual relationships... Persons with disabilities must not be denied the opportunity to experience their sexuality, have sexual relationships and experience parenthood. Taking into account that persons with disabilities may experience difficulties in getting married and setting up a family, States should encourage the availability of appropriate counselling. Persons with disabilities must have the same access as others to family-planning methods, as well as to information in accessible form on the sexual functioning of their bodies.

In the UK, the Equality Act 2010 imposes a duty on public authorities to promote equality for disabled people by treating them more favourably if necessary, and requires the making of reasonable adjustments for disabilities. This could be helpful in arguing that education, information or equipment is necessary for a person to be able to enjoy their right to sexual expression.

So, everyone has the right to sexual expression in private, alone or consensually with others, to have relationships if they choose, and of the type of their choosing. They also have the right to friendship, fun and a social life. Disabled people have the right to be given education and information to support choices about the sexual expression they wish to have in their private lives, and the State must provide such information and support when it is needed for sexual expression. These are powerful rights which should only be restricted when it is necessary to do so, and any restrictions must be proportionate. However, as we shall see, there is much still to be done before these rights are enjoyed equally in practice by all disabled people: other branches of law cause fears of liability which are often unjustified, yet ironically result in potential liability for human rights breaches!

Readers based in the USA should note that, at the time of writing, the UN Convention on the Rights of Persons with Disabilities has been signed (in 2009) but not yet ratified by the USA. A Senate vote in December 2012 narrowly missed the two-thirds majority necessary for ratification. The United States International Council on Disabilities is pressing for ratification of the treaty, but there is a powerful campaign against it, based largely on fears that the Convention would attack homeschooling of children; the sexual autonomy and expression rights of disabled people have not yet become part of the debate. Of course, the ECHR also does not apply in the USA, where constitutional protection of human rights is the key issue, along with specific legislation such as the Americans with Disabilities Act.

So, Table 4.1 sums up the key rights.

Table 4.1 Key rights for disabled people

The right	What it protects	Who and how it helps
Article 8 ECHR	Privacy-related rights, including the right to consensual sexual expression in private.	Anyone championing sexual autonomy, confidentiality, dignity, respect for the forming and maintenance of personal relationships, social lives; the state may also have to provide support for disabled people so that they can enjoy their rights.
Article 10 ECHR	Freedom of expression and the right to receive information, including the public right to know.	The right to receive information and ideas in order to make decisions about our lives, including information about sex and related issues; this helps those campaigning for accessible sex education information, and could be used to challenge some provisions of the Sexual Offences Act 2003.

cont.

The right	What it protects	Who and how it helps
UN Convention on the Rights of Persons with Disabilities	A wide range of rights, based on the principle that people with disabilities must be allowed to enjoy the same rights as others. Unfortunately its protection for sexual expression is implied, not expressly stated. However, a key principle is that people with disabilities should be supported to make decisions about their own lives *themselves*, rather than having other people make decisions on their behalf.	Could be used to challenge various aspects of English law which treat disabled people differently from others, for example the Mental Capacity Act 2005, the Sexual Offences Act 2003, and any court decision or safeguarding approach which prevents a disabled person from making decisions about their own life (including their sexual expression).

The complexity of the criminal law about sex: what does it actually allow, and why is there so much misunderstanding about what it allows?

The aims of this section are to explode some myths (e.g. 'procuring'), to make the argument that healthcare workers are being unnecessarily prevented from supporting clients to enjoy their rights, and that the law allows far more than is currently being done to help people with disabilities. The focus of government and healthcare organizations has given too much priority to protecting those seen as vulnerable, and is bubble-wrapping people so that they are unable to enjoy their lives. As we shall see, there are some surprisingly helpful approaches in existing law: it is not necessarily illegal for a home to pay for a disabled resident to have a sex worker visit them (there are ways of the payment being made which would be legal, and plenty of grey areas in the law which are helpful); the main problem here is that care homes are worried about their funding and public perceptions, so they over-regulate even when it would be lawful to support residents' needs. But if the resident has a mental disability or is under 18, then it is very difficult to arrange legally.

Criminal law is lagging behind human rights law in the way that it perceives disability: it sees people with disabilities as vulnerable potential crime victims and, sometimes, potential wrongdoers, rather than as autonomous individuals with the right to sexual expression. There is a lot of work to be done to reset the balance so that all people, regardless of any disability, can enjoy their right to sexual expression in private. Some aspects of English criminal law are particularly troubling, and we will look at those in particular so that campaigners have a specific line of attack!

The first English law to examine is the Sexual Offences Act 2003 (SOA), which defines criminal offences such as rape and sexual assault, and includes offences of sexual activity with a person who has a mental disorder which impedes choice. Sexual behaviour with consent is generally lawful, unless one person involved is underage or has a condition which affects their capacity to consent. S.74 of the SOA states that 'a person consents [to sex] if [s/he] agrees by choice, and has the freedom and capacity to make that choice'; the wording is not particularly clear or helpful, as I have argued elsewhere.[9] We will look at specific difficulties related to consent, communication disabilities, children, and people with mental capacity issues, in the next section of this chapter. If everyone involved in sexual activity is an adult, not a carer for the other(s) involved, is able to communicate consent by one method or another, does consent freely and has not already been found to lack mental capacity to consent to sexual activity, then whatever they do in private is lawful. The SOA was introduced with the following words: 'None of the measures in the Act are [sic] intended to interfere with the right to a full and active life, including a sexual life, of people with a mental disorder who have the capacity to consent.' Yet fears of criminal liability for supporting the sexual expression of people with mental disabilities/ learning difficulties or mental health problems are very common in the healthcare professions, and so it is unfortunate that the quoted statement and further guidance was not written into the SOA itself. If anyone would like to join my campaign to add such guidance to the SOA, they are most welcome to contact me via SHADA.

The next area of law which causes concern, and about which there are many myths, concerns sex work. In the UK, sex work is legal, although there are many peripheral offences surrounding it. It is not an offence to earn money as a sex worker, nor generally to pay for sex or to arrange for an adult with capacity to enjoy the services of a sex worker. The main offences related to sex work are soliciting, causing/inciting/controlling prostitution for gain, brothel-keeping, and paying for sex with someone who has been coerced or trafficked. In all US states except Nevada, sex work is illegal, which means that care homes cannot legally arrange for clients to meet sex workers in order to enjoy sexual expression. However, sexual surrogacy is a grey area in law in the USA, and so arranging for a client to meet a sexual surrogate is much more likely to be legal.

In the UK, depending on which services a sex worker provides, they may find other legal difficulties: BDSM (Bondage, Domination, Sado-Masochism) may sometimes break the rules of non-sexual assault in criminal law, since the House of Lords in the controversial case of Brown[10] held that it is not legally possible to consent to 'actual bodily harm', which means any injury which has lasting consequences. The most enthusiastic and willing engagement in some activities may, hence, break criminal law if anyone reports it to the police. However, this particular rule looks discriminatory, since the participants in Brown were gay men, whereas in Wilson[11] no offence was committed when a husband branded his wife with his initials; the court in Wilson stated that the criminal law has no place in the marital bedroom. I would argue that judges need to recognize that, if human rights and equality law are to be effective, the criminal law has no place in adult sexual expression in private with consent, regardless of who might be involved in it. Assisted masturbation is generally lawful, unless one person involved is underage or lacks mental capacity. Buying sex toys or (legal) pornography for other people is lawful, depending on their age, and there is nothing in English law to stop a person from phoning a sex worker on behalf of another person. The current law is most unfair of all to deafblind people, since lack of clarity in the criminal law leads people supporting their sex education and sexual expression to fear criminalization, and addressing that human rights violation is one of SHADA's active campaigns.

The easiest way through the maze of all these rules is given in Table 4.2 (page 96).

Now it is time for some discussion of safeguarding. In the last few decades, implied duties to protect vulnerable people have been recognized by human rights law. They are actually more limited than many policy-makers appear to believe – the volume of paper and materials dedicated to safeguarding the vulnerable might make it appear that there are heavy duties on healthcare professionals to protect people from risk, and that bubble-wrapping vulnerable people is the only safe option. One clear factor behind this is that, since it is the State and its bodies which bear the primary legal responsibilities for human rights breaches through failure to protect vulnerable people, it is in the interests of the State and employers to create policies and laws intended to protect people perceived as vulnerable. It is important to make sure that other rights such as dignity, choice and fun are not neglected.

If you work with people whom the law might regard as vulnerable, your main duties are your duty of care to your client, and to assess and report risks to their safety to the police or another authority when appropriate. Your clients, their care workers, and their family members might all be vulnerable and have different rights and needs, which all need to be balanced. A duty of care *must* be carried out in a way which upholds *all* rights, so excessive safeguarding can breach a duty of care owed to a person if it prevents them from exercising choices and freedom in their own life.

Even States have no general duty to protect people from risk, even major risk, in their lives but there might be a specific duty to a specific person if there is a known, real and immediate risk to the life or safety of that person, as seen in the cases of *Z v UK* and *Dordevic v Croatia*.[12] But people with capacity are allowed to decide for themselves how much risk they want to run in their lives; there is only clearly any duty on States regarding risks which people *have not chosen* to run, unless they are in State custody at the time. If a case involving one of your clients ends up in court, the court will have to weigh up both autonomy rights and protection rights, so there needs to be *evidence* about both. The cases which the European Court of Human Rights has thrown out are just as important as those where it has found rights to be violated, since the Court is giving its opinion on whether and when it is necessary for the authorities to protect people from risks. For example, in *Ivison v UK*[13] the duty to look after an underage vulnerable girl who was having sex with older men who had criminal records, and was taking drugs, did not give the authorities free rein to override her own individual sexual and personal autonomy. Hence her mother's claim, that the girl should have been protected by the authorities, was rejected.

Table 4.2 Criminal law as it relates to sex

The law	What it bans	Who it affects
Street Offences Act 1959	Soliciting – loitering or soliciting persistently in a public place for the purpose of offering services as a prostitute	Street-based sex workers.
s.51A Sexual Offences Act 2003	Kerb-crawling	Anybody soliciting a person in the street for sexual services.
Sexual Offence Act 2003 ss. 52 and 53	Causing/inciting/ controlling prostitution for gain	Causing/inciting someone to become a sex worker, expecting gain for yourself or another; or controlling sex workers for gain for yourself or another. These offences do NOT prevent a carer from arranging for a client to visit, or be visited by, a person who is already a sex worker, in spite of the frequently-heard myth that to do so would be 'procuring'.
Sexual Offences Act 2003 s.54, Sex Offences Act 1956 ss.33-36: keeping/ managing brothels	Keeping/managing brothels	A brothel is any place where more than one woman or gay man has sex, for payment or not – hence all hotels, student residences, and many private houses are within the definition. But it is not illegal to sell sex at a brothel, provided that the sex worker is not involved in the management or control of the brothel – a brothel is not criminal in itself, it is managing them that is criminal. This law is not designed to prevent a disabled person from being visited by a sex worker, even if they live in a care home, and does not affect non-penetrative sexual practices.

s.53A of the Sexual Offences Act 2003	Paying for sex with someone who has been subjected to force, threats, coercion or deception	This law is a danger for clients of trafficked or coerced sex workers, since the crime is committed even if the client does not know that the sex worker is 'unfree'. There is a potential human rights issue for clients, and the law will not necessarily help trafficked or coerced sex workers since, statistically, the most likely people to report suspicions to the police have been clients and it is now dangerous for them to do so.
ss.18, 20 and 47 of the Offences Against the Person Act 1861	Causing grievous bodily harm with intent, reckless wounding or grievous bodily harm, and assault or battery occasioning actual bodily harm	BDSM: a person cannot generally consent to be injured in any way which leaves more than transient harm.
Battery	Touching without express or implied consent	May cause problems, for example if a person's disabilities prevent them from communicating consent, but if the person doing the touching believes that there is consent then there is no criminal liability.

To end this section, it is worth repeating that denying an adult with capacity their right to consensual sexual expression in private is a human rights violation, and so is 'breaking the law'. Thus it is sad indeed that some care homes and organizations are so worried about breaking one type of law that they are unwittingly breaking another. A duty of care owed to a client or patient will be broken if it is not carried out in accordance with their human rights.

Current legal problems and grey areas: age-related crimes; communication-related disabilities; mental capacity and controversial decisions of the Court of Protection

This section will outline areas where the law has arguably taken a wrong turn and potentially criminalizes people acting for good motives. It will also assess whether fears of criminal conviction are really justified, and argue for reform. A key point is that the different rules based on age, whether a person is in a care home, and the nature of their disability make the current law so complicated that people do not realize how much assistance with sexual expression is actually legal. The only sensible way forward, so that everyone's rights are protected, is to campaign for greater legal clarity.

The first issue to examine is age-related crimes: the Sexual Offences Act 2003 criminalizes teenage sexual behaviour, and those who assist it, even when they act in the best interests of the teenager. Children under the age of 16 cannot consent to sex or to sexual touching or being touched sexually; hence vast numbers of teenagers are technically committing sex offences by kissing or touching each other with consent, which is a cause for concern. It is also a crime for a person in a position of trust (such as a teacher or care worker) to have sexual contact with a child under 18.

Providing advice about sex, sex lives, sexual health and so on is exempted from liability, but this leaves difficulties for many carers and healthcare professionals who are working with children with complex disabilities which inhibit movement or communication. As the law stands, a child whose disabilities hinder their sexual education or sexual expression (such as masturbation) can only be supported in ways which do not involve touching the child in any way which might be interpreted as sexual. Here the criminal law is in conflict with the human rights of the child. Of course children must be protected from abuse, and from risk of serious harm, but they should not be protected from their own human rights, and it is counterproductive if the law is inhibiting those acting from non-sexual, educational motives, at the request of the young person. This is one of the issues where I will be attempting to encourage reform, so please contact SHADA if you would like to help. At the time of writing there is a political campaign brewing for all children to receive sex education, yet disabled children have not yet been mentioned in the campaign. In order to achieve compulsory sex education, the needs of, for example, deafblind children would require subtle but important changes to the criminal law discussed above.

The second issue is communication-related disabilities: when a person has a disability which affects communication of consent, such as speech or hearing difficulties, the Sexual Offences Act presumes that they do not consent to sexual activity and that anyone who has a sexual relationship with them did not have a reasonable belief that there was consent. Hence it is presumed to be a sex crime: this raises human rights concerns although the law had well-meaning intentions, and causes further difficulties in fields such as sex education for deafblind people. Since everyone has an equal right to sexual expression and sex education, here is another reason why the SOA needs a rethink and a specific exception to protect educators. The definition of capacity to consent used by the SOA ignores equality law and does not appear to comply with the UN Disability Convention. Where a person has communication difficulties, the key issue is evidence of consent; if it is possible for them to communicate consent by any method or technology and they do so, then no crime has been committed.

The final issue which I want to highlight here is that of mental capacity, under both criminal law and the Mental Capacity Act 2005. The current law has unfortunate aspects, to say the least: the Sexual Offences Act potentially criminalizes even longstanding relationships where one person develops a mental health problem, has multiple disabilities or suffers a brain injury; and there has been a string of court cases where the authorities have thought, wrongly, that a disabled person lacked capacity to make decisions about their sexual expression (amongst many other things). Some judges have placed limits on the sexual expression of people with disabilities, including putting them under surveillance to prevent them continuing a relationship. Looking briefly at the Sexual Offences Act, sections

30–33 create offences against a person with a mental disorder which impede choice where that person is unable to refuse due to lack of capacity to choose or inability to communicate choice. Inciting or causing such sexual activity is included. The defendant must know, or could reasonably be expected to know, that the person has a mental disorder and is likely to be unable to refuse. Sections 38–41 create offences of sexual activity by care workers against a person with mental disorder, where the latter has capacity to consent but is influenced by a paid or unpaid carer. Again, causing and inciting such sexual activity are included. Many care workers and healthcare workers are understandably concerned that these offences might be committed when they know that a client or patient is having a sexual relationship, but actually unless they were actively encouraging the sexual behaviour to take place they would not be committing an offence. There is a possibility of being sued for compensation if they knew that sexual abuse was being committed and did nothing to prevent it, but not if consensual sexual activity was taking place.

To discuss the complexities, application and flaws of the Mental Capacity Act in detail would take many hundreds of pages, so I can only outline the current position here. It is important to remember that the Mental Capacity Act 2005 starts from the position that *everyone* is presumed to have mental capacity to make decisions about their own lives, unless and until it is proved that they lack capacity. It also states clearly that everyone has the right to make unwise decisions, and that making unwise decisions does not mean that a person lacks capacity. But the Act goes on to permit making 'best interests' decisions on behalf of other people who do lack capacity to make a specific decision. The Act does not, and cannot, apply to sex, since nobody can consent to sex on behalf of another person, but it is clear that some authorities are using the Act indirectly to control the sex lives of people whom they think lack capacity. For example, an authority might argue that a person lacks capacity to make decisions about with whom they have contact (to which the Act applies); it is very tricky to have sex with someone when you are not permitted to see or meet them. There is also anecdotal evidence that the tests are being applied in an unlawful manner, that is, by deciding what is in a person's 'best interests' when that person has not been shown to lack capacity to make their own decisions. The House of Lords Select Committee on the Mental Capacity Act which reported in March 2014 found widespread evidence that disabled people were having their human rights violated; often violations were the result of misunderstanding the Act and other relevant law, and it is to be hoped that the Committee's recommendations of new laws and new supervisory bodies will soon be put into place. In the meantime, anyone seeking to make decisions on behalf of a disabled person should only do so when the latter is *unable* to make a decision after *all possible support* has been given to them. In our present context, sexual expression, courts have repeatedly made it clear[14] that the requirements for capacity to consent to sex are very basic – a person has capacity to consent to sex if they understand on a simple level (a) the mechanics of the act, (b) that there are health risks involved, particularly the acquisition of sexually transmitted and sexually transmissible infections and (c) (if relevant to them) that sex between a man and a woman may result in the woman becoming pregnant. If there is anything which could be done to enable the person to have that basic understanding, then it must be done. It is not lawful to prevent an adult from having consensual sexual expression in private, alone or accompanied, unless they have already been found to lack capacity to make decisions about sex.

The future: enabling rights

If I ever ran for political office, my manifesto would read: 'rights not bubble-wrapping'. That does not mean that I am advocating abandoning vulnerable people to the risks of life at all – simply that the right to protection and the autonomy-based rights need to be weighed up against each other. Some people need support to exercise their rights, and sexual expression is no exception. The reform agenda to make that possible for everyone involved is as follows: when Person A has physical disabilities which prevent them from fully exercising their right to sexual expression, alone or with others, then Person B who is merely compensating for the disability by providing assistance or support must be seen as acting lawfully. The same applies whether Person B is a partner, healthcare worker or sex worker. Any law or professional Code which bans helping people to express themselves sexually must be reformed.

The assumption that all people with disabilities are vulnerable must be challenged, and bubble-wrapping all the enjoyment out of some people's lives must end. If you spot initiatives, risk assessments or substituted decision-making going too far into autonomy rights for people with disabilities, advocate for change (or contact an organization which will!). There is a pressing need for a human-rights-based rethink of existing English law and professional Codes; disability rights have moved on, and the law needs to adapt. At the time of writing, Ireland is pressing forward reforms with the aim of becoming the first country in the world whose law fully complies with the UN Convention on the Rights of Persons with Disabilities, and it is to be hoped that other countries will follow their lead. In Canada, British Columbia has also introduced a model of supported decision-making under which people with capacity issues are supported whenever and in every way possible to make their own decisions, rather than anybody making decisions on their behalf. With creative models such as these, and concerted effort from disability rights advocates on the issues highlighted in this chapter, small changes could make a world of difference towards ensuring that everyone has an equal opportunity to enjoy their right to fun.

Resources

1. Sir James Munby, Re MM 2007, EWHC 2003.
2. House of Lords Select Committee on the Mental Capacity Act. Report of 13 March 2014. Available at www.parliament.uk/business/committees/committees-a-z/lords-select/mental-capacity-act-2005, accessed on 15 October 2014.
3. *Pretty v UK*, application no. 2346/02, European Court of Human Rights, 29 April 2002.
4. *ADT v UK*, European Court of Human Rights 21/07/2000; and *Dudgeon v UK*, European Court of Human Rights 1981 ECHR 5.
5. *X v UK*, case no. 7215/75, European Court of Human Rights 1978.
6. *Handyside v UK*, 1976 European Court of Human Rights ECHR 5.
7. United Nations (2006) *Convention on the Rights of Persons with Disabilities*. Available at www.un.org/disabilities, accessed on 8 July 2014.
8. United Nations (1993) *Standard Rules on the Equalization of Opportunities for Persons with Disabilities*. Available at www.un.org/disabilities/default.asp?id=26, accessed on 8 July 2014.
9. Elliott, C. and De Than, C. (2007) 'The case for a rational reconstruction of consent in criminal law.' *The Modern Law Review 70*, 225–249.
10. Brown 1994 1 AC 212.
11. Wilson 1996 2 Cr App R 241.
12. *Z v UK*, European Court of Human Rights 2001 ECHR 333; and *Dordevic v Croatia*, European Court of Human Rights 2012 ECHR 1640.
13. *Ivison v UK*, application no. 39030/97.
14. See for example Re AB 2011 Court of Protection, EWHC 101.

C H A P T E R 5

SUPPORTING YOUNG DISABLED PEOPLE AND THEIR PARENTS

As long ago as 1978, Alex Comfort (of *Joy of Sex* fame) wrote: 'Sexual education for disabled children should begin at the same time as sexual activity – at birth'[1] and it seems other experts agree.

The book *Holding On, Letting Go*[2] emphasizes the point, saying that, when things go wrong with learning impaired clients, such as when they start behaving inappropriately, professionals wish someone had taught the person about sex from the very beginning. If only they had listened when the child expressed sexual desires, and supported them, then the individual might not be so angry or outrageous now.

This chapter outlines ways in which health and social care professionals can, and sometimes do, support parents and young people to be sexually enlightened. I don't claim to be an expert but feel really strongly about this, so offer you some inspirational examples I have found, together with encouragement and some ideas of my own.

One of our young female Outsiders members, Claire, came to us very needy, wanting to go on a journey to lose her virginity and experience everything she'd missed out on. She called Outsiders her 'main mentor in life'. She certainly went for it and, one day, we realized what the hurry was: Claire met the death that both she and her mother knew was coming. She was still in her early twenties.

This made me wonder what it had been like for Claire's mother, to watch her wheelchair-using daughter take risks, demand privacy, move out of the family home, and find a boyfriend. So I asked if I might interview her for this book. What came out of this conversation amazed us both.

One of the most ridiculous misunderstandings was that Claire complained to us that her mum never knocked before coming into her bedroom. Her mum told me she knocked as loud as she could but, getting no reply, would enter, only to be confronted with live interaction via a webcam on the computer, and a semi-naked daughter. We laughed, because we could both see how easy it might have been to work out that Claire's deafness called for a flashing light instead of a knock, and all would have been well. Plus, maybe a lock on the door.

Mum said that the psychological part of Claire's condition waxed and waned, so that she was sometimes gutsy and capable of running her life, but at other times vulnerable and incapable. This made sex a real worry for mum – she wanted to let go, and not interfere, but the next thing was she'd be needed by Claire to support her through the mess she'd landed herself in.

When I asked what support mother and daughter had received from healthcare professionals, mum told me that the only time Claire and she ever visited one together was at appointments with the consultant. 'Right,' I said, 'it was the consultant's job to ask how things were going with Claire's adult life, sex included, and offer or recommend some support.' But no: sex had never been mentioned. Consultants please take note.

Trust and good communication throughout childhood enables much more open and honest discussion during puberty and adulthood. Professionals should support parents to encourage their child to express their fears, doubts, troubles and worries, physical, emotional and sexual. They should bear in mind that children and young people find it difficult to articulate their problems, and may begin with a small worry, then build up to what's really troubling them. The parents may also invite you to listen to them and discuss how to support them. This might prevent the child from growing up feeling let down, undervalued, and perhaps going off the rails.

Discourage the parent from disapproving of their child's sexual feelings, because this will produce anxiety, perhaps leading to depression, self-harming or thoughts of suicide. Emphasize that nearly all the sexual problems which disabled people experience would not have happened if respect for dignity and sexuality had been considered right from the time of their birth.

If a young disabled person cannot talk to their parents about sexual issues, they may ask you. You could try facilitating the parents to listen, but, if they cannot, *it is your duty of care to do so.*

I have personally learned how our members were affected by their childhood experiences. Apart from being bullied, teased, feeling left out, and being abused by adults, their sexual confidence was dented by negative comments and lack of support. One of Outsiders' chairwomen who had spina bifida talked about how her father was cross if she made stomach sounds or farted at the dinner table, which gave her a lifelong complex about her bowel problems.

In the book *Queer Crips: Disabled Gay Men and their Stories,*[3] co-editor Bob Guter (also founder of the disabled gay man's website Bent) described how he was not shown to his mother for a week after birth, and then she had a nervous breakdown. Throughout his childhood, he heard both his parents blaming each other for his impairments. He writes about how he was often in a complete rage during his childhood. In cultures where disability is believed to bring shame to the family, both the family and the disabled offspring need even more support from others.

Such cruelty seems so unkind when a child is vulnerable and perhaps suffering with pain and teasing outside the home, so to feel hostility within their own families must feel unbearable. Disabled children really need extra encouragement at school to be assertive and to seek help when being mistreated not only because they should not suffer, but because abuse in childhood so often leads to abuse in adult relationships.

Now I am going to make suggestions for improvements in supporting young people right from the start. I would also recommend the wonderful guidance given in the Contact a Family booklets.[4]

When parents first find out that their baby has a disability, they may be shocked, scared and disappointed not to have the 'perfect' baby they dreamed of. They need all the support they can get, with information and advice. It's good for them to join a support group of mothers and fathers who have been through this process and assure them that their baby will bring them pleasure and pride. It is excellent if the support group helps the parents to become demonstrably loving, because babies build on their sexuality by suckling and mouthing things, and touching their own and other people's bodies and being cuddled, gaining enormous satisfaction from warm, physical contact. It provides them with trust and the ability to eventually learn to receive affection and to be affectionate with others. Supporting them at this stage will gain their respect for when you start advising them to communicate about sexuality.

Mothers of babies initially kept in an incubator should be encouraged to make up for lack of loving contact when they come out. If a parent is having difficulty in feeling total love for their child, because he or she is disabled, ask if they would like to talk this over with a counsellor to give them support and encouragement. Remind them that what happens to their relationship with their baby will have an impact on its future life, including its sex life, so it is important to seek help. Suggest that they read the book *Reconstructing Motherhood and Disability in the Age of 'Perfect' Babies*,[5] meet other parents in the same situation, and join a local support group or register on the website of the Parents of disabled children – Special needs forum support group.[6]

When you get the opportunity, advise the parents to speak about sex openly at home, and to show affection for each other in front of the child, so that the baby learns that demonstrable love and sex are normal, acceptable functions.

When a baby grows into a toddler, you may need to support the parents to stop their child feeling shame around their behaviour or body. Encourage the parents to offer admiration, allowing the child to feel loved. If the disabled child has spent time being examined by doctors and nurses, they may not develop a real concept of privacy and nudity appropriateness, so this may need to be taught at home.

If they are totally or partially blind, deaf or deafblind, time needs to be spent encouraging them to discover everything that other little ones learn and observe, and this is covered in Sytske Brandenburg's work at the Theofan Institute, Holland.[7] She says that a blind toddler may need to touch other children's bodies, their mother's, and their own, to learn what sighted toddlers can see. Play can be organized to give the visually impaired children a chance to experiment with the role of man and woman and to discover their own and someone else's body through play. All this needs to happen before touch becomes taboo. Appropriate or inappropriate environments or situations for self-stimulation need to be taught.

It might help children with visual impairment to receive a (non-sexual) massage, in order to experience positive awareness of their body. This could help to make them feel wonderful in their own skin, and more at ease with being touched. You can find how to massage an infant online.

If you read Helen Keller's autobiography, you learn that it is possible for a deafblind person to become socially active and popular. She wrote, 'You receive one body. Whether you love it or hate it, it's yours for life, so accept it. What counts is inside.' Deafblind pioneer Lex Grandia, who married and became the Secretary General of the World Federation of the Deafblind, claims in his paper *Sexual Development of Young Deafblind People*[8] that many deafblind children lack stimulation and expression. He writes that when he was little, he was living in a dream world, rather than reality, because he was afraid of reality. Lex was not encouraged to think for himself, and he didn't learn the barrier between his and other people's bodies, because it was forbidden to touch other people. People without barriers are easily abused and many deafblind children report abuse. If touch were included with smell and taste in their education, they would know about barriers. Lex is in favour of deafblind children being able to touch live models (models brought in specially for the class, and not teachers or family members).

The UK national organization Sense[9] is developing creative ways of supporting deafblind people to learn about their bodies, and about gender and sexuality. A yoga teacher guides them to touch each other's bodies in the non-sexual areas and helps them understand why they cannot touch other people's bodies in the sexual areas. They are helped to find out about clothing so they can choose their own, which helps them build up their sexual identity. A music club attracts deafblind members and this has led to parties and a summer ball where they can meet each other.

For children with unimpaired sight, mirrors are very important because, by the age of two, the child will recognize the mirror image as a reflection of themselves, thus gaining self-image. Mirrors are important tools at all ages, allowing parents and carers to discuss the disabled person's body with them in a positive way. Support the parents in this. Disabled children will begin to notice if they look different from other children. Support the parent in efforts to help the child grow up without a feeling of having 'something wrong with them', which will save them from lack of confidence in dating and relationships. You could also support the family by offering to introduce them to other parents of similarly disabled infants who live locally, so that the children can play together, and feel as if they look 'normal'. Becoming accustomed to mixing will help them use peer support throughout their lives.

Once children begin to ask about sex, it's time to provide the early stage of sex education. Encourage parents not to leave sex out of conversations, and dismiss any ideas they may have that disability will mean their child has no sexual feelings or desires, or that nobody will want them as partners. Disabled girls sometimes start periods earlier than others, and puberty can start earlier in both genders, so they need to be prepared by the time they are seven.

It was interesting to see the documentary *A Brief History of Mine*[10] which was screened on television in Britain on 7 December 2013. In it, an old school pal of Stephen Hawking told of how, when he shared a meal with the Hawking family, he was amazed to discover that the children were included in discussions around the table on such topics as sex and abortion. Stephen is a good example of the outcomes of witnessing family sex chat, as he went on to enjoy two marriages, producing two children of his own.

Children can be highly affectionate and enjoy hugging other children and adults. However, if the child uses a wheelchair, cuddling may be difficult. You can discuss physical interaction with games with other children on the floor, and in places where the child can be out of their chair, so that they don't miss out. Hugs with the family on the sofa are to be encouraged.

Parents can be supported to do their best to prevent their disabled child being left out of forming friendships, playing games such as doctors and nurses, and openly discussing sex with other children. At the same time, encourage the parents to prepare their child for nasty comments about their impairment or appearance, because young children soon begin to internalize these messages. For this, they may need discussion and confidence building, and a counsellor might be brought in, perhaps to see youngsters in a group.

Parents may need extra support when their child reaches adolescence, because they may be accustomed to caring for their child and so, all of a sudden, feel rebuffed. The adolescent may still need to have things to be done for them, such as having to have parcels opened for them, or to be washed in the bath when they have fully formed breasts and genitals. This will reduce their privacy, and you might be in a position to listen to the adolescent, to see if they feel that things could be done better for them. There is a very good Dutch paper, *Sexuality of young adults with cerebral palsy:*

Experienced limitations and needs,[11] stressing that many young people find it difficult to discuss sexuality, so it is the responsibility of adults to raise the issue.

There are things the parents themselves cannot physically support their child with, such as masturbation, but conversations on the subject are not illegal with underage children. You may be able to explain how the disabled youngster can pleasure themselves. If they are too physically impaired, this could be by using fantasies, rubbing themselves against a mattress, and playing with the erogenous zones of the body which they can reach. Some mothers say to me on the helpline that they don't want to have anything to do with this, and yet that they are getting no support from elsewhere. Please offer mothers of disabled teenagers that support.

Some disabled women may have difficulties with enjoying sex, and exercising their Kegel muscles (pubococcygeus muscles and perineal muscles) can help them have orgasms. Disabled girls who are taught to exercise them from an early age may well appreciate this later in life. The exercise is best described as squeezing on the muscles which they use to stop peeing. Some mothers do teach their daughters, and it's a good idea to encourage it.

Sytske Brandenburg[7] worked in a special school for visually impaired children, where parents came twice a year to make and evaluate the individual education plan with the care staff. Sexual development was one of the topics discussed. Sytske writes:

> On one hand, we have to make sure from time to time that the responsibilities between parents and care staff are defined properly... On the other hand pupils are more open nowadays about, for instance, incest experiences, so that, within our institution, we have to discuss how to deal with this phenomenon and how to recognize its signs.

This is tricky, because no child wants to testify against his or her family, but of course, once the subject is out in the open, it can become explosive. Care needs to be taken to protect the child at all costs.

Sytske encourages teenage workshops with sighted teenagers so they can learn the impact that certain hair styles, make-up, and behaviour have on others. Gail Bailey's book *What Can You See?*[12] offers tips for social and emotional teaching and how to inform all pupils about what it means to be visually impaired, and the articles

Teaching Your Blind Child About Sexuality[13] and *Teaching Sex and Relationship Education to Pupils with Vision Impairment*[14] are also helpful.

Sytske's school also uses mixed groups with partially sighted and blind students to support blind students to gain the social skills to overcome lack of eye contact, asking pals to describe how others may be looking at them adoringly, or strangely if their eyes don't look 'normal' – which is why some visually impaired people wear dark glasses.

Sytske is keen that all blind children be taught sexual values and standards necessary for sexual enjoyment. They need instructions on sexual and non-sexual touching so that they don't allow others to touch their sexual parts until they are old enough, and that even then they need to consent. She insists that education includes learning about such things as cuddling, hugging and kissing, and social skills for asking first. In his school, they are encouraged to take dancing classes and other activities with sighted children, to support their social skills and confidence in dating.

Visually impaired young people need to learn to be assertive and confident, to ask people to be respectful and, for example, not to leave without saying they are departing.

Deafblind children benefit from having 'communication partners' to interact with who can help them discover who they are, throughout their education. Sense Scotland works with a system whereby communication partners develop shared understanding with the deafblind child, allowing the child to grow so that they can move on to the next stage of knowledge. Throughout this, the deafblind child leads, and can learn about themselves, the world, relationships and personal development. Partners are encouraged to view deafblindness in a positive way.

At the Chailey Heritage Foundation, as part of a Personal, Social and Health Education (PSHE) Positive Body Awareness Programme which they were piloting, they allowed teenage girls (over 16) with profound and multiple learning difficulties, and perhaps a developmental age of as little as 6 months, to choose a bikini top and matching shorts. They dressed them in these matching outfits and showed them a reflection of themselves in the mirror. Most gave enchanting smiles of pleasure at themselves in the looking glass.

The recognized professional tasked with training children in sexuality in Britain is the school nurse, and I was pleased to learn that the Royal College of Nursing (RCN) says that it is unacceptable for school nurses to opt out of sexual healthcare: if the nurse is finding it difficult, he or she should speak to the school nurse team leader or manager. The RCN is in favour of working in partnership, and offers advice on the use of written guidelines.[15] However, it is obvious that nurses are not trained to have the knowledge which young disabled people say they need, and complaints are ignored. One of the Outsiders members said that sex education does not teach you much about the real world, leaving you feeling abnormal. Schools should be using a sexual health professional, and for this the best plan would be to bring in someone from Brook. I have already voiced the opinion that a sex therapist, a parent, and perhaps a sex worker who sees disabled clients should be part of the team. Certainly something has got to change.

From what I hear about children throwing around aggressively hostile remarks of a sexual, racial and discriminatory nature, it seems essential that regular classes be held at schools, finding out which words they have heard and/or are now using, and what they think they mean, and then teaching them the true value or implications of those words and thus the effect that using them may have on other people. It was really horrid to hear about a nine-year-old daughter of a friend of mine who heard 'I am going to kick you up the vagina' shouted at her in the playground by an older boy. It was even more terrible to hear that *the school did nothing about it*! Such lessons could go under the 'anti-bullying' label which, it seems, is more acceptable than sex, and saves all the debates over improving sex education and making it compulsory – which never seem to get anywhere, despite huge national campaigns. Role-play, such as making the culprits look different, and the other kids making fun and doing cruel things to them, might help them learn. Something needs to be done, and I am impressed by the work on behaviour of the ICU Transformational Arts project in Birmingham.[16]

At the same time, all kids, especially disabled kids, need to be educated on how to retaliate in creative, non-violent ways, and trained to stand up for themselves. This may be much more difficult with people with learning difficulties and those with sensory impairments, but it will set them on the road to self-preservation throughout their lives.

Many young adolescents enter a phase where they reject advice, share inaccurate information about sex, look at porn and may engage in sexual texting. A disabled teenager may need to have an adult they can trust, with whom to discuss things they have learned and got involved in, to prevent them from feeling confused and losing confidence. You may be that person.

Education about using porn is very important at an age before they start to look at it, because porn is about fantasy, not reality, and it is *not* educational. Bad things can happen if young people are not told this, while there are serious gaps in sex education. For example, young people see couples in porn happily (and easily) engaging in anal sex. Anal sex is rarely included in sex and relationship education (SRE) in schools. Young people tend to copy porn and try it out, the girls feeling obliged to carry on even if they are in pain when the boys do not take care to see that the girl is ready for penetration.[17] Anal sex needs to be taught properly and not copied from porn.[18] This may be more important for disabled girls, who could find they are able to feel most pleasure from anal contact – just like disabled people may discover all kinds of alternative sites of pleasure.

The London School of Economics carried out some research in 2013 into what 5–16-year-olds worry about when searching online, and whether they tell their parents about frightening and upsetting things they see. The outcomes were encouraging. The young people interviewed said they can tell when something repels them and avoid it. Although teenagers are curious, they won't venture beyond what they enjoy. When these young people do get upset by something they see online, they want to discuss it with a trusted adult, and they will select an adult who is least likely to 'blow their top' and initiate bans and rules on them. So, if a parent wants to be that trusted adult, he or she must prove him or herself to be non-judgemental – explain this to them.

Disabled youngsters complain that they get excluded from gossip around sex with the others at school, so they may not even have heard of anal sex. When they do hear about something like that for the first time and suspect that the others in their age group have known about it for ages, they can then get a feeling of low sexual self-esteem because they are suddenly aware of being more ignorant than their peers. Parents may well worry about the consequences of their child learning too much about sex, especially if they have a learning disability and/or are vulnerable in other ways, but ignorance is never good.

Disabled pupils can also be excluded from so many of the activities of young people, and this separates them even more from their peers, which is extremely damaging to their lives. It is important that they stay connected through activities they can take part in. Encourage parents to arrange parties at home where all the activities are fun and accessible and the disabled young person can excel at them. Outsiders runs a competition called 'Human Snail Racing' where four competitors are bound in cling film and have to reach the other side of a slippery mat, and physically impaired people often manage to win. Persuade the school to run inclusive events. Explain to staff that disabled pupils should not be made to feel left out all the time.

Adolescents may feel a strong need for conformity and acceptance, so having a physical or behavioural difference can make them feel unacceptable unless people demonstrate their acceptance. I run body-image workshops in Outsiders, described in Chapter 2.

Disabled people approaching adulthood may express the need for more privacy and tolerance. You could suggest to parents that they consider providing a carefully selected PA so that some of the intimate care is not done by themselves. This may help the adolescent grow, in terms of their intimate thoughts and desires. You can support the youngster in dealing with their personal worries over things such as gay and lesbian desires, and dealing with homophobia. You could explain that sexual identity can sometimes be a transitory phase. More about sexual diversity will be found in Chapter 9.

Intense idealism about love and partner selection, which people often feel when young, means that many disabled young adults assume that they will form a relationship with a non-disabled person, perhaps like their parents and their friends. This is normal, and often continues throughout their twenties. However, if the young disabled person has grown up valuing peer support, they may continue to mix with disabled peers and thereby benefit from self-acceptance and acceptance of disability.

I know a wonderful gang of disabled lads who enjoy fun together being adventurous, going out dressed in animal onesies. They support each other to be assertive, and make the most of life, saying that if disabled people are assumed to be childlike, they may as well enjoy some juvenile fun!

A Guide to Getting It On![19] is a very good resource both on explaining sex to young people and in discussing sex and disability. It is a book which covers most things which young people need to know about sex.

The fpa (Family Planning Association)[20] offers advice to parents, schools and others about sexuality and disability. Brook[21] supports under-25s in their sexuality, and offers sex and relationship education to young disabled people.

The charity Kids[22] supports disabled children and young adults in gaining the confidence to discuss relationships and sexuality with each other, in order to enable young people to make more informed choices in their lives.

ParentBooks'[23] website section Disability, Puberty & Sexuality lists (expensive) books which may be of use.

Parents of learning disabled children can be helped by reading *Holding on, Letting Go*,[2] which is a great resource to help them strike a good balance as their child becomes more independent.

When disagreements between you and the parents you support occur, for example where parents do not want their child to have sex education, your best argument should always be that discussion and knowledge makes their children less likely to get themselves into trouble.

Resources

1. Comfort, A. (1978) *Sexual Consequences of Disability*. London, UK: Lippincott Williams and Wilkins.
2. Drury, J., Hutchinson, L. and Wright, J. (2000) *Holding On, Letting Go – Sex, Sexuality and People with Learning Disabilities*. London, UK: Condor/Souvenir Press, Human Horizons Series.
3. Guter, R. and Killacky, J.R. (eds) (2003) *Queer Crips: Disabled Gay Men and their Stories*. London, UK: Routledge.
4. Contact a Family booklets: www.cafamily.org.uk/search-results/?s=growing+up.
5. Landsman, G. (2009) *Reconstructing Motherhood and Disability in the Age of 'Perfect' Babies*. London, UK: Routledge.
6. Parents of disabled children – Special needs forum support group: www.parentsofdisabledchildren.co.uk.
7. Brandenburg, S. (1998) *Sex Education, who is limited? Knowledge, skills and feelings of both parties in Sex Education and Young People with visual impairment*. Proceedings from the conference 25 March 1998, Scottish Sensory Centre, University of Edinburgh.
8. Grandia, L. (n.d.) *Sexual Development of Young Deafblind People – Moments of sexual development of young deafblind people and the involvement of the surrounding family and professionals*. Available at www.wfdb.org/sexual_development.text.shtml, accessed on 8 July 2014.
9. Sense: www.sense.org.uk.
10. Hawking, S. (2013) *A Brief History of Mine*. Available at www.channel4.com/programmes/stephen-hawking-a-brief-history-of-mine, accessed on 8 July 2014.

11. Wiegerink, D., Roebroeck, M., Bender, J., Stam, H., Cohen-Kettenis, P. and Transition Research Group South West Netherlands (2011) 'Sexuality of young adults with cerebral palsy: Experienced limitations and needs.' *Sexuality and Disability 29*, 2, 119–128. Published online. Available at www.ncbi.nlm.nih.gov/pmc/articles/PMC3093545, accessed on 8 July 2014.

12. Bailey, G. (2009) *What Can You See?* London, UK: Royal National Institute for the Blind.

13. Lesner, J. (n.d.) *Teaching Your Blind Child About Sexuality.* Available at www.wonderbaby.org/articles/teaching-your-blind-child-about-sexuality, accessed on 8 July 2014.

14. Royal National Institute for the Blind (n.d.) "Teaching Sex and Relationship Education to Pupils with Vision Impairment" in National Curriculum 2014. Available at www.rnib.org.uk/sites/default/files/National_curriculum_guide_2014.doc, accessed 26 September 2014.

15. Royal College of Nursing (2003) *Signpost Guide for Nurses Working with Young People: Sex and Relationships Education.* London, UK: RCN.

16. ICU Transformational Arts: www.icu-transformational-arts.com.

17. Morin, J. (2010) *Anal Pleasure and Health: A Guide for Men, Women and Couples.* San Francisco, CA: Down There Press.

18. Marston, C. and Lewis, R. (2014) *Anal Sex Among Young People and Implications for Health Promotion: A Qualitative Study in the UK.* Available at www.bmjopen.bmj.com/content/4/8/e004996.full. See also *10 Rules of Anal Sex* by Jack Morin, available at www.scribd.com/doc/86887/10-Rules-of-Anal-Sex-by-Jack-Morin.

19. Joannides, P. (2013) *A Guide to Getting It On! A Book About the Wonders of Sex.* Waldport, OR: Goofy Foot Press.

20. Family Planning Association (fpa): www.fpa.org.uk.

21. Brook Advisory Service: www.brook.org.uk.

22. Kids: www.kids.org.uk.

23. ParentBooks: www.parentbooks.ca/Sexuality_&_Disability.html.

CHAPTER 6

COMMUNICATION

This chapter starts with the reasons, revealed through research, why many health professionals avoid discussing sex, followed by some of my own observations, with suggestions for how the reasons can be addressed.

Then we look at how you can phrase your approaches to disabled people, so that you will feel confident and they won't feel you are intrusive, being patronizing or making assumptions. Hopefully you will see how simple it can be.

Finally, I discuss the importance of teaching communication skills to disabled people so that they have the language and confidence and feel empowered to ask for the things they need in order to enjoy a happy sex life.

Why health professionals don't talk about sex

Profound and highly productive writer Darja Brandenberg wrote that sexuality is a very private and sensitive topic in most cultures today.[1] We are all different in the degree to which we feel comfortable to openly discuss sexual themes with loved ones in our own lives, so it is not surprising that we find it difficult to find a way of raising the subject with clients and patients. She claims that most healthcare professionals rate sexuality as one of the most difficult subjects to raise with their patients, alongside spirituality and death.

John Drury, Lynne Hutchinson and Jon Wright, co-authors of a treasure of a book called *Holding On, Letting Go*,[2] say that health professionals find sex a problem to discuss candidly because none of us likes our vulnerabilities and insecurities exposed.

Lorna Couldrick, in her research,[3] expresses the view that professionals should, where possible, work in a team, as different professionals such as occupational therapists and physiotherapists bring different skills. It's also a good idea, she says, because there will always be some members of staff who will not, because of their personal views or religion, enter discussions on sex with clients.

Health and social care professionals who don't often work with disabled people and want to feel more comfortable communicating with them might use the great resource, *Disability Etiquette*.[4]

In a 2012 paper *Why don't health professionals talk about sex?*,[5] the authors Kerry Dyer and Roshan das Nair found 24 excuses which have been put forward. These were:

1. Fear of opening a can of worms

2. Worry about causing offence

3. Need for permission from parents and staff

4. Expecting the service user to raise it first

5. Personal discomfort

6. Language barriers

7. Service user may sexualize the consultation

8. Concern about own knowledge and abilities

9. Access to training

10. Lack of recent experience

11. Lack of time and resources

12. Lack of availability of written information

13. Lack of availability of policy guidelines

14. Not their responsibility

15. Communication problems between professionals

16. Not being given 'permission' to raise the issue

17. Assume it is not an important issue

18. Lack of awareness of the range of sexual issues

19. Assuming the cause of the sexual issue.

Some themes were particularly marked, relating to the sexuality of:

20. The opposite gender

21. Black and ethnic minority groups

22. Older people (40s and over!!!)

23. Non-heterosexual service users

24. Clients with intellectual disabilities.

I'll deal with these one by one:

1. *Fear of opening a can of worms.* Most people are reticent to speak about their private lives, let alone to tell you a long history of events, and you can always interrupt by saying you are not the expert, but can find one, if they would like.

2. *Worry about causing offence.* Any intervention can be preceded with the words, 'Please tell me if anything I ask is causing you offence, as I am only trying to help you', or 'Would it offend you if I asked about your social, and even sexual life? If so, I won't ask.' There are service users who do not want health professionals discussing their private lives, and prefer instead to sort out their own problems. You could offer a hand-out from the Sexual Respect Tool Kit[6] so that they have the relevant specialist resources.

3. *Need for permission from parents and staff.* You don't need anyone else's permission to discuss sex with someone who is 16 or over.

4. *Expecting the service user to raise it first.* This has been proven not to work. Research shows that service users believe it is the professional's role to start the conversation. Plus they are worried that they might embarrass the professional or that it is irrelevant to them, so tend to avoid it.

5. *Personal discomfort.* You could start by saying something like 'I find this as uncomfortable as you might, but it's really important to ask you how your condition is impacting on

your social and sexual life and sexual happiness.' Practice helps by desensitizing you. You could also access training or practise role play with your colleagues or supervisor.

6. *Language barriers.* If this means the service user not speaking English, then translators can interpret. If it refers to the language for sexual terms, each can agree to stop the other at any stage if it seems that you are not understanding each other, to clarify what is being said.

7. *Service user may sexualize the consultation.* This is most unlikely to happen unless the service user has a mental health condition. However, it is important that hypersexualized behaviour is addressed as this may place the service user and other people at risk. The professional should state their professional boundaries, and send for another member of staff to come in as a witness in case of trouble, to calm things down, and perhaps to help end the consultation.

8. *Concern about own knowledge and abilities.* It is totally unnecessary to have either; just ask an open question, listen, and refer on as necessary. The Sexual Respect Tool Kit resources are there to be referred to. The editors of this paper I am discussing here were delighted with the arrival of the Tool Kit and even did an evaluation of its film for us.

9. *Access to training.* You need to find training, otherwise there is a lot of information available from the resources I mention in this book.

10. *Lack of recent experience.* It's time to catch up!

11. *Lack of time and resources.* Outsiders' research demonstrates that the average length of time required for discussion is three or four minutes, and no follow-up required. Resources were dealt with above.

12. *Lack of availability of written information.* There is plenty listed in this book and more is being produced every day.

13. *Lack of availability of policy guidelines.* This objection may be justified, and getting sexuality guidelines in place should be a priority for all health establishments, professionals and

therapies. See Chapter 7. If your place of work has no policy and guidelines, suggest they create some.

14. *Not their responsibility.* It is part of holistic care. At the very least, the professional can print the hand-out in the Sexual Respect Tool Kit and pass it to the client.

15. *Communication problems between professionals.* There should be discussions about sexuality in all group practices, and sexuality needs to be brought into discussions wherever it may be relevant.

    If one member of staff causes a fuss about sexuality being discussed within the practice, there needs to be strong leadership with determined positive views. Graham Jowett, head of Treloar College, started his job by only employing staff who approved of students being allowed sexual expression. There are several ways to help staff see why they need to leave their personal views and beliefs at home, and the Values Workshop is available under Training in the Resources section of the Sexual Respect Tool Kit.

16. *Not being given 'permission' to raise the issue.* You may feel you don't have permission, either from your governing body or from your clients, unless they have come to ask specifically about a sexual problem. But sexuality belongs in holistic care, and the law forbids discrimination against disabled people which prevents them enjoying the same things as others can enjoy in the privacy of their own homes. You also probably know that sexual dysfunction can also be a symptom of a medical condition such as diabetes, so asking about sex can be a diagnostic tool.

17. *Assume it is not an important issue.* It is very important to talk about sex, not only as a diagnostic tool but because sex plays a vital role in health and life. On the Yahoo! Answers website, the favourite answer to whether sex was the most important thing in life was 'When all is said and done, Yes! Sex is the most powerful force on this planet. It has altered life throughout the uncounted ages and will continue to do so for many more to come.'

    The importance of sexual expression has best been outlined in the American white paper *The Health Benefits of Sexual Expression* published by the Planned Parenthood Federation of America,[7] also available on the Sexual Respect Tool Kit website.[6]

The paper lists 25 reasons why sexual expression is important. These are that it enhances:

- longevity

- reduction in heart disease and strokes

- decrease in breast cancer due to oxytocin levels rising

- reduction in prostate cancer

- higher immunity levels

- better sleep patterns

- increased youthfulness

- better fitness

- fewer incidents of endometriosis

- better fertility rates

- more regular menstrual cycles

- relief from menstrual cramps

- safer pregnancies

- ability to carry on having sex for longer, with improved sexual satisfaction and fewer problems of erectile dysfunction

- fewer migraines

- relaxation

- better emotional heath

- fewer psychological illnesses

- less depression and reduced likelihood of attempts to commit suicide

- reduced likelihood of being violent

- reduced likelihood of getting stressed

- higher self-esteem

- more enjoyment of intimacy

- social health in that they bond more easily with partners and have better relationship satisfaction

- people's commitment to each other through the association of their sexuality with spirituality benefits.

I hope this convinces those who once doubted!

18. *Lack of awareness of the range of sexual issues.* You won't need any special awareness in order to ask the question if the disabled person is having problems, and then to discuss what they would like to do about it. There's a choice of discussing the problems with an expert (a helpline, a sex therapist, or someone in your practice); of reading more; or of looking online. Mostly, your client will be happy that they are not alone, and will be pleased to be asked and taken seriously. You can reassure them that, if they have a problem, there is usually a solution.

19. *Assuming the cause of the sexual issue.* Nobody can assume anything when it comes to sex.

20. *Opposite gender.* If you feel that sexual attraction may get in the way of serious discussion, you should suggest that the patient see someone else to take over the discussions.

    A GP once joined Outsiders because he was an amputee fetishist and was worried that he might have a female amputee patient arrive in his surgery, and not be able to cope. He met some amputees, and realized he was in full control of his actions. He was grateful for the experience, and left Outsiders. Such things should, of course, be discussed in medical training.

    Some health and social care professionals feel that the service user might be more offended or that the discussion would be more uncomfortable if there is a gender mismatch. They can, of course, usually be offered a choice.

21. *Black and ethnic minority groups.* It is racist, so unacceptable, to treat different groups and cultures differently. Because some cultures may react differently to sexual discussions, perhaps ask clients how they would like to be approached and, before you ask the question, say that you would welcome their honest reply but that they don't need to provide an answer if they don't want to.

22. *Older people.* It would be ageist to treat older people differently. Some older people continue to enjoy sex throughout most or all of their lives.

23. *Non-heterosexual service users.* Be respectful, don't make assumptions, and treat people with sexual diversity with the same respect as everyone else. See Chapter 9.

24. *Clients with intellectual disabilities.* It would be discriminatory to treat them differently, but you do want to be sure that they understand the discussion. It's important that they listen and understand. Use short, clear sentences; and speak clearly, checking that they have understood at every stage. Be patient, even if you may be running out of time. If time is an issue, ask direct questions to get straight to the heart of their difficulties. There may also be additional risk issues due the client being more vulnerable to abuse and exploitation. Professionals obviously need to be aware of these in order to safeguard appropriately. The course 'How to turn Dreams to Reality' run by the fpa[8] is for people with learning difficulties, and might be relevant. The fpa will run any course on sex and disability that you ask for.

Kerry Dyer and Roshan das Nair, who wrote the paper we've been discussing, went on to investigate how much traumatic brain injury health professionals discuss sex and this is soon to be published.[9]

When the Sexual Respect Tool Kit was evaluated, a new observation emerged: the more severely disabled the patient, the less likely nurses are to initiate conversations around sex.

I guess the nurses imagined that the disabled patient is unable to enjoy sex, and perhaps that they might be shocked to have been asked.

I do hope this book will help all its readers to see that the severely disabled person would be totally delighted to know that somebody is considering their sexuality. They may need a tiny piece of advice, or medical help with, for example, adapting the procedures used for continence, or breathing arrangements, for sexual activity. However severely impaired the person is, they still have sexual thoughts and dreams, can probably enjoy masturbation, and are capable of having happy sexual relationships. Some severely impaired people work out ingenious lifestyles for themselves. They may, for example, enjoy wonderful sexual affairs with people which are not full-time, but involve seeing each other regularly.

My observations

The findings above did not include the worry that some health and social professionals have, especially GPs working in small remote communities. Some patients fly to far-away cities to see a sex therapist or doctor with their intimate problems, fearing that these might become common knowledge in their community. The GP could reassure their patients of absolute confidentiality, and then remind them that sexuality is not shameful, and should ideally be included in their holistic care.

Neither did Dyer and das Nair's paper demonstrate that patients may show a distrust resulting from past experience of being judged negatively over their sexual orientation or tastes. Of course, reassurance that you will always be completely non-judgemental needs to be stressed.

I am surprised that speech impairments were not amongst the items which health professionals found off-putting. Certainly, those with speech impairments in Outsiders say that they were never asked about their social or sexual lives by health professionals. When you cannot talk very easily, unless you are incredibly outgoing, this will have a profound effect on your social and sex life. An Outsiders member with a speech impairment, who was not asked about her social or sexual life by her speech and language therapist, was actually helped along by a professional in the job centre, who insisted that a local supermarket give her a chance serving on the cigarette counter. This gave her the social boost she needed, and she still works in a supermarket: she loves chatting to customers, and is quite happy that she is often asked to repeat what she says. She is now thinking of applying for a job as a flight attendant!

Communicating with people who use AAC (augmentative and alternative communication) may be facilitated by a PA, who can teach you the basics if your client needs a private chat. AAC includes pictures and symbol communication boards and electronic devices, and using the body to convey messages, perhaps by gestures, body language and/or sign language. Many people with cerebral palsy, whose speech is difficult to understand until one becomes accustomed to it, use an iPad or a machine such as a lightwriter, which is basically a typewriter which may have a screen where you can read what they are typing, or translates the message to become the sound of a voice. Some do not mind you finishing sentences for them, which speeds things up; and they can usually nod yes or no. One of our Outsiders members told me that using her machine is a bit slow, and that people get impatient. In social situations, they may wander off, never to return to see what she had typed! In a clinical setting, more time may need to be allocated.

People with little movement or verbal speech may only be able to manage to communicate 'yes' and 'no' through eye movement or facial expressions, so that you have to ask questions requiring yes/no answers until the question which the person needs to have answered has been reached.

Symbols are sometimes used by those who are non-verbal. The Widgit website[10] is very helpful, and has a useful section on communication, pictured on pages 126–8 (Figure 6.1). Sadly, symbols for sexual parts and activities leave much to be desired and I shall shortly be working on a project to ensure they are improved. The symbols you select for use can be put on a central resource, a Widgit word processing package, so that you simply type the word into your computer and the symbol appears on-screen.

The Chailey Heritage School for severely disabled students with learning difficulties created a 'communications book' on sexual matters. The students decided what they wanted to talk about, and found ways – using pictures and non-verbal languages when necessary – to express themselves. The book was written by and for the students in a Personal, Social and Health Education (PSHE) class (at their request) with Helen Dunman, the teacher, and a speech therapist facilitating them and physically putting the book together, with them, into a user-friendly format. All staff working with older students are encouraged to get involved and use this book if students want to chat using it. Training has been given to both students and staff about how to use the book and parents have been informed as well. Coming to a residential school means to most students that they will be living away from their parents, with a group of peers for the first time, so this sexual communication programme was extremely welcome to many of them.

People who stammer usually say they don't like sentences being finished for them. Most of them find situations like seeing a health professional stressful and stammer-inducing, whereas when relaxing with friends they may not stammer at all. So, offer them options, like writing down what they need to say. Telephone conversations may be very difficult. Advise your stammering clients to explain in advance to potential dates and people who intimidate them that it will be difficult until they settle into a conversation, and please just stay with it, maybe until after taking a break, to start again!

FIGURE 6.1 'COMMUNICATIONS BOOK' USING WIDGIT SYMBOLS

Good Communication

It's not always what you say, but how you say it that counts.

Begin by making eye contact.

Be aware of your body language.

Be non judgmental.

FIGURE 6.1 *(CONT.)*

Good Communication

Communication is two way.

After you have spoken, stop, listen,

and look for feedback and clues of understanding.

Do not butt in when the other person is speaking.

Good Communication

To communicate well is to understand and be understood.

If you understand each other,

are pleasant and respectful,

you can still have a successful exchange.

FIGURE 6.1 *(CONT.)*

Finally, to help convince you that people with speech impairments can enjoy sex, I'd like to quote from the Motor Neurone Disease Association leaflet *Sex and Relationships: For people living with MND*[11] which says:

> Sex is often a time when people can express themselves without having to talk, so in one respect it [sex] might not be such a problem. However, you might want to develop a sign language or a personal code that has a special meaning for you as a couple. Or you could write or record your thoughts and feelings to your partner in advance. This is less spontaneous but could be helpful.

There was no mention, in the paper discussed above, about the difficulty of communicating with people with sensory impairments and I'll deal with these here.

Visually impaired people usually have some sight, and it is very useful to know exactly what they can see. If there is more than one person in the room, you need to specify who you are talking to, maybe touching their arm to alert them that you are addressing them. If you wish to move with them to another part of the room or another room, offer them your arm to hold. You can also place their hand on the back of a chair so they know where to sit. You don't necessarily need to guide them everywhere but it is important to let them know of any changes you have made with layout, for example. If you are giving the person prescriptions or things with written instructions, ensure that they have someone to read them, or read them out loud yourself. They may wish to record what you say.

If blind people are going to use injections, ensure that there is a really safe way for them to avoid overdoses. I know one blind man who lost his capacity to have an erect penis ever again, by injecting too large a dose of papaverine into his penis.

Some deaf people use lip-reading, some use sign language, some use hearing aids with loop systems, and some use a combination of these. Many sighted deaf people use the two-handed manual alphabet used by deafblind people, perhaps as a back-up. Hands-on Signing is used by British Sign Language users whose vision no longer allows them to see sign language and they therefore 'feel' sign language by resting their hands on the communicator's hands.

Many people who are losing their hearing avoid using hearing aids for as long as possible because they don't like the artificial sounds produced; so you may need to speak up, but don't shout.

When communicating with a deaf person, sit straight onto them with the light on your face, so they can see you, your lips, and any signing you use. You may not know signing, and they may need to bring their own signer.

People with tinnitus find it very distracting and they may be depressed because there is no medical remedy.

Obviously, texting can be a godsend to deaf people for communication. In a consultation, use note-writing to make sure everything is clear, providing the deaf individual uses words.

Deafblind people mostly communicate using the manual alphabet which is very simple and easy to learn – see the chart below (Figure 6.2). You tap the palm of the hand twice to say 'yes' and wipe the hand across the palm to say 'no', and for erasing an error, changes in the conversation, new paragraphs, and so on. There are demonstrations on YouTube.

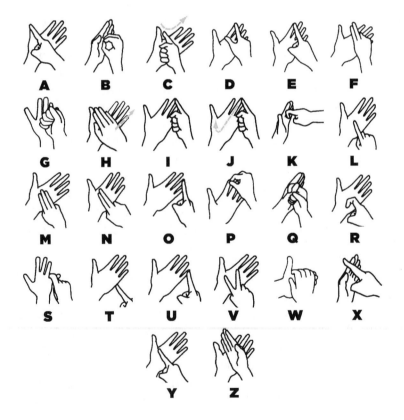

FIGURE 6.2 DEAFBLIND ALPHABET

If you have a service user with Tourette's syndrome, accept their idiosyncrasies such as swearing and rude words. Wait for them to stop, or invite them to exit the consultation for a while until the build-up of the impulse to come out with irrelevant profanities dies down.

Disabled people may simply seek your reassurance and permission to go ahead with their own plans with someone they have started to share intimacy with, because they have been led to believe that they will never find love, and they can't believe their luck!

Opening lines and discussions
Broaching discussions

If you were brought up in a family where sex was never talked about, you may well find it difficult to talk about it now, but professionals have found that practice brings confidence. If you feel too inhibited, start off by asking the other person how their social lives are faring. This then can slowly lead to questions about pleasure, satisfaction and sex. You'll be astounded at how delightful a journey this can be.

Take a leaf out of the sex therapists' book, and try to sit in a chair the same height as the client, with no other furniture in the way, at an angle of 75 degrees. Then you won't be staring straight at them, dominating them or looking up to them, and you can both read each other's body language which, sometimes, tells you more than the words they use.

It is usually helpful to tell the client how long you have, but also to say that there is no hurry, because there can be other opportunities to talk. This is particularly important when, as often happens with disabled people, they bring up the subject of a sexual problem in passing, when you are least expecting it, and may have little time to spare.

As you progress, double-check that you have really understood each other, because people might not be accustomed to talking about sex, and may not understand all of the words you have used. If a client uses the word 'sex', you need to ask them what they mean by it, as the word can mean different things: gender, intercourse and the whole gamut of sexual activities. You may need to check what a woman means when she says she can't feel inside her vagina. She may mean she can't feel her genitals at all, yet the only word she knows is vagina. I do reassure females that women don't have many nerve endings inside the vagina (except the G-spot), so she's not losing out much if she cannot feel inside. On the other hand, having no feeling in her genitals may mean that she needs to search elsewhere on her body to find places where she can enjoy sexual stimulation. Individuals and couples can have fun checking this out.

Ensure that your questions don't exclude people. For example, simply asking a person their 'marital status' is not sufficiently inclusive and does not tell you as much as if you ask such questions as to whether they have a partner and who they live with, because the answer to the latter might not be their long-term partner. Similarly, 'What form of birth control do you use?' makes the assumption that they have heterosexual, penetrative sex, so it is better to ask, 'Do you use birth control and/or protected sex? If so, which methods do you use?'

Research has shown that asking about 'sexual concerns' is preferable to asking about 'sexual problems'.

Another important thing to bear in mind always is that *how* a client says something may be more important than *what they say*. Men, especially, use bravado to cover up things which are going wrong for them. If they hover when leaving the room, ask if there is something else important to add which has been too difficult to talk about. If they can't articulate the problem, and you suspect it is of a sexual nature, you could offer them one of the Sexual Respect Tool Kit's hand-outs.

In order to find out about a client's sex life and to really get to the truth, don't ask them 'whether' they do certain things, but 'how many times' or 'when they started' doing them. For example, 'When was the last time you were intimate? What happened? How often do you make love at the moment? How does that compare with before? What effect does this situation have on your life?' In fact, using such open-ended questions is always more productive than using closed-ended ones, where the answers are simply 'yes' or 'no', because they may well, out of caution, say no.

You will need to reassure the client that anything they say will be kept in strict confidence, and this should be emphasized again before you finish. Mind you, my experience with disabled people is that, to most of them, confidentiality is the least of their problems, and they don't care who knows about their private life, so long as it improves!

Preparing for the moment you bring the topic up

Sometimes, it's best to use an introductory statement and question:

> 'In order to understand your difficulties better, and to try to help you, I would like to ask a few direct questions about what happens in the bedroom and whether any difficulties appear. You don't have to answer anything if you don't want to.'

or

> 'I will be asking some personal questions that will help me to help you.'

Assure the patient/client that these are questions you ask everybody. Once they have answered, tell them how useful the answers are; for example, you might say, 'Thank you for sharing that; it helps me to see options on how to move things forward with you.'

Ask the service user to let you know if a question makes them feel uncomfortable, and say you'll find a better way to discuss things that makes them feel more at ease.

Finding your own style and vocabulary

It is important to appear genuine, but try not to look nervous, embarrassed or guilty. If you are feeling apprehensive, you can admit in your opening words that it's always a little tricky talking about intimate matters.

Find words you are comfortable with. There are many terms: 'private life', 'personal pleasure', 'intimacy', 'love-life', 'what you do in the bedroom', and so on. If you have a personal favourite gem, don't be afraid to use it; this will confirm to the client that they are talking with a nice human being. Having said that, it's sometimes essential to copy your client's language for sexual parts and activities. Plain talk works best.

If you feel stuck, here are some easy options about moving forward:

> 'I'm certainly not an expert, but I wonder if we should bring a relationship therapist in to help you sort where your priorities lie.'

'I might not be the best person to discuss your private life with – is there any member of our team that you might feel more comfortable with? (a woman or a man?)'

'There is a member of my team who specializes in…'

Opening lines

Sue Lennon, cancer nurse, in our Sexual Respect Tool Kit film is great to watch, as she says the following in such a relaxed and inviting way:

Many patients in your situation have reported a sexual impact from their illness… Is that something you've experienced?… Are you able to talk about it?… Would you like to talk about it now?'

The phrase 'a sexual impact' can be adapted to include social impact, or name the usual sexual impact which people with the same impairment as your client sometimes experience. Your aim is to give them permission to be open about what is bothering them.

Don't worry about having to cope with the answers. You can always refer them on. If they ask you what to do, you can ask what they think they might try, followed by, 'I am not sure, but I'll ask my colleagues and find out.' Then you can call the Sex and Disability Helpline, if you like. I like tricky problems!

Here are some other questions, including some more direct and specific ones:

'If you have a sexual relationship, how has it been affected by your illness?'

'When you masturbate or are in a sexual situation with someone, how often do you become sexually excited/lubricate/get erections?'

'How often do you experience orgasms?'

'Do you ever have any problems with pain or mobility when trying to be intimate?'

'What are the ways you've tried for overcoming these?'

'If you have ever tried having intercourse, how did it go?'

If you find yourself in a situation that feels just too difficult, don't give up – or get half-way through a sentence and look uncomfortable. Find a positive way of backing out. For example: 'There is a member of our team who specializes in discussing personal issues, and I would like to make an appointment for you to see them, if that's OK? In the meantime, here is a leaflet which you might find useful.'

Couples with cerebral palsy are sometimes difficult to both understand and support with their complex struggles with overcoming stiffness, spasticity and lack of control. A sexual advocate[12] can be suggested.

If you miss an opportunity to open dialogue during a consultation, make a note of it and bring up the subject the next time.

Using models

A special model was created long ago for discussing sex with clients. It is called the PLISSIT model.[13] PLISSIT stands for:

> **P**ermission-giving (letting your client know it's OK to discuss sex and/or the topic they are concerned about)

> **L**imited **I**nformation (like saying that most people have sexual desires, many people masturbate, and would like to fall in love and enjoy a sexual relationship)

> **S**pecific **S**uggestions, and

> **I**ntensive **T**herapy recommended.

However, Lorna Couldrick, an occupational therapist based at Brighton University[3] has critiqued the PLISSIT model as unsuitable for disabled people because:

1. Disabled service users may approach health and social care professionals, sometimes in places and situations where discussions on sex would be difficult, and yet they must find a way to allow the discussion to take place. It is not, therefore *always* necessary to provide permission to disabled people.

2. It assumes the worker recognizes and accepts that the disabled person is a sexual being with sexual needs.

3. The PLISSIT model lacks exploration, often required to dig around to find exactly what the disabled person needs. Issues for disabled people may range from establishing and maintaining a relationship, adapting to changes in roles with a lover/carer, and not just problems within the human sexual response cycle. Without exploration, professionals will not be able to identify appropriate support and help.

4. Taking a team approach, responsibilities can be shared so that each member can bring their own expertise and those who find certain things difficult are compensated for by their colleagues.

5. Finally, very few disabled people who are seeking support require intensive therapy.

Instead, Lorna proposes the Recognition Model for use with disabled people.[3] It can be seen on the SHADA website.[14] The Recognition Model lists five stages of interaction:

1. Recognition of the service user as a sexual being

2. Provision of sensitive, permission giving strategies

3. Exploration of the sexual problem/concern

4. Addressing issues which fit within the team's expertise and boundaries

5. Referral on, when necessary.

Working together

Teams working together need clear guidelines to ensure everyone is working in a coordinated way. Guidelines may include such things as:

- boundaries

- ensuring clients can have private time for masturbation

- how staff should approach conversations about sex with clients

- when they are unsure about anything, to bring it to the attention of those in charge

- induction training for all staff on policies and guidelines

- refresher courses regularly laid on for existing staff

- managers in different areas monitoring and supporting staff in following guidelines

- current topics and problems around sexuality not being left out of meetings

- discussions around sexuality becoming the norm and enjoyable.

If you are working in a residential home group practice, you need to ensure that the staff are trained to become relaxed with conversations around sex, to create an open and uninhibited atmosphere. Discuss with other staff issues such as how you will all cope with this work emotionally, perhaps using Schwartz Rounds. A 'round' of issues which practice staff have met whilst supporting their service users will allow sharing of embarrassing or difficult cases. It could also be the time for joint decisions on individuals who need group agreements for their support to move forward. They can identify their mental barriers to including sexuality in holistic care. Brook or the fpa could provide a trainer. Look for other specialist training guidelines which are listed in the resources of the Sexual Respect Tool Kit. Assure staff that they won't be required to be experts or have special knowledge, just the confidence to use common sense, and to understand and accept that they must not inflict their own values or beliefs on others while doing their job. A good strategy is to ask each of them what opening line they would feel comfortable with using when initiating a discussion on sex with a client. Tell everybody that practice will help them gain confidence.

There may be some members of staff for whom sex-talk just flows off the tongue. By all means make the most of these people, but it is important not to rely on them exclusively, as they may leave. Much better to ask them to lead discussions in practice meetings, to normalize conversations around sex. Then, you can all share their skills.

Helping disabled people communicate about sex

Teaching disabled people how to communicate their sexual feelings and needs gives them invaluable tools which they can take with them and use throughout the rest of their lives.

You could start by putting up one of the posters we supply on the Sexual Respect Tool Kit website.[6] Some of the posters use disabled models, including a wheelchair user with a catheter showing between her legs. The message is 'Sex is Talked about Here'. You might like to show clients the training film available from the Sexual Respect Tool Kit, especially the last section, as this is about peer support, and is very moving.

Following this, it might be good to explain to clients that everybody is on a journey with their sexuality. As people learn and mature while progressing through life, they sometimes develop new tastes and preferences. For example, some people realize they are gay quite late in life. As disabled people become less frantic to have sex like everyone else, they will find that just enjoying the pleasure of pleasing a partner and being pleasured, perhaps just using tiny movements around an erogenous zone, can bring the them both to a state of delightful bliss.

Training disabled people to ask health professionals for support with personal issues with confidence and without embarrassment can be empowering. They can learn to ask about confidentiality, to be assertive about reporting abuse, and to state their needs assertively.

Equally, training in procedures for hiring the right sexual services for them to meet their needs at various stages in their life could be of great benefit. Once you have read Chapter 8 on sexual services, you could look at the Sexual Advocacy website[12] to see the support which the advocates offer. Training could encourage your disabled clients to learn more for themselves. You might suggest they read the TLC Trust website,[15] so that they can see what is on offer. Organizing a local escort to come and talk to your clients may help to put the work into context.

Training disabled people to discuss sex and relationship difficulties with their lovers and partners will set them on the road to successful affairs and partnerships. Relationship break-ups are more difficult for disabled people, especially if their partner is their carer too, so some stay in unhappy relationships as they see no alternative.

Here are some simple tips and tools which they could find invaluable.

1. BECOME ACCUSTOMED TO TALKING ABOUT SEX

In order for couples to evolve together, they do need continuous, frank and honest communication between them, and this is usually more important for disabled people, who may have to find alternative ways of enjoying sex. I often quote the example of Erica Jong, who wrote that what kept her happy with her fourth husband was the fact that, every morning, he would ask her what her sexual fantasy was that day. Such a simple idea, but potentially so effective! If couples talk together about their sex life and emotional ups and downs every day, they become closer and happier.

2. BE TOTALLY OPEN ABOUT VULNERABILITIES AND FEARS

If a person is feeling worried that they don't live up to their partner's expectations and needs, then it is sensible for them to spend some quiet time together to ask precisely what their expectations and needs are, and to discuss how they can be met. In other words, suggest your disabled clients become accustomed to talking about how they are coping, or not, and about their successes and their failures, so that they can live in harmony with partners.

3. BECOME KNOWLEDGEABLE

Books I recommend are *A Guide to Getting It On* (great for young people),[16] *The New Joy of Sex*,[17] *The Sex Book*,[18] *The Ultimate Guide to Orgasm for Women*[19] and *The Ultimate Guide to Sex and Disability*.[20] They all include things of use to disabled people, and can expand their horizons. There seem to be no equivalents for people with learning difficulties.

4. DISCUSS PROBLEMS IN A POSITIVE WAY

I advise people to begin all sentences with 'I' not 'you', for example 'I am feeling neglected' rather than 'You never give me any attention.' Pointing the finger makes people go on the defensive, but saying how you feel invites empathy and negotiation.

5. MEAN WHAT YOU SAY

It is worth reminding clients that telling a partner over and over that you will break it off if the partner tells lies, or otherwise lets you down, won't work. It's better to break it off. The partner may think twice after having been given a space and then a second chance.

6. BE CLEAR ABOUT NEEDS

If a couple are experiencing sexual misunderstandings, they should get into the routine of both taking turns in stating what they want during sex, or other times when they may be struggling.

7. WHEN A PARTNER IS ALSO A CARER

The couple could discuss strict cut-off times when the carer becomes the lover, even if they may need to do a bit of caring during the love-making. One idea is for the person needing care to sometimes invite a friend in to become their 'bedroom companion', supporting them to get ready for sex and maybe also stay during the initial parts of the love-making to help position them.

To make being both carer and live-in lover even more difficult, the carer may resent having to share their space when PAs are around, day and night, which can feel intrusive. Time therefore needs to be set aside for negotiating what will work for both parties.

Invite your disabled service users to make suggestions for interesting discussions and follow-ups. There is a lot to teach disabled people, so enough time needs be set aside. While sex and relationship education is so sadly lacking for disabled people, it may be up to you, so do your best!

Image credits

Thanks to Widgit for their kind permission to use these four pages from their website. They can be found on: www.symbolworld.org/articles/1105/screen/1.

Deafblind manual alphabet courtesy of Action on Hearing Loss (the new name for the RNID).

Resources

1. Brandenberg, D. (2013) *Sex and Young Disabled People with Progressive Conditions.* Sexual Respect Tool Kit. Available at http://sexualrespect.com/Darja.pdf, accessed on 15 July 2014.

2. Drury, J., Hutchinson, L. and Wright, J. (2000) *Holding On, Letting Go – Sex, Sexuality and People with Learning Disabilities.* London, UK: Condor/Souvenir Press, Human Horizons Series.

3. Couldrick, L., Sadlo, G. and Cross, V. (2010) 'Proposing a new sexual health model of practice for disability teams: The Recognition Model.' *International Journal of Therapy and Rehabilitation 17*, 6, 290–299.

4. United Spinal Association (2009) *Disability Etiquette – Tips on Interacting with People with Disabilities.* Available at www.unitedspinal.org/pdf/DisabilityEtiquette.pdf, accessed on 8 July 2014.

5. Dyer, K. and das Nair, R. (2012) 'Why don't healthcare professionals talk about sex? A systematic review of recent qualitative studies conducted in the United Kingdom.' *Journal of Sexual Medicine 10*, 2658–2670. Available from http://onlinelibrary.wiley.com/doi/10.1111/j.1743-6109.2012.02856.x/abstract, accessed on 8 July 2014.

6. Sexual Respect Tool Kit: www.SexualRespect.com.

7. Planned Parenthood Federation of America (2007) *The Health Benefits of Sexual Expression.* Available at www.plannedparenthood.org/files/3413/9611/7801/Benefits_Sex_07_07.pdf, accessed on 8 July 2014.

8. fpa (Family Planning Association): www.fpa.org.uk.

9. Dyer, K. and das Nair, R. (2013) 'Talking about sex after traumatic brain injury: Perceptions and experiences of multidisciplinary rehabilitation professionals.' *Disability and Rehabilitation.* Epub ahead of print available from http://informahealthcare.com/doi/abs/10.3109/09638288.2013.859747, accessed on 8 July 2014.

10. Widgit: www.widgit.com.

11. Motor Neurone Disease Association (2014) *Sex and Relationships: For people living with MND.* Information Sheet 20A. Available at www.mndassociation.org/Resources/MNDA/Life%20with%20MND/Information%20sheet%2020A%20-%20Sex%20and%20relationships%20for%20people%20living%20with%20MND.pdf, accessed on 8 July 2014.

12. Sexual Advocacy: www.AdvocacyProfessional.com.

13. Annon, J. (1976) *The PLISSIT Model of Sex Therapy: Behavioral Treatment of Sexual Problems.* New York, NY: Harper & Row Medical.

14. The Sexual Health and Disability Alliance (SHADA): www.SHADA.org.uk.

15. TLC Trust: www.TLC-Trust.org.uk.

16. Joannides, P. (2013) *A Guide to Getting It On! A Book About the Wonders of Sex.* Waldport, OR: Goofy Foot Press.

17. Quilliam, S. (2008) *The New Joy of Sex.* London, UK: Octopus.

18. Godson, S. and Agace, M. (2002) *The Sex Book.* London, UK: Cassell Illustrated.

19. Heart, M. (2004) *The Ultimate Guide to Orgasm for Women.* San Francisco, CA: Cleis Press.

20. Kaufman, M., Silverberg, C. and Odette, F. (2007) *The Ultimate Guide to Sex and Disability.* San Francisco, CA: Cleis Press.

CHAPTER 7

SPECIFIC PROFESSIONS AND THE ALLIED THERAPIES

I hope this chapter not only encourages you to consider including the support of sexuality in your services to disabled people, but also demonstrates the range of services which could be ideal for disabled people in your care. You may never have thought of suggesting to someone who seems blocked in their sexuality that they might try art therapy, for example, but this may just be what they need.

I hear the same complaint from colleagues across the whole range of the professions, that they feel let down by their governing bodies which have no training, policies or practical guidelines to support and guide them. Thus, many don't feel confident enough to deal with speaking to disabled people about sex. My advice is to complain to your governing bodies, and prove to them that it is necessary. You could even create a petition which has their legal obligations listed, to be signed by the relevant professionals.

Although having the governing body policy and guidelines is the ideal, you don't need to be knowledgeable in order to ask the question. Some of your clients or patients will be feeling desperate to speak to someone about their troublesome personal lives, so you can be the start of a process by listening, taking them seriously, reassuring, discussing and sending them elsewhere for more help if necessary.

Many health and social care professionals do not realize that they can join the Sexual Health and Disability Alliance (SHADA)[1] and gain from it, even if you cannot attend meetings. You can stay updated on what we are doing and can send questions, ideas and news to the group. You can join SHADA groups abroad and international special interest groups. If you *can* attend the meetings in London, you might not realize that they are designed to support those members who attend, so I always say to people who are coming, do ask for support on what you are stuck with/need to know, in advance, and we'll reserve some time and aim to have the experts there to support you. Many pioneers are regular attendees. There is also always the option of calling our Sex and Disability Helpline.[2]

I have spoken to a wide range of disabled people who speak of missed opportunities: typically, of the health professional or therapist they *did* see when they were young, who failed to ask about how they were coping in their social or sexual lives. For example, a dentist who pulled a number of front teeth from the mouth of an 11-year-old boy only spoke to his parents about how this might affect his face and, as a result, his subsequent social acceptance. Sadly, neither the parents nor the dentist ever supported the boy to feel confident about his looks. The result was that he always covered his mouth with his hand and was shy and uncomfortable in company. Now, years later, he still finds mixing with people a real challenge.

So please take this responsibility seriously, and don't be put off because at the outset you may feel ill-equipped to cope. You may not want to look unprofessional but, remember, one of the great things about sex is that there is always something new to learn, and nobody can be expected to know everything. Indeed, just saying that itself to a patient or client will make them respect you for your honesty. Together, you can find a way.

In most services, and especially in mental health, questions about sexual expression are not included in the initial assessment, which is very outdated, ignoring duty of care; and very sad, when so much more could be done. It is helpful to mention to the client before the assessment takes place that any worries of a personal or intimate nature can be discussed.

I am going to start by discussing nursing, which has been viewed as being at the vanguard of acceptance of sexuality in person-centred care. The RCN (Royal College of Nursing) was the first, and is still currently the only, professional body to have written a document for nurses to support their patients, including those who have disabilities, with their sexuality. Sadly, this 2000 document was made redundant in 2013; more on that later. The College of Occupational Therapists has been talking about a policy document, and the College of Social Work, being new, says it has an open mind on the idea. The British

Medical Association (BMA) Junior Members' Forum voted in favour of medical students being trained in sex and disability.

Starting with the medical professions, my list then takes you through the major therapies and social work, followed by the more specialist, less conventional and mixed therapies, peer support and my newly created body image therapy.

Nursing

It may be thanks to the wonderful book written in 1985 by Jean Glover, *Human Sexuality in Nursing Care,*[3] that nursing got off to a good start. It is still a very useful and pertinent book, currently out of print, though you can find second-hand copies online. Jean was one of my sex therapy teachers and wrote the book before she'd met me, so the section on disability is tiny, but at least it's there.

The 2000 RCN document *Sexuality and Sexual Health in Nursing Practice: Discussion and Guidance* was the first and only document on sexuality to include disability produced by any professional body in Britain. It did not lay out a policy but suggested that each nursing or medical establishment did. It made suggestions rather than offering guidelines, but at least it was a start. I was told that it was made obsolete in 2013 and is no longer available online, although there are still a few copies which can be viewed in the college. Other publications on sexuality[4] have since been produced, but none address the management of sexual health where it is impacted by disability and there are very few policy guidelines on offer. In 2014, SHADA was invited by the RSN to write a short paragraph on sex and disability for the Sexual Health page on their website.

Nurses are, of course, accustomed to dealing with people's genitals and with the reality of all kinds of people trying to find a bit of privacy for sexual pleasure and release, and many say that little bothers them. However, in these days of under-staffing, they may be less likely to sit down at a patient's bedside and listen to their private fears. Such fears may simply be about how their attractiveness or functioning might be affected by illness or treatment, and worries about whether sex will actually be possible for them. They may wish to express their total sense of isolation over the way an operation or progressive condition may impact on their sex lives. Any conversation, even if the nurse does not have the answers, can start the process of preventing a sexual problem arising.

Sexual health clinics are often disability-friendly places where the nurses are usually experienced and respectful with disabled patients. They can be experts at educating disabled people and their partners around the sexual side-effects of illness and disability, and can advise on how to make sex better. Thus, if other health professionals feel stuck with nowhere to send a disabled client for help, these clinics are an option.

Midwives can make a great deal of difference to the mental state of pregnant women and of mothers who have recently given birth who are at a very vulnerable stage of their lives. The midwife might tell them what many other women complain of, which can be a starting point for open discussions. They can suggest coping mechanisms which can both help with existing difficulties and prevent future sexual problems arising. Midwives should not be afraid to discuss sex with single mums, surrogate mums, lesbian mums and disabled mums.

A woman's rectum and vagina can be damaged by a bad delivery during childbirth, and if this happens, she may blame herself for subsequently having painful intercourse and/or a leaking rectum. When left untreated, the anal sphincter atrophies and things get worse. The woman has literally become disabled as a result of childbirth, yet very few will choose to have a stoma. Follow-up support with post-natal women could do more to support them. Mike Lousada[5] is a London-based trauma therapist who does body work with such women in London, but what they probably need is surgery.

The liability and blame culture in nursing in care homes, mentioned in Chapter 3, is having a damaging effect on person-centred care, which is very worrying, but, I hope, with pressure from pioneers in SHADA, this will improve soon.

Doctors and other medical staff

Medical schools sometimes provide training about sexuality as part of their core curriculum, but this does not include disability. The problem is that the General Medical Council (GMC), when asked about adding something into the curriculum, in return ask what should then be removed.

Doctors are trained to make people better, and have traditionally felt deeply uneasy with patients they cannot cure. Disability is something they cannot cure, so doctors have felt ill-prepared to treat disabled patients. In addition, sexuality is not considered a priority, and it does not sit very happily in most doctors' agendas. They find it 'fluffy medicine'. Most medical staff have 'heard it all before' with patients coming to them with strange objects stuck up their rectum, for example. Such things are considered amusing, and they can cope. But when someone comes to them with a delicate personal sexual problem, most shy away.

Reasons given in medical texts say that doctors feel they lack training, fear being intrusive, and fear they have only inadequate knowledge. Doctors often make common assumptions, for example that a visibly impaired patient is innocent of sexual desire and unlikely to find partners.

Uncertain of whether or not anything can be done to improve a disabled person's sexual plight, a doctor may decide not to mention sex at all. But the best possible route is when the patient feels comfortable talking about everything with their GP or consultant, including sex. So, whatever their sexual tastes or whatever the impairments of the patient, please ask, listen, take interest, and *take them seriously.*

The Institute of Psychosexual Medicine in London provides education, training and research in psychosexual medicine for qualified medical practitioners. Practitioners around the UK are listed on their website.[6] Their Annual Scientific Meeting in 2014 was entitled, 'Allied Health Professionals and the IPM' and I have suggested another on disability.

Gynaecologists sit somewhere in between the sex therapist and other doctors, and ought to be better at discussing sex with patients, but regrettably they seldom are.

Doctors need to maintain respect from their patients, so remember: you may be laughed at if you are prudish, or if you shy away from sexual matters. You are doing a professional disservice if you leave vulnerable people unhappy in the area of their lives which may be the most important to them.

Consultants, surgeons and GPs have a duty of care with a disabled patient to discuss the implications of their condition on sexual activity. If they are planning to conduct an operation or procedure, or to prescribe medication that might impact on the patient's sex life, they need to *discuss* this with them. People deserve to know and do worry, so bring the subject up, and offer choices.

Many disabled patients have problems with their continence and sexual function. For example, when preparing for the insertion of a supra-pubic catheter, it is essential to discuss its siting and sexual implications. The Sexual Respect Tool Kit Training Film[7] shows a young lady with MS describing how her catheter was sited low down to enable her to sunbathe, and she told her surgeon, 'Actually, I prefer sex to sunbathing.' He then moved the catheter to a higher position on her body, which she herself had selected. But even then, no real discussion ever took place about where would be the ideal siting. The second procedure, moving the site (which was also not in the most ideal place), would not have been needed at all if the surgeon had discussed the situation with her fully in the first place!

Also in the Sexual Respect Tool Kit film, GP Daniel Atkinson says, 'Thinking about talking about sex is more frightening than actually doing it'. Dr Atkinson had been selected to talk at our conference on sex and disability by the Royal Society of Medicine, where the conference was taking place. Having agreed, he thought he had better make a concerted effort to speak to his disabled patients about the topic. He was scared, but determined; and he reached this conclusion as quoted above.

The Sexual Respect Tool Kit provides instructions on how to initiate discussions around sex, which only takes three minutes to read because we were told that doctors will not read anything which takes longer. If you are a doctor and still reading this book, congratulations! I don't expect you have time to support your patients in all the ways I suggest in this book but, learning what needs to be done, you can refer on and delegate.

In the Canadian textbook *Sexual Medicine in Primary Care*,[8] the author Dr Bill Maurice says that what most patients want to know is that they are normal and not alone.

Sex and disability is not, at the time of writing, taught in medical school, although a medical student who belongs to SHADA,[1] Natalie Barclay-Klingle, who is also a member of the BMA Junior Members Forum, proposed there that it would be good to look at unifying the quality of teaching given to all medical students about sex, sexual health and disability. The motion was passed, and was then taken to the Medical School's Council for a decision on how to take it forward.

Natalie wrote this:

As a medical student, I am taught to communicate with and treat individuals as whole beings, with emphasis on physical, mental and social well-being. However, I find that the amount of information I am given throughout the medical curriculum regarding disability and sexual health is virtually non-existent, and not enough to make a difference to disabled people in medical practice. SHADA has taught me so much in this area and I would like to be able to share it with my colleagues, since I believe that medical education should allow qualified doctors to confidently speak about the importance of sex with every patient, and especially with those with disabilities. I am passionate in trying to make this a mandatory part of the medical curriculum.

There is a Program in Human Sexuality in the University of Minnesota's Medical School,[9] which claims to be one of the largest clinical, teaching and research institutions in the world specializing in human sexuality.

Doctors have much to contribute by encouraging their disabled patients to enjoy sex in any way they choose (so long as it's legal) and ensure that their impairments, fatigue, pain, incontinence, lack of movement, spasms or medicines and so on, which may adversely affect their sex lives, have as little negative impact as possible.

Social workers

Some social workers are really good at supporting people with their sexual expression, seeing it as part of a holistic approach to their work. But this is patchy in learning disability services, ignoring, for example, older clients.

The government is ultimately responsible for social policy, which local authorities put into practice. Although policy on sexual well-being is necessary, there are, as yet, no policy guidelines from the College of Social Work, nor is there training. This means that most social workers still feel ill-equipped and unsupported in having a sex-positive attitude to their work. The importance of sexual well-being needs to be in the training curriculum, so students have it in mind when they get out into practice.

Social workers usually meet people in crisis; so, for example, someone who has been sexually abused may present in mental health crisis, or having self-harmed. Or an older person with dementia might self-harm through excessive masturbation using household objects. The social worker needs to provide positive support, but this does not have to overshadow their work dealing with the more positive benefits of sex and intimacy.

Some statutory social workers undertake needs assessments for benefits for disabled people, which sometimes includes money to buy sex toys, hoists, visits with sex workers, make-up, and others. An official in the personal budgets at the Department of Health agreed with me that this should happen, but budgets have been cut and often all the social worker can do is signpost on to other sources.

It would be a shame if the only concern of the state were with safeguarding, making sure disabled people were not a risk, rather than allowing them full autonomy.

Mental health professionals

In mental health professionals we include psychiatrists, psychiatric nurses, clinical psychologists (MSW or MSSW), clinical social workers, mental health counsellors, and others.

I have heard complaints from people who work in mental health that sexuality is rarely included in their work, and there is sparse literature on the subject. Sexual difficulty can itself be a key aspect of a deterioration of mental health. Dr Bill Maurice,[8] with his background in psychiatry, talks about how the treatment of mental illness can affect sexuality and that some psychiatric disorders are of a sexual nature.

A bipolar volunteer of mine described his therapist as wanting him to be a square peg fitting a round hole, and being fobbed off with platitudes.

The best coverage I have found is the Canadian *Sexuality, intimacy and mental health: How do we include sexuality as a part of recovery and rehabilitation? How are relationships affected by mental illness? And what is healthy sexuality? When is it a problem?*[17] It is a lengthy treatment, ranging from dating to sexual phobia, and the effects of medications.

Geli Heimann[18] says that 'positive psychology' explores a person's strengths and resilience both as an individual and within the couple/family unit, rather than their weaknesses and dysfunctions. This has been used to support disabled people with their sexuality.

Alzheimer's patients may be confused and attempt to have sex with the wrong person by mistake, or no longer differentiate between private and public spaces. This is rather like the situation of those with learning difficulties, where health professionals are forced to deal with sexual problems, and may have training. I list a helpful publication covering this topic.[19]

As sex is an important part of people's lives, mental health workers need to include sexual feelings and activities in history-taking, and ask about any problems the client may be experiencing in socializing and intimacy. Safer sex and other knowledge may be needed by the client to keep them safe and give them confidence. This type of thing is often sadly lacking yet is very important for people with mental health problems living in the community.

Many disabled people suffer from anxiety caused by anger, resentment, repression and frustration. Their sexual urges, if unexpressed, may trouble them to such an extent that they display bad behaviour and have thoughts of suicide

The most useful book I have read on mental health and sex is Chad Varah's *The Samaritans: Befriending the Suicidal.*[20] Chad started the Samaritans because he came across a young girl who was feeling suicidal because she was pregnant. It was his non-judgemental openness about sex which caused him to eventually be thrown out of his own organization! His book explains how when somebody is depressed, just one disaster in their lives can make them give up. This disaster may well be of a sexual nature, and something that they've never been given permission to express before their Samaritans phone call. I hope this helps you see why it can be so important for you to offer such a discussion with your client.

In my research, I approached all the professional bodies to find out how they support clients in their sexuality, and disabled clients in particular. Routinely, phone calls were met with 'Please put this in an email' and the email subsequently ignored. I just hope my questions might have made them think, and realize that they might need to consider this gap in their provision!

Occupational therapy

In America, occupational therapists include sexuality as part of a routine evaluation of clients, and it is considered a safe place for sexual concerns to be discussed. A really good account of the ways that this can happen with disabled people is written in the American Occupational Therapy Association's fact sheet, *Sexuality and the Role of Occupational Therapy.*[10] A more recent American paper which can be found online, *An Occupational Therapist Perspective on Sexual Health,*[11] provides more insight.

Sadly, the UK lags behind. British Occupational Therapy pioneer Lorna Couldrick has long argued that the impact of disability on sexual expression should be included within any holistic occupational therapy assessment. OTs (Occupational Therapists) are, after all, dealing with all other activities in their clients' lives. However, many are uncertain about their role in this area and lack confidence and competence. Lorna has asked the professional body, the College of Occupational Therapists (COT), to write a discussion and guidance document. This would really support OTs and encourage them to seek post-registration training if necessary. Basically, a professional body must write its own policy for it to be convincing to those people asked to abide by it and to feel meaningful ownership of it. In addition, having done their own work, the policy would be more likely to then be put into practice. However, at the time of writing, there is no evidence that COT intend to create a discussion and guidance document to support their members.

OTs know, only too well, how important it is for people to enjoy activities which they relate to in everyday life, and how their mood and mental health affects their capacity to enjoy these activities. Support with sexual issues should simply be part of what OTs do, and they should be able to tell their clients that it is part of what they do.

OT Amy Parkin focused her MSc research, in conjunction with Leeds Metropolitan University, on the views and practices of OTs in the United Kingdom. She found that 87 per cent of OTs working in physical areas of practice believe that sex is a valid domain for occupational therapy, yet only 28 per cent reported that they directly ask clients about sexual issues within their practice and 63 per cent are rarely or never approached by clients for support with sexual difficulties. The implication of this is that patients are not getting the support they may require from their OT.

Where occupational therapists did say that they regularly addressed the issue of sex with clients, it was described as a natural extension within their practice. Exploring the impact of a disability on a relationship in terms of roles was felt to be especially important: OTs said that some of their clients felt that too much emphasis was put on the mechanics of sex, with neglect of the emotional side of things, and OTs are very skilled at exploring and appreciating occupational roles (partner, worker, etc.). Within the sample of OTs who did address the issues, the most common intervention was giving out information leaflets, followed by equipment prescription, and advice on pain, fatigue and positioning.

The right setting was also an emerging theme, with a community setting suggested by some. Obviously it is best if the conversation cannot be overheard, and the more private it is, the better, but Lorna Couldrick found in her research[12] that sometimes disabled people ask sexual questions at the most unexpected times and in the most unexpected places, and thus the practitioner must find a way to take questions seriously, discuss the urgency of the question, and how best it can be dealt with. It was with this in mind that she wrote her Recognition Model[13] for use with disabled clients, to replace the established PLISSIT model, both described in the previous chapter. Amy Parkin's sample spoke of various factors that hindered their ability and confidence to address clients' sexuality within conversations and assessments – namely the lack of university and in-service training, and the disappearance of services and personnel they may have referred to. Hopefully, OTs will form a closer working relationship with SHADA in the future, once OTs are aware of the available support such as the Sexual Respect Toolkit.[7]

Amy's sample included some really good examples of occupational therapists facilitating 'quiet' private time on hospital wards for younger inpatients, when they could masturbate if they wished, and the suggestion made that clients should be aware of available support services before being discharged from acute care. One of Amy's sample recommends massage, post-amputation, to reduce phantom pains and to help with intimacy. Amy says this is a good example of how professionals can extend their traditional interventions supporting couples to come to terms with change and accepting body/sexual transitions.

Only 37 per cent of Amy's sample of occupational therapists had received any training and most wanted more. Some suggested that they should not be alone in this venture: that the supporting of clients with sexual difficulties should be multidisciplinary. This would certainly help the various professions to work together. Knowing who specializes in what aspect of sexuality and emotional support as a service pathway would be useful.

Amy, among many other occupational therapists, fully supports publication of guidance in this area by the College of Occupational Therapists, and she is now contributing to the visibility of what therapists feel they need, with the hope that this encourages the

College of Occupational Therapists to resume the writing of their policy guidelines.

I have seen a suggestion in the leaflet *Pleasure Able – Sexual Device Manual for Persons with Disabilities*[14] that occupational therapists could adapt sex toys so that they can be used by their disabled client. It would be useful if they could make a clamp to hold a sex toy in place for a disabled person with little or no bodily movement to use when they want to masturbate. They could also teach a friend, family member or care support worker to position the sex toy when required. The clean-up after ejaculation should be viewed as being just like any other task in the daily care routine.

Physiotherapy

Physiotherapists support people with their movements, agility, comfort and pain management. Therefore there is plenty of work to be done with disabled people who may struggle to get into positions, to feel comfortable enough to enjoy masturbation and partnered sex, because they have spasms, and suffer from pain, stiffness, lack of balance and so on. Sadly, it seems, physiotherapists are not normally trained to support clients in facilitating sexual pleasure, only to move their bodies better for walking and doing other daily tasks. There is only one area of support I found: pelvic floor physiotherapy does support clients in the treatment of bladder and bowel problems and genital pain, which may be experienced during sex.

Physiotherapists should realize that all they need to do is ask the client if they have any sexual problems, then describe what is happening in their body to bring these about, and discuss how the person can adapt and move forward.

Speech and language therapy

Speech and language therapists (SLTs) are responsible for ensuring that those people who find speech difficult or impossible are offered the best possible means of communicating. It is they who advise on who needs to use which symbols, so they should be aware of the topics needing to be discussed around sexuality and ensure that the symbols provide them with accurate descriptions. I think they have recognized the need but have been a bit shy of really providing clarity.

SLTs are also required to advise every disabled person who needs a device to help them communicate about which type would best fit their requirements. This, of course, may be necessary for their socializing and relationships. However, SLTs have no way of knowing which devices may be best for various types of impairments, lifestyles, and so on. Joe Reddington has provided independent advice on augmentative and alternative communication (AAC) devices for SLTs on his disability blog.[15]

SLTs are sometimes used with transsexuals who need help with speaking more like their newly acquired gender. It seems that sex and socializing are otherwise excluded from the SLT agenda. I have already mentioned how this let down a girl with a speech impairment, as her social life was not discussed in her professional consultation.

SLTs and speech coaches could support disabled people who need to develop their voices and gain confidence in speaking assertively, in order to discuss sex with partners and perhaps to compensate for their lack of mobility. This may be highly beneficial in order for them to enjoy the type of sex they wish to engage in. Joanna Crosse's book *Find Your Voice*[16] talks about empowerment through becoming more assertive in language and voice. It also includes a section about one Outsiders member, a disabled girl with cerebral palsy and a severe speech impairment.

Cognitive behavioural therapy

Cognitive behavioural therapy can be used to retrain the way people think in order to change their behaviour. Thus, somebody who acquires an impairment which changes the ways they can enjoy sexual activity, but who is finding it difficult to adapt, could be helped to change the way they think of sex. They can be taught to start having sex without aiming for goals such as orgasm, and develop a new attitude to realize many new pleasures.

Drama therapy

Drama therapy can be used to help people feel more relaxed when talking about sex. It is a back-up therapy in spinal units, used to help people come to terms with their new bodies. It could be used to support disabled people to become more assertive in stating their sexual needs to a partner, and in learning to invite their partner to do likewise. Those with Asperger's syndrome have told me that they have found drama helpful with socializing. It can, for example, give them practice in expressing feelings such as 'I feel confused about what you want to do with me and my body. Please tell me how you feel and what you want.'

Art therapy

There is no training, and there are no policies, on the use of art therapy to support disabled people in their sexual lives, which is a shame because art therapy offers the opportunity for expression, and can be particularly helpful to people who find it hard to express their thoughts and feelings verbally or are aphasic. People who have used art therapy say they gained new insights about themselves.

But art itself is used outside the art therapy profession to support disabled and sexually troubled people. Sarah Berry runs Fannies Rule[21] for women who have problems accepting their vulvas. Using a mirror, the group draws their own vulvas and find, for example, that their labia are not unusually long or short, and each woman is not alone in her insecurities. This helps them move forward. Sarah is welcoming of disabled people in her group.

Katie Sarra[22] is an art therapist who deviates from what she was trained to do by painting disabled people nude, in oils, to provide them with positive attention and an image of themselves looking beautiful, which helps them gain sexual self-confidence. Esther Bunting runs Spirited Bodies[23] involving relaxed, private sessions where disabled people can join in life modelling and drawing, which provides similar support. There is more about such work at the end of this chapter under body image therapy.

Preventive therapy

Preventing obesity means that the person will become more active, attractive and sexy and less likely to have diabetes – which can lead to impotence. Preventing smoking means that the person will be more likely to attract a partner because they don't smell like an ash tray. Preventive therapy might persuade diabetics to control their condition and avoid amputation. With sex being the second strongest human drive (after survival), this therapy could be better and more extensively promoted as sexy to encourage people who struggle to defeat unsexy habits.

Trauma therapy

Trauma therapy can support people in their sexual relationships after war injury, accidents, birthing problems and sudden changes due to disability.

Music therapy

Music therapy can transport people out of their everyday lives, bring a unique joy, and lift their spirits. It can be relaxing, or lead to excitement, such as sexy or romantic feelings. This can open up discussion. It can also allow people to express themselves in a medium other than words. Like art therapy, it can bring a disabled person to a place where they feel in touch with their inner selves and feel a better connection with people around them.

Mixed therapies

These are increasingly used by occupational therapists and other professionals to support their clients and are listed below.

Creative arts therapy

Creative arts therapy uses a mixture of therapies: writing, drawing and drama, for example, to empower people to feel more responsible for themselves and gain self-confidence and self-esteem. It is used in the ICU Transformational Arts project,[24] mentioned in Chapter 5, which involves engaging, multidimensional programmes and workshops in schools, to effect long-lasting and holistic change in the behaviour of young people.

Recreational therapy/therapeutic recreation

These use a mixture of therapies to enable disabled people to continue to follow their creative interests by helping them with their confidence to become more involved with others. It is an avenue whereby single people might find a partner. The therapy could help to bring back sexual functions which were lost, and enable the person to become more capable of enjoying sex and meaningful relationships.

Activity therapy

Activity therapy uses a collection of therapies such as exercise, beauty, games and crafts to allow disabled and elderly people to live full lives. There is no reason why they cannot include partner dancing, flirting, and things which keep their sexual spirit alive and help participants share the knowledge that sex need not stop with impairment and old age.

Peer support, counselling and group therapy

Peer support is highly effective and takes place in both a structured and an unstructured way in the Outsiders club. The club helpline is answered by people with disabilities and they pride themselves on the way they talk like a friend rather than as a professional, with some positive influence from the Samaritans. Outsiders' V Group, mentioned in Chapter 1, provides excellent peer support. There is also the unstructured support which members provide each other online, in our Clubhouse, and in person, sometimes in practical and other times in personal ways, in their everyday lives. It also happens at our lunches and events.

Peer support is also provided in spinal injury centres. Spinal injured sex therapist Michelle Donald runs workshops in various units, covering sexual topics. Peer support is the essence of some private online disability groups, and they may or may not include sexual matters. We need more disabled people to support those with similar impairments and become sexual counsellors and therapists.

Peer support can be done one-to-one or within groups. Groups can be very powerful, as you probably know. What health and social care professionals can do is to set up, or simply encourage the formation of, groups for adults and children with the same impairments, so that they can gain confidence from being with each other and learn the value of peer support. They may naturally want to include sex in their topics of discussion, or welcome your suggestions. I am told that groups are more difficult with people with learning difficulties, as they may all have varying levels of ability to grasp information. What can work well with people who feel anxious or depressed is having a community space where they can mix with other people and start to support each other. A good example of a peer support group is Young People For Inclusion[25] based in Kentish Town in London, which truly inspires its disabled members to live eventful lives.

Body image therapy

When Esther Bunting gave her brilliant presentation on her project, Spirited Bodies,[23] at the Outsiders Jamboree in 2013, I realized that she and many other artists and practitioners I know are all working with the same goal in mind: to support people with their body image and sexual self-confidence. Esther's life-drawing classes include disabled people, and one of them was there to speak of the benefits he had gained.

Simply giving the disabled person positive attention to their bodies helps them gain a feeling of worth, and sets them on the road to being able to enjoy bodily pleasures. I know many individuals who offer their different skills to achieve this effect, and thought that they might perhaps benefit from being in touch with each other. So, I drew up a list of such practitioners and, with their permission, put them on the Outsiders website, calling the group Outsiders' Partners. There is now talk of a conference and perhaps group events. Practitioners include those who use art, photography, costumery, hairdressing, massage and various kinds of body work.[26]

Ashley Savage has been photographing disabled people since 1996, and has a gallery of his work on his website Savage Skin.[27] He says that he empowers the disabled model to state how they want the picture and how they wish to present themselves so they have control over the session. I have witnessed immediate improvement in the confidence and happiness of Outsiders members who have been his subjects. Photography and filming are well known to bring sexual confidence to people – some women decide to appear in porn movies to this end. Those who pose or appear in film report that, somehow, it feels as if the lens is making love to its subject. Most of Ashley's subjects (including Mat Fraser) have leapt ahead, enjoying sexual adventures in life.

Estelle Robb[28] is a Scottish girl in Aberdeen, who shares her experiences of cancer with her mother and grandmother. She is also a hairdresser, and provides a free hairdressing service for those experiencing cancer and chemotherapy, styling wigs for them to make them feel fabulous.

D. Fisher runs Second Coming[29] in London, using dramatic costumes she has collected in charity shops – which she may adapt – to dress people, including disabled people. She makes them look spectacular in their own individual style, which brings a change in the way they see themselves and feel inside. D. dresses the models in the Outsiders' Tactile Fashion Shows mentioned in my preface.

Val Rusco, through her service Channelled Bliss,[30] offers people of all orientations, abilities and degrees of mobility a way to delve deeper into the sensuality of their bodies through the channelling of energy, breath work and the gentle touch. Through breath work, she teaches clients how to enjoy full body orgasms without touch.

I hope that learning about these artists, craftspeople and professionals will inspire other professionals and therapists, and I look forward to a time when their work will perhaps become incorporated in established professional practices.

Resources

1. The Sexual Health and Disability Alliance (SHADA): www.shada.org.uk.
2. The Sex and Disability Helpline: 07074 993 527, 11am to 7pm weekdays.
3. Glover, J. (1985) *Human Sexuality in Nursing Care.* London, UK: Croom Helm.
4. Royal College of Nursing publications: www.rcn.org.uk/publications:

   002 469 *Sexual health competences: An integrated career and competency framework for sexual and reproductive health nursing across the UK* (2009)

   004 136 *Older people in care homes: Sex, sexuality and intimate relationships* (2011)

   002 021 *Signpost guide for nurses working with young people: Sex and relationships education* (2005)

   004 368 *Genital examination in women: A resource for skills development and assessment* (2013)

   004 122 *Competences: For nurses assessing and counselling women who request and/ or receive long-acting reversible methods of contraception (LARC)* (2011, currently being updated)

   002 018 *The nursing care of lesbian and gay male patients or clients. Guidance for nursing staff* (2003).

5. Mike Lousada: www.MikeLousada.com.
6. Institute of Psychosexual Medicine: www.ipm.org.uk.
7. The Sexual Respect Tool Kit: www.SexualRespect.com.
8. Maurice, W.L. (1999) *Sexual Medicine in Primary Care.* St Louis, MO: Mosby.
9. University of Minnesota Medical School Program in Human Sexuality: www.phs. umn.edu.
10. American Occupational Therapy Association (2013) *Sexuality and the Role of Occupational Therapy.* Available at www.aota.org/en/About-Occupational-Therapy/ Professionals/RDP/Sexuality.aspx, accessed on 8 July 2014.
11. Tanner, B. (2012) *Competent and Confident: An Occupational Therapist Perspective on Sexual Health.* Available at http://soundideas.pugetsound.edu/ms_occ_therapy/55, accessed on 8 July 2014.

12. Couldrick, L., Sadlo, G. and Cross, V. (2010) 'Proposing a new sexual health model of practice for disability teams: The Recognition Model.' *International Journal of Therapy and Rehabilitation 17*, 6, 290–299.

13. The Recognition Model: www.shada.org.uk.

14. Naphtali, K., MacHattie, E. and Elliot, S.L. (2009) *Pleasure Able – Sexual Device Manual for Persons with Disabilities.* Disabilities Health Research Network. Available at www.dhrn.ca/files/sexualhealthmanual_lowres_2010_0208.pdf, accessed on 8 July 2014.

15. Joe Reddington's Disability Blog: www.joereddington.com.

16. Crosse, J. (2009) *Find Your Voice.* London, UK: Piatkus.

17. Ellery, D. (ed) (1999) 'Sexuality, intimacy and mental health: How do we include sexuality as a part of recovery and rehabilitation? How are relationships affected by mental illness? And what is healthy sexuality? When is it a problem?' *Visions (British Columbia's Mental Health Journal) 8*, Spring/Summer issue. Available at www.iusmm.ca/documents/C%C3%89RRIS/cerris_cmha_sexualite.pdf, accessed on 8 July 2014.

18. Geli Heimann: www.geliheimann.com/healingspace/positive-strengths-psychology-plus-a-holistic-systemic-approach.

19. Bamford, S.-M. (2011) *The Last Taboo: A Guide to Dementia, Sexuality, Intimacy and Sexual Behaviour in Care Homes.* London, UK: ILC-UK. Available at www.ilcuk.org.uk/files/pdf_pdf_184.pdf, accessed on 8 July 2014.

20. Varah, C. (1988) *The Samaritans: Befriending the Suicidal* (7th revised edition). London, UK: Constable.

21. Fannies Rule: www.londonsexcounselling.co.uk.

22. Katie Sarra: www.katiesarra.com.

23. Spirited Bodies: www.spiritedbodies.com.

24. ICU Transformational Arts: www.icu-transformational-arts.com.

25. Young People For Inclusion: www.ypfi.org.uk.

26. Body Image Therapy: www.outsiders.org.uk/partners.html.

27. Savage Skin: www.SavageSkin.co.uk.

28. Estelle Robb: estelle.robb@sky.com.

29. Second Coming: secondcomingclothing@hotmail.com.

30. Channelled Bliss: www.channelledbliss.com.

CHAPTER 8

SEXUAL SERVICES

This chapter explains differences between the various types of sexual services on offer:

1. **Sex therapy**, also called **Sex and relationship therapy** and **Psychosexual therapy**, which is primarily therapeutic, usually educational, and uses talk without sexual touch.

2. **Body work**, which is also primarily therapeutic and is educational, but is experiential and includes sexual touch.

3. **Body image therapy**, which offers techniques to provide sexual self-confidence and may include sexual or non-sexual touch.

4. **Sexual advocacy**, which is facilitation using talk and education, sometimes including non-sexual touch and enablement.

5. **Striptease**, which is performance, usually without touch or any bodily contact.

6. **Sexual surrogacy** and **Sex work**, which primarily provide various kinds of pleasurable and satisfying sexual activities, including intimacy, and can also provide education, emotional support and nice company.

1. Sex therapy (also known as Psychosexual therapy)

Sex therapists are professionals who see people, usually couples, who are experiencing a sexual problem. The therapist normally already has had some academic training before starting their therapy training, which takes a minimum of two years part-time at a medical or other professional establishment. Most training establishments are able to provide an accredited diploma, and accredited sex therapists are listed on the College of Sex and Relationship Therapists (COSRT) website.[1] Sex therapists specializing in seeing people with sexual diversity appear on the Pink Therapy website.[2]

Sex therapy includes a range of therapeutic techniques so that the sex therapist is fully equipped to respond to their clients. Clients are usually given home work, lovely things to do which magically take the pressure off, and allow them to function as they want, and to enjoy sex again. My own personal experience of seeing clients was enormous fun, and it was great to support couples in becoming happier. Even when all they really needed was permission to separate, you could see the new optimism in their eyes.

What a sex therapist may *not* do is use their hands on the clients' bodies. Only if they also have a medical qualification can they touch, but not in a sexual way.

Common problems treated are lack of desire, lack of erection, inability to reach orgasm, reaching orgasm too fast or slowly, or they have stopped having sex. Good information about sexual problems is given on the COSRT website.[1]

If you have a client who complains about a lack of desire, erection or orgasm, it is best if they go to their doctor first. The problem may be caused by medication, or it may indicate the onset of a condition. For example, lack of erection may indicate the onset of diabetes. Once these options have been dismissed, you can discuss an appointment with a sex therapist.

Many British people say they don't want to go for therapy, especially if they are a partner who doesn't wish to engage in sexual activity, and perhaps don't feel able to talk about sex. Most sexual problems are caused by relationship difficulties and reluctance to talk. Once a couple get to the therapist, they are both usually eager to tell their stories, because they feel supported and safe.

I find it tragic that a patient might go to their doctor with a sexual problem such as not being able to get an erection, and have medication such as Viagra, Cialis or Levitra prescribed, when the problem might be resolved by a sex therapist for life by the person having as few as four hour-long sessions of sex therapy. It's as if sex therapists have been ousted by pills! I keep saying that they need to do a better PR job on themselves, and make the service more attractive and modern.

There are still many very conventional sex therapists who are only really happy with conventional couples, rather than lesbian, gay, bisexual, transgendered, queer and intersex (LGBTQI) people, those into BDSM (bondage, domination, sado-masochism), those who enjoy an alternative lifestyle, or need to see a sex worker. Dominic Davis who runs Pink Therapy,[2] the agency for sex therapists catering specially for people with sexual diversity, writes, 'Counselling and therapy programmes in Britain are genuinely still ridiculously uninformed about differences experienced by gender and sexual minorities.' Relate training even instructs the students who train with them not to recommend sex workers to their clients!

COSRT,[1] Pink Therapy[2] and AASECT (the American Association of Sexuality Educators, Counselors and Therapists)[3] all have great websites where local accredited sex therapists can be found. AASECT even has an international directory covering Canada, USA, South Africa, India, China, Australia and New Zealand.

Michelle Donald is a spinal injured Relate-trained sex therapist with a good grasp of disability issues. She trained because she received no support around sex when she broke her back, and she is certainly changing that around in the spinal units today. Michelle is excellent at supporting men who are cock-centric and cannot conceive of the idea of enjoying sex if they can no longer get an erection. She runs workshops on the subject in spinal units. It would be great if all disability support centres could employ trained peer sex therapists.

Although most sex therapists are happy to see disabled clients, few specialize in disability. I've mentioned Michelle Donald above; Maxine Aston specializes in people with Asperger's, and Sue Newsome and Mitch Tepper (also spinal cord injured) in America see people with physical impairments. Dominic Davis, founder of Pink Therapy, and Simon Parritt, the last director of SPOD (Sexual Problems of the Disabled), are both disabled sex therapists who take a special interest in disability generally.

Clients are advised to talk to the therapist over the phone before booking an appointment, because they may need a certain chemistry, and confidence that their particular impairment or lifestyle is to be adequately understood.

It is also a really good idea for health and social care professionals to meet their local sex therapists at some stage (perhaps inviting them to come and make a presentation) so that they feel confident in themselves about making referrals or recommendations.

2. Body work

There are many types of body work, and I am covering only the basics here, including both accredited practices and those which are not. Many use techniques taken from ancient yoga, Tantric or Taoist practices. There is a new style of sexual therapy which includes working with the body, as well as talk. It started with Sexological Bodywork[4] where students train under Joseph Kramer, based at the Institute for the Advanced Study of Human Sexuality in San Francisco. In London, there is Psychosexual Somatics[5] where Mike Lousada runs a course.

Sexological Bodywork was officially approved as a certified and licensed profession for trained sexologists by the State of California in 2003, and people come to train from all over the world. Joseph also travels and a training session took place in the UK in 2014. The work may include internal and external genital and/or anal touch, although touch is strictly one-way, with the worker remaining clothed and wearing surgical gloves.

Some practitioners call themselves sex coaches, and Sexological Bodywork includes coaching in body awareness, communication skills, and self-touch/masturbation skills for increasing self-awareness and erotic potential. Sessions are personal growth learning experiences that help clients learn more about their own physical and emotional life. A common theme is healing shame, and recovering natural joy in the body. The work is said to provide a nurturing environment in which the client can feel safe and explore erotic energy.

Psychosexual Somatics was created in London by Mike Lousada, who is now the chair of the accrediting body, the Association of Somatic and Integrative Sexology (ASIS). They are working towards becoming accredited from a university, and setting up a sex-positive centre where they can be based, perhaps together with other similar professional groups.

Clients are men, women and couples, and therapy uses four stages:

- Awareness of blocks through psychotherapeutic processes

- Removal of emotional and physical blockages through physical therapy

- Re-connection to and awakening of the body through sensual touch

- Enabling sexual empowerment and cultivating orgasmic response through bodywork.

Surgical gloves are also used in Psychosexual Somatics, but the work differs from the Sexological Bodywork in that it expertly supports people who have suffered trauma, both physical and mental. Mike has seen disabled clients, those with phobias, and many women disabled by damage during childbirth.

Sexual massage

Sensual or sexual massage focuses on sexual pleasure and usually orgasm, as opposed to massage *therapy* which focuses on muscle problems. It can be of assistance to disabled people, including the massage experience and teaching how to orgasm through breath, as described in Chapter 2. Here are the various types:

- *Tantric massage* often includes some coaching and support in breath, relaxation and use of erotic energy. It includes massage of the whole body, and may lead to orgasm.

- *Taoist erotic massage* combines intense breath work and full-body massage techniques which can produce a heightened erotic state.

- *Four-handed erotic massage* is when two practitioners work on a client at the same time, pampering simultaneously as they create a flood of sensation all over the client's body. This overload of stimulation makes it easier for the receiver to let themselves go. It might help a disabled person to feel so overwhelmed with pleasure that they forget their negative attitudes to their body, and perhaps the pain which it brings them. It may also be good for people with athetoid cerebral palsy, because two people might be better placed to deal with the client's body.

- *G-spot massage* is massage focused in the lower front wall of the vagina, where the sensitive G-spot sits. Massage can result in the release of female ejaculate also known as amrita – a clear, sweetish liquid which comes from the Skene's glands and exits in a spurt via the ducts around the urethra (where urine comes out). Physical and emotional release frequently result. This massage could perhaps teach a disabled woman who has trouble enjoying genital pleasure to feel it from around her G-spot.

- *Prostate massage* involves an internal massage of the prostate gland (reached through the anus). This area of the body is rich in nerve endings, and will lead to orgasm. I recommend prostate stimulation to disabled men, those with spina bifida in particular, who find it difficult to reach orgasm by masturbating the penis, or whose orgasms are weak.

- *Taoist approaches* (also sometimes written, and always pronounced, Daoist) focus on becoming aware of the circulation of energy through the body, including sexual energy, and learning to direct that flow at will.

Breath work

Placing attention on the breath and using different rhythms of breath can be an amazingly powerful experience, particularly in conjunction with sexual energy. As discussed in Chapter 2, orgasmic states can be reached solely with breath work. I have personally been in a women's group for a workshop led by the famous American pioneer, Annie Sprinkle. We stood in a circle all breathing together, and I, with some other women, broke into spontaneous orgasm – quite extraordinary!

Many professionals work with the breath in some form, even if only to help their client relax. Learning to breathe properly is used as a method, along with relaxation, to calm the mind and body. Correct breathing is important for the health of tissues, allowing proper oxygenation, and therefore the proper functioning of muscles. Pursed lip breathing (PLB) could be used to reduce muscle spasms in people with cerebral palsy, for example, so that intercourse may become possible for women whose spasms make vaginal intercourse impossible or very difficult.

Tantra

The word Tantra means 'thread' – which is woven into the cloth of everyday life. It was originally a style of meditation and ritual that arose in medieval India and Tibet before the 5th century AD. Tantra is an approach to life, including a sexual life. Modern western Tantra is very popular for many reasons and it provides people who want to develop their sexual techniques and sexuality with the opportunity to do so at gatherings called Tantric workshops, which sound less threatening than sex events. Some believe Tantra to be a corrective force to western repressive attitudes about sex.

Sue Newsome,[6] mentioned previously as a sex therapist, is also a Tantra teacher specializing in disabled clients. She spoke about Tantra at one of our Outsiders days for disabled people, and described one very important aspect of Tantra which is, I think, useful for some disabled people. That is, increasing your awareness and clarity of the here and now, and enjoying goal-free sex. It encourages disabled people, therefore, not to worry about 'having sex like everybody else' or 'trying to reach an orgasm' but enjoying every tiny moment of erotic bliss for what it is.

Tantric training helps practitioners feel extremely comfortable to both discuss and use touch to help disabled people feel more accepting of their bodies. One spinal injured girl I know hired Sue to help her over her newly acquired dislike of her genitals since her spinal injury, with its resulting paralysis and the insertion of a supra-pubic catheter. Seeing a Tantric practitioner seemed to her to be less threatening than seeing a sex worker, and much more satisfying than sitting in a clinic discussing the matter only in theory. In a mirror held for her, she saw that her vulva was beautiful and that, with lubricant, it glistened and, in the end, she realized that she liked it.

3. Body image therapy

Body image therapy is the facilitation of a shift in the way disabled clients feel about their bodies. Practitioners may use a wide range of very differing techniques and disciplines; this is covered at the end of Chapter 7.

4. Sexual advocacy

This is a service for both health professionals and the public who need someone to train or support them, or mediate between them on sexual issues. Advocates can also advise clients on using sex workers. They can enable disabled couples to enjoy sex together, including the placing of hands, mouths and genitals as instructed, without getting otherwise involved. Details of this service are on www. AdvocacyProfessional.com.

5. Striptease

Striptease is creative performance which can be enjoyed by both male and female viewers, whatever the gender of the performers. Disabled people, in my experience, can gain uplifting pleasure from watching a striptease performance by a dancer who is capable of beautiful erotic movements. It can be aspirational and sexually inspiring – even soothing – for them.

Male, and female, and transgendered strippers are not necessarily traditionally beautiful, but they are talented at displaying their bodies in a creative, seductive, beautiful way. They are usually self-taught. Striptease artists do not engage in sex with clients. Unlike burlesque dancers, they do generally strip naked and expose their nipples, genitals and bottoms, as this is what many audiences want to see. They usually work in pubs, collecting donations amongst the pub's patrons before their act, and can also be hired to come and strip for your disabled friends or residents.

They are sometimes called lap dancers, but lap dancing clubs are rather soulless places where performers have little say over what they wear, the music they dance to, or how they dance. They may even have to pay to work there, and have a hard time raising enough to come home with money in their pocket. They will be chatting up clients to take them to private rooms to do a more intimate dance, perhaps including hand jobs and rubbing of bodies together to earn more money.

My reason for spelling this out is that when I have spoken to health professionals about their clients wishing to go to a sex show, they have been pointing them in the direction of the large lap dancing clubs rather than the strip pub. This is fine if the clients want more than a show, but normally they prefer to be in a sexy, friendly environment rather than a sterile commercial one.

Some deafblind people find the idea of full-on sexual contact too overwhelming with a sex worker and prefer a stripper, even though they cannot see them. The stripper dances close, giving off the aromas of their body, the stroke of a soft garment, and the deafblind client has the performance described to them using the manual alphabet by a third party. You can see pictures of such a show on the SHADA website in the Conference section.

If the disabled residents of your residential home decide to have striptease as their entertainment, some are listed on the TLC website, and you can find strippers locally either through an agent or by dropping into a local strip pub.

6. Sexual surrogacy and sex work

Sexual surrogacy

Sexual surrogates support people with sexual challenges, including disabled people. Sometimes the service includes sexual intercourse, but it may be simply learning to touch, or to communicate desires or define boundaries. Surrogates see people who are still virgins, as well as people who have not been able to enjoy sex for a long time, and those who need an experience of sex to make them feel whole.

The difference between surrogates and sex workers is that surrogates traditionally (and officially in the USA) work in conjunction with a therapist or doctor. The therapist or doctor can find out what the client needs, prepare them by explaining what to expect from the surrogate, and structure the sessions.

In most parts of America, sexual surrogacy is legal (but not in some states, such as Massachusetts), whereas prostitution is illegal almost everywhere. Disabled people in America therefore usually have a choice: to either visit a therapist and surrogate team, or hire a sex worker who is working outside the law.

In Britain, some medical personnel and therapists do hire experienced sexual surrogates (usually they are escort sex workers) to work with them and their single clients, or clients when the partner refuses to attend. This may not work, because the surrogate/client relationship is not an 'emotional, soul-mate or love' type of relationship and, as already stated, most couples' problems stem from relationship difficulties.

Some UK sex workers call themselves surrogates, even though they do not work with therapists, because they feel this gives their service a more respectable, serious image, and avoids being seen as a sex worker. They may or may not provide a service which is more considered and structured than is usual with sex work.

The International Professional Surrogate Association (IPSA)[7] is based in Los Angeles. Cheryl Cowen, the fabulous sexual surrogate on whom the film *The Sessions* was based, was one of their earliest members. She has done this work for 40 years and you can see a short film about her life called *Cheryl Cowen Greene: Sexuality & Disability – A Seat at the Table.*[8] The title of this film is based on what her client

Mark (portrayed in *The Sessions*) had said to her when they first met: that he felt like he was always looking into a restaurant full of people enjoying eating together and that he would never be allowed in. She had replied, 'You deserve a seat at that table.'

Sex work

This section describes what is widely considered to be a controversial topic. Some people find the selling of sex unacceptable, and some still believe it to be degrading. I agree that nobody should be forced to do any work they don't want to do, but I am not discussing that side of the business here. The sexual services described in this section are done by professionals who chose this line of work, and specialize in seeing disabled people. They provide a much-needed release, as well as sexual education, confidence and pleasure. I am a strong supporter of the practice, and so are an increasing number of people in Britain. This is exemplified by the screening of positive TV programmes such as Rupert Everett's Channel 4 documentaries, *Love for Sale*.

However, it is beyond the scope of this book to delve into these broader aspects. The fact remains that for many disabled people, use of sex workers in a controlled, professional environment provides them with much-needed and much-deserved release and pleasure, and for this reason I am a strong supporter of the practice.

Sex work is the term used for a professional who engages in physical sexual activity with a client for money (or favours). Sex work is the name the workers choose, rather than prostitution. They want it to be recognized and respected as legitimate work. Most of the people who engage in sex work with disabled people do a sterling job and are very different from the public image of prostitutes working in the street, perhaps to support a drug habit.

The buying and selling of sex is, and always has been, legal in the UK but illegal in most states of America (the exception being Nevada, where a dozen counties allow it). Canada is currently reconsidering its laws against sex work.

Where sex work is illegal – or when health professionals *think* it is illegal, as is common in the UK – it is very hard on the disabled person who is dependent on care. Whereas other people can buy sex via an underground route, the disabled person may have their options blocked, because their care staff are not allowed to break the law. Illegality, real or imagined, also makes life much more dangerous for the sex worker, because they have no protection from the law.

In Britain, the law forces sex workers to work alone in isolation, although they can, if they can afford it, employ a maid. Consider this: the sex worker is working in secret, in isolation, often with a new client they have never met before, naked, with no support for their safety at all. How brave is that? How many of us could cope with such a challenge? You may assume that they do this out of desperation, but no: it's usually a career choice. Some have left other professional jobs to enter this work, because they know they have the skill, and enjoy using their talents. It must feel good to work in a trade where the need/market is always there, and you are admired all day by appreciative clients, and happy in your work. Some have wanted to be sex workers from an early age, have gone into it while at university, and carried on with it after graduation. Others choose the work as a fabulous alternative to jobs in unscrupulous companies and departments, or dreary office or farm work.

Sex workers look after many of our populace's intimate needs, often providing a shoulder to cry on, and a long-sought-after vagina or penis, with sexual wisdom and compassion which none of the rest of us could come anywhere close to. They deserve professional respect, instead of the stigma which they currently have to deal with. I often find, when I talk to them about their work, that they never stop talking, like lonely people often do. This is because they have so few people they can actually talk to about their work, and rarely with their family, neighbours or new people they meet.

You may have seen lurid tales about sex work in the media, and feel nervous about embarking on professional dealings with people who sell sex. The media use a ploy which we pro-sex activists call 'double pornography'. They tell a story in sordid detail to turn the reader on, then say how bad it all is, to keep the reader feeling self-righteous, yet eagerly awaiting the next instalment. Then they buy the same newspapers/watch the same news channel.

The terrible stigma surrounding sex work is based on unsound statistics, misconceptions and misinformation promoted widely by anti-sex radical feminist and religious campaigners, then propagated by the media and government. Their strategy is to get sex work and performance banned altogether. Campaigners against the selling and buying of sex, striptease, lap dancing and pornography use a myth of wildly over-inflated statistics on trafficked women, and the false notion that sex work is violence to women – even though many sex workers are male, and most sex workers say they are in full control of their lives. Sex workers are furious with the feminists who seek to snatch away their employment, ignoring the academic work which, amongst other things, proves that criminalization only drives the trade underground, which makes it more dangerous for everybody. Back-up for what I am saying can be found in the 'Naked Anthropologist' blog, written by Dr Laura Agustín,[9] the much-ignored book by statistician Dr Brooke Magnanti (aka Belle de Jour) called *The Sex Myth*[10] and The Global Network of Sex Work Projects, based in Edinburgh.[11] There are already laws against kerb crawling, paying a trafficked sex worker and trafficking, so we don't need more laws to ban the buying of sex.

Disabled people can be badly affected by all this negativity. They phone up the Sex and Disability Helpline in tears, fearing that the next threatened ban would bring the end of their sex lives. The propaganda makes them feel bad about wanting to see a sex worker at all: they say they don't want to end up feeling grubby. I reassure them by telling them they should look upon the experience as *education*. They should request that they be taught what pleasures their own bodies are capable of feeling, and how to please a partner and become a great lover. That way, they will be all set up to find a partner.

In this book dealing with disability, we are focusing on the sex workers who call themselves escorts who specialize in disabled clients. They are earnest and highly professional people who want to do a good job and see their clients go away with big smiles on their faces.

At the end of this chapter I include two interviews: one with a disabled girl who used an escort to learn how she could experience sexual pleasure, and the other with an escort who sees disabled clients.

Escorts

Escort is the name used by most independent men, women and transgendered people who sell sexual services on their own terms. They are listed on specialist websites, advertise themselves with their own websites and may use an escort agency to help bring in more custom. To find one, simply type the name of your nearest town, plus 'Adultwork' or 'UK Adult Zone' into your search engine. It is not illegal to order one on behalf of your disabled client if they need such support, and this can usually be done by phone or email. Some websites such as Punternet offer user reviews, and many mention their work with disabled clients in their profiles. Some escorts who specialize in disability appear on the website which I set up for disabled men and women to access responsible sex workers, the TLC Trust.[12]

The TLC website also offers advice for disabled clients and sex workers seeing disabled clients. The site runs itself – although the co-founder, who is an escort herself, vets the escorts' profiles before they can be featured. Incredibly, the only complaint I have ever received from this site was from a sex worker complaining that a disabled ex-client was using threatening behaviour. Touching Base[13] in Australia is a long-established organization which facilitates links between people with a disability, their support organizations and the sex industry.

Escorts only offer safer sex, that is, using condoms during intercourse; and having regular check-ups to ensure that they have no sexually transmitted infections. More than a person you pick up in a bar, they can be relied on to be safe. They do not work if they have a cold or other infection, and they expect their clients to postpone their appointment if they are unwell.

Long ago, I discussed disabled people hiring escorts with the manager of a residential home for disabled people, who was having trouble with members of staff who were earning extra cash by selling sexual services themselves. Naturally, this was not good for the dynamics of the home, and the manager was delighted to find an alternative. She wanted to know more, as I expect do you.

Escorts usually offer a wide range of services including sexual intercourse, oral sex, anal sex, kissing, cuddling and being a shoulder to cry on, plus kinkier things. They will usually have boundaries, saving certain activities for their private lives. In a word, they will provide almost anything the client asks for, so disabled people should not fear about being really open and honest. Whether your client simply needs to lie in a pair of warm arms, or has a complex set of intimate requirements, his or her needs will be taken seriously.

An escort really can help a disabled person gain knowledge about their own body's sexual capabilities and sensitivities, as well as learning how to please another person and gain sexual self-confidence. Many males say that losing their virginity 'makes them feel like a man'. It can help a disabled individual reclaim their body from the medical profession. This is, of course, also all true of the work which surrogates and some Tantric practitioners do.

Many disabled women say they would love to pay an expert to help them explore and learn what their bodies are capable of enjoying, but they rarely make a booking. Disabled men, on the other hand, may claim they are really looking for love and affection, but then book an escort when they feel horny! Lesbian and other women hire female escorts who see women, and I advise women to be careful not to hire an amateur male. I recommend they examine their website carefully and talk to them seriously beforehand. Sometimes it's sensible to hire a couple who work together: the female to look after her and the male to introduce her to heterosexual pleasure.

I recently spoke about my work at a sex workers' conference, and I said that I had been told that many disabled men don't have a clue about using an escort and turn up with unrealistic expectations, going away disappointed. The escorts at the conference told me quite plainly that many non-disabled men are like that too, which seems a shame. What we have done is provide guidelines on seeing an escort on our website www.AdvocacyProfessional.com. Our advocates are happy to discuss the whole journey with a disabled person in advance or you could look at the site and have that discussion yourself, or suggest your client read the guidelines.

Some escorts work from home, others from a flat they use for work. Others only visit the client in their own homes, perhaps, or in other people's homes or in a hotel. Most do all of these. When the escort has to travel, it can be a more expensive service to cover the cost and perhaps a charge for a driver who sits outside waiting to take them home, and ready to rescue them if they signal they are in danger. One escort told me she travels 500 miles to visit a disabled man living in a remote part of Britain, once a year when his parents are on holiday!

A few enterprising disabled men club together and hire an escort to come and work with several of them in one of their homes, one after the other, to save money. One group of amputees with no legs hire a girl to come and lap dance for them (even though they don't have laps!).

Escorts also provide girlfriend/boyfriend experiences, which involve having a date as well as sex, perhaps even spending the whole weekend or holiday together. For most disabled people, being seen out with a beautiful sexy person can provide a much-needed ego boost.

Escorts are allowed within the law to employ a maid to answer the phone and help with the chores (but not appear to be controlling or involved in the management of a brothel). It is not allowed by law in the UK for more than one sex worker to work in the same building, because that constitutes a brothel. This is not necessarily a good thing, because working together is less isolating, and safer for everyone. However, it may mean that escorts really look forward to clients arriving and having their company!

Many people think that hiring an escort is over-priced, but it is actually about the same as any professional might charge for specialist work. It takes time and costs money to furnish the flat they use, purchase fetish and sexy outfits and keep them clean, wash their hair and body between appointments, and cover overheads. Many offer a drink and both male and female escorts have been known to routinely cook their client a roast dinner!

Escorts often relate closely to disabled clients, because both they and disabled people are stigmatized in society.

Most escorts have worked with elderly, disabled and even dying clients. They enjoy meeting a wide range of people in their work, and helping them explore their intimate desires. They lead extraordinary lives which some find totally satisfying, so it's sad that they can rarely share these experiences with the world and those around them.

Sexual assistants

Sexual assistants look after the sexual needs of disabled people. In Europe, this initiative was started in 2003 by Nina de Vries, a Dutch sex worker who, in 1997, began offering erotic massage to those with learning difficulties and brain damage in Berlin. In 2003, Nina was asked to train sexual assistants for disabled people in Zurich. Now, institutions exist in Germany, France, Switzerland and Italy. Training is provided, and sometimes intercourse is included. In 2014, Inès Olhagaray and Charlotte Boitiaux, both French journalists, started making a webdocumentary on sexual assistance around Europe.

Sexual assistance is different in Japan. A business-like Niigata-based national organization called White Hands was established in 2008. A young lady visits a client, takes off his pants, wipes him down, then his condom-covered penis is masturbated. The procedure lasts 5 to 10 minutes. There is no mention of female clients. You can watch the procedure in an online film called *Medical Sex Workers In Japan! (Helps Men With Severe Physical Disabilities With Their Sexual Needs)*.[14]

Brothels

Brothels are illegal in the UK, and most parts of America. However, Nevada is famous for its brothels and they thrive legally in other parts of the world. Asta Philpot and other disabled people in Britain campaign for brothels for disabled people with access and special facilities such as hoists and a menu in braille. This is especially important because so many escorts work upstairs in inaccessible flats, and the disabled person may not want to invite them into their family or residential home. Some brothels in Germany and Australia have features for older and disabled clients, realizing that, by doing so, they increase their client base.

Some brothels in Britain do thrive, but it is often the best-run houses that get closed down, and the most underground unsavoury places run by greedy criminals that continue. Being found guilty of running a brothel can be a very expensive experience, as all assets may be seized. When Cynthia Payne's luncheon-voucher brothel in Streatham was (famously) busted, two wheelchair-using Outsiders members were inside, and I was disappointed that they felt they could not speak out to support Cynthia.

Brothels could provide opportunities to chat and dance with the sex workers, and find out whether they have any chemistry with, before deciding which one to pick. An Outsiders member with Duchenne Muscular Dystrophy, who had given up on finding a girlfriend because of his deteriorating condition, told me how his favourite escort was the one he ended up seeing regularly, because they 'had a certain chemistry'.

Brothels provide a place where sex workers can work together and support each other. This works best as a collective of sex workers where they all take some responsibility, or when the brothel is run by a former sex worker who understands their mindset.

The Women's Institute investigated brothels around the world, and a feature film was made about this, *Love Ranch*, starring Dame Helen Mirren. Most conclusions of the investigation were positive and Dame Helen came out with the much-quoted remark, 'I am a complete believer in legal brothels'.[12]

Sex workers as teachers

In 2013, a residence for learning disabled adults in England informed me that they had found a suitable escort on the TLC site to perform the role of teacher for a learning disabled resident who could not be taught how to masturbate by using words, pictures or film. The selected escort stated on his TLC profile that he had worked as a volunteer support worker in a few independent living situations, so seemed eminently suitable. The staff are having to go through many hoops to get this procedure passed, and last time I heard, were thinking of employing the escort for a few weeks as a care support worker, to let him get to know the client and learn how to communicate with him. I am advising them when asked.

Sauna workers

In England, 'sauna' tends to be the name given to gay sex establishments, which may be for paid or unpaid sex, or both. In Scotland, it is the name for licensed commercial sex parlours, giving sex workers a safe environment in which to work. However, in 2014, there was a series of raids in Edinburgh where these licences are currently, after 30 years, being threatened.

Massage parlour workers

Great massage parlours emerged in the UK around the National Exhibition Centre near Birmingham after the planners for the centre told the government there was no point in creating such a centre if there were no places nearby offering girls selling sex. This gave rise to the glamorous and high quality Birmingham parlours.

These days, massage parlours are licensed heterosexual establishments in England, Wales and Northern Ireland. The masseuses massage their customers, which the customer has paid for on entrance, and then she adds a sexual service for extra money, usually keeping this cash for herself. If the sexual service does not include penetration, just a hand-job or 'happy ending', then no law is broken.

As mentioned earlier in this book, one of our Outsiders members, who is blind, goes to massage parlours to 'see' women with his hands. He massages them and doesn't want any massage in return!

Massage parlours usually also do outcalls. using their a driver to deliver the lady to the client's address, wait in case she calls for help, and drive her back again.

Massage is sometimes offered for sale mid-week in other establishments such as naturist resorts and swing clubs, but how much sex is on offer is rarely stated, and simply enquiring can have a visitor either welcomed or thrown out. If people understood the law which states that non-penetrative sex can be sold by more than one practitioner from any establishment quite legally, then perhaps the British could be clearer about what is on offer and where.

How to tell if a sex worker is trafficked

As it is illegal in Britain to purchase sex from a trafficked person, and those clients suspecting a person is trafficked should report it to the police, you may wonder how a customer can tell. Well, for a start, you can ask questions about her willingness and freedom of movement. Trafficked sex workers are nothing like the escorts with profiles on the TLC-Trust website for disabled men and women to hire. Unless you visit the street, a massage parlour, brothel, or a flat which is obviously not the sex worker's, you are unlikely to encounter one. She may (or may not) seem vulnerable rather than confident. For more information, read *Sex at the Margins*[15] or the 2013 report by the UK Human Trafficking Centre (UKHTC).[16]

Hotel worker

In the old days, British hotels ran their own team of sex workers and that practice still happens in various places around the world. Nowadays, the story in London is that there are only five of the big hotels which allow escorts to sit in the bar, available for hire. Restrictions on this are in place in other hotels, for fear of scandal. What may be of interest you is that no hotel will turn away a disabled person who arrives in the daytime, with the escort arriving separately.

Professional dommes, doms and subs

Professional dominatrices/dommes, male doms, and submissives work in parlours called 'dungeons' or 'playrooms'. They are highly professional, skilled people, full of fun and imagination, totally misrepresented in the media. They cater to clients who arrive with all kinds of requests, which need to be administered with care and respect. The clients may be submissive or dominant, and may get off on a variety of things, including pain, mental humiliation or domination, fear, bondage, suspension, enemas, and fantasy enactment.

So long as these professionals do not provide penetration (in the mouth, vagina or anus) they can legally work together in the UK in a dungeon or playroom, which cannot be prosecuted as constituting a brothel. Playrooms thrive in America, and Pandora's Box is a famous New York establishment.

The experience of surrender can be exquisite and domination is a skill which professionals take great pride in. It can be 'heavy', using whips and chains, or 'light' with silk scarves and words. Contrary to what it may seem, the dominant is actually at the service of their submissive client, leading them along their own individual previously agreed path in an experience of surrender.

These professionals also take great pride in their elaborate implements, such as collars, paddles, whips, floggers and saddles; and playroom owners are likewise proud of their equipment such as a dentist's chair, cross, dog kennel, queening stool, cage or stocks. They may have an enema room, a place for water sports and scat play and/or a degradation chamber.

The session usually ends with the client experiencing an orgasm, which may happen automatically because this is their fetish, or from masturbation, maybe using a range of implements including anal vibrators and nipple clamps. Some say, 'A good scene doesn't end in orgasm; it ends in catharsis.' This is all legal, but the dominant may have to be careful of the potential liability under criminal law, if any physical injury is caused which is more than temporary, since the law does not currently allow people to consent to being injured.

Fantasy role play is very much part of BDSM. Indeed, there are organizations which specialize in certain types, for example kidnapping. If you want a peek inside a BDSM parlour, look at Susan Meiselas' beautiful photos of Pandora's Box online.

Some playrooms are accessible, the owners often spending money to ensure this, as most dungeons are, by their nature, in the basement. Disabled people may visit a playroom for any of the reasons anybody else would. One female lesbian Outsiders member visited a domme to get dressed up in a corset and 'learn the ropes' of being a domme herself.

Outsiders had a member with athetoid cerebral palsy who drove himself from Paris (before the tunnel) to see a top London dominatrice, sometimes coming to our lunch during the same trip. He told us that, when he reached home, his mother, on seeing the whip marks on his body, could never understand how he could be paying for receiving even more suffering in his life!

A call on my helpline came from a care worker in a residence for learning disabled people who was worried that a male resident wanted to enjoy BDSM without having a relationship. He thought he was gay and sub. My response was to ask a dom I knew to visit both her and the resident, run through commercial and non-commercial options and perhaps provide a service too. You could find a dom near you online. Speak to them first to see if they are suitable. There is more on disability and BDSM in Chapter 9 on sexual diversity.

Adult baby services

Some professionals specialize in certain fetishes such as adult babies. One Outsiders member, a man with cerebral palsy, has such a fetish. He lives at home and keeps his taste secret from his parents and friends. He has always been treated well by his 'Mommies' who put him in nappies, perhaps in a large cot with toys and a dummy, and change his nappies as necessary.

Webcam sexual services

Professionals provide flirtation and stripping live online, to the clients' wishes, so they have virtual sex together while the client sits in the comfort of his own home, and masturbates to orgasm. Some unsavoury websites squeeze more money out of paying clients before more sex can take place, so you may need to alert your disabled clients to this. Perhaps the two safest sites currently offering this services are ifriends and Cam4. Cam4 includes men and trans people as well as girls. Some of the performers are disabled – they sit on the bed and are watched looking sexy even if they cannot walk, and thus earn money without having to go out to work. They do have to be self-assured and tough to do this work, but disabled clients might prefer them. Relationships can be built up so a web worker knows their client's requirements and how to get them off. Other interactions can also be very impersonal, leaving a disabled client feeling uncared for, but really it's up to the client to form a good relationship.

Phone sex operators

These are people skilled at turning clients on verbally till they orgasm. They cut to the heart of their clients' fantasies, and take them on exaggerated erotic journeys in their head.

Street worker

This is not to be recommended, because many girls on the street are supporting a drug habit and you cannot tell which ones are, and which are healthy. They are also risky since they might also have unprotected sex for extra money, or rob clients.

Truck-stop worker

This is not too common in Britain but more common in third-world countries. The British comedienne Kate Copstick went to Kenya and taught the truck-stop ladies to offer 'cleavage sex' in order to decrease their risk of catching AIDS!

Pornography

Pornography is a huge subject, often judged negatively. To the uninitiated, porn may look alarming – for reasons ranging from ignoring safe sex practices to sexual politics – but it operates according to certain codes and activities represented. The regular porn viewer will probably have subtle preferences for types of porn. Porn's subtleties are as broad as the diversity of human desire.

In general, porn represents not reality but fantasies. It creates a hyperbolic world where people who represent physically desirable types (not necessarily traditionally glamorous types – see below) have energetic sex in positions which are geared more to camera visibility than physical satisfaction, comfort or real life. It does not tend to represent the everyday, responsible aspects of sex. It certainly should not be used as sex education.

For example, condom use is not commonplace in straight porn and there are numerous 'bareback' gay films. According to the adult industry, customers do not want to see 'mundane reminders' of reality.

With the growth of the internet as a medium for distribution, porn has come to represent every type of appearance, from the traditional pin-up, through girls next door, to mature women (so-called MILFs), BBW (big beautiful women), and 'natural and hairy' (unenhanced breasts and unshaven pubic areas). Porn does not dictate, but rather reflects, its viewers' sexual desires. However, with all the piracy which goes on today, people who once created expensive productions can no longer afford to do so.

UK law is messy. Porn cannot legally depict underage or animal sex, or 'extreme porn', which is anything that is life-threatening, or an act which is likely to cause serious injury to breasts, anus or genitals.

I am often asked to recommend porn, especially by people who believe all porn stars are trafficked, and I can recommend quality directors here, some whose porn has been enjoyed by disabled friends. The best creators of porn in my view are: Maria Beatty (especially with her film *Silken Sleeves*), Joybear, Erica Lust, Abby Winters, CarryOnMouse for exotic porn comedy, Jean Daniel Cadinot for male gay sex, and the East Van Porn Collective for student porn. A website overview can be found on PVVOnline.com, and Indie Porn Revolution shows queer porn. A reliable supplier is yourchoice.co.uk.

Young People and Pornography – A Briefing for Workers[17] was produced in 2009 by Brook, Centre for HIV and Sexual Health, and fpa and is available online.

The Chailey Heritage Foundation produced some guidelines for the staff of their school for severely disabled students, called *Pornography/Sexually Explicit Material*. In it, they recommend that any young person using a magazine must be able to access it her/himself or use an electronic page turner, with a switch if necessary.

Obviously, in adult residential care and educational establishments with students over 18, it is important that the web access system used by residents is not blocking porn sites.

You may find a disabled client wishing to *become* a porn star, in order to present disability to the porn-viewing public as sexy. This is admirable, and all I can say, as somebody that was tempted (twice) to be in porn, is that it really is very, very difficult, and requires good acting skills and many other specialist skills – which I certainly didn't have and which are rare. Most men find it difficult to perform in front of a camera and its crew.

As mentioned earlier in this book, Canadian Loree Erickson made an erotic film starring herself, a queer woman with a disability. This is available from femmegimp.org. Other films starring disabled people can be found on www.sexualrespect.com/resources.html#films.

Sperm production assistant

Hospitals now invite sex workers to come in and assist disabled men with progressive conditions to produce sperm, to be put into storage for later use.

Supporting your clients to enjoy sexual services

You can read more about supporting disabled people seeing escorts on the Sexual Advocacy website, www.AdvocacyProfessional.com. In order to be able to support your disabled clients with a sex professional, you may need to convince your board of trustees, as mentioned in Chapter 3. Convincing your Trustees and Board of Governors that escorts can make a useful contribution to a disabled person's sexual happiness can be most easily done by bringing an escort into the next board meeting to answer questions. My advice would be not to list this on the agenda if you want to be sure board members will actually turn up!

I accompanied one of the TLC's sex workers, 'D', to a meeting at a care home. We were there to answer questions from the board (who failed to attend) but the staff asked questions and 'D' replied to these, with her irresistible, candid charm, thus:

Q: 'What would you do if a student with cerebral palsy bashed you on the head with an arm?'

D: 'Duck.'

Q: 'What would you do if they threw up over you?'

D: 'Clear it up. That's what I do as part of my job: dealing with pee, poo and sick!'

Q: 'What would you say if a student did not want a session with a stranger, and needed visiting in advance?'

D: 'I would come down on the train from London and meet them free of charge beforehand, and allow them to make up their mind.'

'D' had them mesmerized and she won the staff over.

Having escorts coming into a hospice, school or residence to work with a disabled resident might seem risky, but is not, and can easily go unnoticed. Contrary to what you might imagine, escorts dress demurely when not in action in the bedroom, and would look like just any other visitor.

I normally advise against residences and schools paying for sexual services, as disabled people need to understand the value of this service to really differentiate it from a love affair in their minds. On top of this, the residence paying makes the transaction legally complex, depending on where the sex takes place and whether or not the disabled individual has the capacity to consent.

Interviews

Why I went to Andrew Rosetta, by Sophia

Sophia is a London-based young lady with cerebral palsy who uses a wheelchair. In answer to my questions, she said:

> I had never had pain-free intercourse and I could not open my legs wide without pain. At school I had been shown a picture of a woman's vulva, which had really upset me and I could not bear to look at such images, or accept my own genitals.
>
> I went to see Andrew Rosetta, a male sex worker living in Covent Garden, who had been introduced to me by Tuppy. Having no money, I swapped typing for his sexual services. He would greet me on arrival, offer me a cup of tea, and we'd have a chat. He helped me get undressed. Usually, he massaged me first and sometimes, especially in the beginning, it was only massage or chatting in a relaxed, friendly way.
>
> For intercourse, he would help me get into position lying on the bed. He took care to get us both into exactly the right position for my comfort: he eased his body between my legs and was very gentle, patient and understanding. I'd only ever had intercourse with another disabled man, who had been impatient and inconsiderate. The difference with Andrew was amazing: Andrew was so gentle, confident, friendly and genuinely caring.
>
> Now I have become sexually confident and am enjoying all kinds of sex with my partner. I have even, slowly, been able to accept my genitals and look at pictures of other women's bits.

Andrew Rosetta wrote a book which included this experience: *Whatever She Wants.*[18]

'D's questionnaire

When I was running the fundraising Erotic Awards, we sent questionnaires out to the sex worker nominees, because we wanted to know all about their work. The last winner of the Female Sex Worker category of the Year 2012 was the very same 'D', which is how I first came to meet her. Here is her completed questionnaire:

NAME
'D'

HOW WOULD YOU DESCRIBE YOURSELF?
My preference is for the catch-all term 'sex worker'. Not that I shun 'whore' (as you can see from the photo I took of the red umbrella I embellished) or 'prostitute'...but they are only really used by people who spit them out as an insult or to degrade us. They're never neutral words, when they're coming from non sex workers...

If you're not an actual whore, then don't use it! They're our words to use and address each other with, they've been reclaimed. So I call myself tart, hooker, whore, prostitute, escort, floozy, strumpet, sex worker. In my dreams, I like to think I have things in common with history's grand courtesans too...and then I wake up. Haha!

WHY DID YOU ENTER THE BUSINESS?
I was always and forever fascinated by the subject, and around 1989 I found a book in a second-hand shop called *Working – My Life as a Prostitute* by American sex worker Dolores French.[19] I couldn't get enough of it, and it set the cog wheels in motion. I didn't need persuading from a book, I just KNEW that I was the right type of person to do it well. That book sort of jolted me, though. I absolutely hated living in my small 'Hicksville' town with no job prospects; even though I was fairly academic and did well at school, I wasn't going to get anywhere if I stayed there. I needed to be self-employed, whatever I was going to choose. So, I have been lucky. I have succeeded in being self-employed at something I like, and that feels good.

APART FROM THE MONEY, WHAT MOTIVATES YOU?
Even after all these years, I still get all excited at meeting a new visitor, and every time feels like it's the first time. That sounds completely cheesy, but I know, for me, it's true. It's a pretty exciting job that never

feels like a job because it's the right one. I always sort of equated the word 'job' with something that I didn't like, but that's only because I had loads of dead-end awful ones before! I love meeting new people, hearing about their lives and having fun with them too. Some of their stories are mesmerizing! I can't deny that it's also an empowering ego boost to see a person really enjoy themselves sexually, and be part of that. Everyone likes to think that they're a fabulous pleasure giver, me included! I would never have met some of these guys in any other way, and I'm quite close to some of them. We can say things to each other that we can't say to anyone else. I like our secret nudges and winks in company, hehe...

WHAT DO YOU ENJOY MOST ABOUT BEING A SEX WORKER?

One of the best things ever is seeing shy guys and virgins gaining confidence and becoming more relaxed and happy, especially after they've been so nervous and convinced that there's something wrong with them.

There's been tears and laughter! It's very rewarding though.

It teaches you things about people, things you wouldn't learn anywhere else. They tell me stuff they would never tell anyone else, so it's nice to be trusted like that.

I like being independent and self-employed, choosing how and when I work, and I like having sex! I do have orgasms with people.

I remember being in a parlour and the maid looking at my flushed face and saying 'Do you *really* like this?' and I said yes. She said that she felt disgusted if she had an orgasm (when she was active), and she thought I was weird for liking it. Being made to feel odd for liking sex, wow!

WHAT DO YOU ENJOY LEAST ABOUT BEING A SEX WORKER?

Stigma, the ridiculous legislation and laws made by men and women who ignore our lived experiences, the media, the stereotyping, the misperceptions, people who have never been sex workers telling me what my life is like and campaigning to make it more dangerous for me despite being shown and told numerous times that their personal feelings and moral crusading has a negative impact. Prohibition has never worked and never will. Being told that I'm 'not representative' and that I'm 'privileged'. I became educated and privileged *because* of sex work.

HOW LONG HAVE YOU BEEN A SEX WORKER?

Well, my first booking was summer 1990! I was 24. I'm still 24 now. Haha! In my head. I was almost discovered so it was a short-lived dalliance, but I knew I was going to find another way.

I came to London in 1993 and worked in a parlour for four years whilst at university. I loved that place. I finished up there after graduating but discovered that the internet was teeming with websites and forums in 2005.

God, it was like Christmas finding that! I was so excited. I got a website sorted out and threw myself into it all.

WHAT DO YOU SEE YOURSELF DOING FIVE YEARS FROM NOW?

I decided long ago that I would be a sex worker until I'm not physically able to! It's a huge part of my life and I won't give it up for anyone. I do other things and earn money at them, but I absolutely feel that being a sex worker is right for me. I'm quite a good photographer now, and I've also started making money at that too.

WHAT ARE YOUR SPECIALITIES?

Well, I'm no pornstar! I'm not that fit! I'm more of a 'GFE', a girlfriend experience. More intimate than porn, I'd say. I love kissing! Kissing is the ignition key for me. People tell me I make them feel relaxed and make them laugh. It all sounds like a Benny Hill/ Carry On film. Sometimes, it is, haha.

HOW DO YOU FIND CLIENTS GENERALLY?

Internet. I write everything myself, market myself, advertise, write a blog, swap links and banner adverts and put it all out there. I use some paid advertising too. Punternet and Adultwork bring most hits, I study the analytics stats on my sites. TLC obviously brings some too!

WHAT IS THE AGE RANGE OF YOUR CLIENTS?

21–93 years. Yes, 93. He's a sprightly young thing, full of beans! I see all sorts of people, but on average, most are married and 30–60 years. I'm a cougar to some and a sugar baby to others, haha.

WHAT ARE YOUR BEST CLIENTS LIKE?

I'm very lucky, I attract what I want to attract: just really nice people. Smart, interesting, polite, kind, generous, clean and tidy. And they seem to appreciate my brain as well as my body. I think, haha. Nobody wears a dirty raincoat, though non-sex-workers always seem to tell me they do. And they should know, eh?

WHAT ARE THE MOST IMPORTANT REWARDS YOU RECEIVE AS A SEX WORKER?

It's an education that you just wouldn't get in any other way, and in sharing such personal things, I feel very honoured and a bit special. That feels nice!

Being emailed by a very socially awkward guy (at first) telling me he was getting married! He was a virgin when we met.

Learning amazing things from people who can't walk/talk/move freely. I'm a lucky girl to meet the people I meet.

An orgasm is a reward too! Not the most important, but a good incentive!

HAVE YOU DONE ANY TALKS? PRESS TV APPEARANCES?

No, a journalist quoting me in a newspaper without my knowledge was enough to get me in trouble. I can't for personal reasons, and (right now) because of the negative attention it brings.

DO YOU CAMPAIGN FOR SEX WORK LAW REFORM?

I'm more of a supporter and ally, though I shake my fist online a bit. Maybe one day I can be more active than I am now, I hope so. I do read and keep up with the amazing sex workers who are active and am eternally grateful for their hard work. It's frustrating to not be able to join in completely.

WHAT ARE YOUR DREAMS/IDEALS/PLANS?

Well, it would be great if the day came where saying 'I'm a sex worker' wasn't received as if you've just said 'I've murdered your entire family.'

To have decriminalization, enabling us to be safer in our chosen work. We pay taxes, we should have the human and labour rights that other working people have.

To carry on being a sex worker because I think it's the right thing to do. When people ask 'What do you really want to do?' I feel insulted. As if this isn't good enough. I'm already doing what I really want to do!

The use of escorts in your work

It does strike me that escorts are very much under-used by health and social care professionals and they could serve many more useful roles. They could be used much more in sex education, as teachers, and acting as live models for deafblind, blind, learning disabled people, and others.

Your first step is to find a local escort (or perhaps two: a man and a woman), who is intelligent and discerning. You can start this process by reading the TLC website and reading the profiles to see if any suitable workers work nearby. Your selected worker/s can be invited to come and talk to you all, so you can begin to feel confident about them working with your vulnerable clients. Discussions can include the rates they would charge for each of the tasks you may need doing. If one seems unsuitable, don't give up, but search until you find someone suitable.

Tasks may include working with several clients in a residential home who are too impaired to masturbate. The sex worker could come in weekly to 'lend a hand', hold a sex toy, or strap a sex toy on the genitals of each of the residents who want these services. This could raise the feeling of happiness of those visited, and indeed raise spirits in the home. The costs can be divided between the clients and, so long as the residents involved agree, it's a big step forward.

Sex workers can also be used to talk to the residents who want to discuss sexual issues with someone who is not a member of staff. They can teach disabled people of any age more about sex, and help them fathom out ways to find more pleasure.

Acting as a life model, they can teach disabled people with visual impairments and learning difficulties all about the body, and how it works; and they can demonstrate all types of masturbation, and warn them about what is dangerous to do (like sticking sharp objects inside themselves).

Long ago, when the famous sex activist Annie Sprinkle was a sex worker seeing clients in New York, she told me how she loved her disabled clients. Annie moved on to become a performance artist and run workshops and events. I went to hear her speak at the ICOP (International Conference on Prostitution) in Los Angeles in 1997, where I'd been invited to speak on sex work and disability. In her talk, Annie spoke about how, before a client entered to see her for a sexual service, she would psych herself up to really feel and express love for them for that hour. I am telling you this to remind you for the last time in this chapter about just how amazing sex workers can be.

Resources

1. College of Sex and Relationship Therapy (COSRT): www.cosrt.org.uk.
2. Pink Therapy: www.pinktherapy.com.
3. American Association of Sexuality Educators, Counselors and Therapists (AASECT): www.aasect.org.
4. Sexological Bodywork: www.sexologicalbodywork.com and www.sexological bodywork.co.uk.
5. Psychosexual Somatics. Clients searching for therapy can go to www.MikeLousada. com and people wishing to train can go to www.psychosexualsomatics.com.
6. Sue Newsome: www.sexandrelationshipcoaching.com/SueNewsome-SexCoach-Tantra.asp.
7. International Professional Surrogate Association (IPSA): www.surrogatetherapy.org.
8. Greene, C.C. (2013) *Cheryl Cowen Greene: Sexuality & Disability – A Seat at the Table.* Available at www.youtube.com/watch?v=gds2RvmCBKE, accessed on 8 July 2014.
9. The Naked Anthropologist blog by Dr Laura Agustín: www.lauraagustin.com.
10. Magnanti, B. (2012) *The Sex Myth – Why Everything We're Told Is Wrong.* London, UK: Weidenfeld & Nicolson.
11. The Global Network of Sex Work Projects: www.nswp.org.
12. TLC Trust: www.TLC-Trust.org.uk
13. Touching Base: www.touchingbase.org.
14. World Star Hip Hop (2013) *Medical Sex Workers In Japan! (Helps Men With Severe Physical Disabilities With Their Sexual Needs).* Available at www.worldstarhiphop.com/videos/video.php?v=wshh9pq3l1jTZ6V1IwMN, accessed on 8 July 2014.
15. Augustín, L. (2007) *Sex at the Margins.* London, UK: Zed Books.
16. UKHTC and SOCA (2013) UKHTC: A Strategic Assessment on the Nature and Scale of Human Trafficking in 2012. Available at www.nationalcrimeagency.gov. uk/publications/15-ukhtc-strategic-assesssment-on-human-trafficking-in-2012/file, accessed on 8 July 2014.
17. Brook, Centre for HIV and Sexual Health, FPA and The National Youth Agency (2009) *Young People and Pornography – A Briefing for Workers.* Available at www.sgcyp. org/LinkClick.aspx?fileticket=oOrgQMeHg%2FU%3D&tabid=414, accessed on 8 July 2014.
18. Rosetta, A. (2009) *Whatever She Wants – True Confessions of a Male Escort.* London, UK: Ebury Press.
19. French, D. (1989) *Working – My Life as a Prostitute.* London, UK: Victor Gollancz.

CHAPTER 9

SEXUAL DIVERSITY

Sexual diversity includes people who are lesbian and gay, bisexual, transgendered, queer, intersex and asexual, collectively often referred to as LGBTQIA. It also includes sexual preferences, behaviours, and lifestyles such as BDSM, fetishes, swinging, and polyamory.

I am offering you here, in this chapter, a whistle-stop charge through some of the most common sexual practices which take place in the name of sexual diversity. I hope that those of you who are unfamiliar with sexually diverse people can learn, and feel comfortable and confident in working respectfully with them. If sexually diverse people make you feel uncomfortable, work on yourself to find acceptance. Read the books and watch the films recommended here and perhaps invite a Pink Therapist[1] to come and talk to you and your colleagues. I hope that, if and when the need arises, you can also support parents to become accepting and understanding of any sexual difference of their child.

People who feel, experience and enjoy sexual diversity would prefer to be both accepted and respected in society. This is especially true in places where they may feel vulnerable, such as at school, in hospital, at the surgery and in residential homes. I quote here a young, highly intelligent, disabled, polyamorous, transgendered, queer member of Outsiders, who told me this about their experiences after being seriously injured in a road traffic accident:

Practical support can come with a big weight of oppression. It would have been nice to be dealing with healthcare professionals who had a greater awareness of diversity, and actively brought non-oppressive attitudes and practices into their words and actions. It would have been nice to be fully met as an individual in a way which enabled me to feel safe enough to be myself.

The two threads – disability and sexual diversity – twining together, leave a complex weave of, at times overt prejudice, at other times systemic bias and ignorance, and at times complete erasure and isolation. (*eirwen*)

Thankfully, in 2003 the Royal College of Nursing brought out strong guidelines for nursing staff, at least regarding lesbians and gays.[2] The wonderful booklet on lesbian and gay people with learning difficulties, *Secret Loves, Hidden Lives?*[3] came out in 2005. However, much sexual diversity remains unmentioned in disability texts. Some of your clients may be sick with worry about their desires and feelings, and may really need someone to talk to. Others who want to keep their sexuality as private as possible still need to know that, if they need your guidance or you otherwise find out, you will be accepting.

People who don't identify as sexually diverse are referred to as 'straight'. However, many straight people actually venture into sexually diverse fantasies or flirt with the idea of group sex. They may find themselves in a same-sex encounter or realize they have a fetishistic preference.

I hope we are all grown-up enough to know that to be gay is not a sickness, sadism is not violence, and masochism and submission are not being weak nor posing a dangerous risk to the person.

Human sexuality can be highly misrepresented in the media and in most people's minds. It is not only about the kind of sexual activity we enjoy, for example what we do when we have sex, but also the way we feel about ourselves, how we wish to be seen, and the gender and sexual orientation of people we find sexually attractive. It is thus a combination of sexual behaviour, identity and orientation. Our sexuality is not something we choose, and fighting it makes people stressed and unhappy. Remember, you cannot tell just by looking at someone what their sexuality is like, so it is important never to make assumptions.

It is interesting to note that sexual behaviour, identity and orientation can all evolve, wax and wane – sometimes slightly and sometimes dramatically. So labels may be misguided and temporary, rather than fixed. Even within the broad categories, everybody is a little bit different. There is no one definition of 'gay', for example, because a man may identify as gay but not have sex with men. Or perhaps he usually has sex with men, but sometimes with women.

Some people who enjoy being sexually submissive may have known this about themselves all their lives; others suddenly realize later in life. Submissives may confine their submissive pleasures to their master/mistress but enjoy traditional sexual intercourse and non-submissive activities with their husband or wife. More and more wives are leaving their husbands in later life and finding a female partner with whom to enjoy intimacy.

Disabled people who may have had little chance to experiment or express their sexuality may start off on their journey not even knowing if they are gay, and may not realize their true sexual identity until later life. You can support them to explore, both online and perhaps going to clubs, and offer discussion to help them realize their potential. Other disabled people, on the other hand, may have felt certain from a very early age what their sexual orientation, identity and tastes are.

You must remember that your clients' needs will never be exactly the same as your own, because each person is different. If the disabled person senses that you might disapprove of their orientation, lifestyle, identity or tastes, then they are unlikely to open up and state what needs they have. This can make them feel isolated and defensive, trapping them into unsuitable situations, and even depriving them of a sex life. So, be sure to make it clear that you are open-minded and unprejudiced by using open questions, saying things like, 'What kind of sexual partner might you like?' rather than 'Do you wish you had a girlfriend?'

You may find that, after listening to disabled people starting to express their sexual feelings, they worry about their desires. Simply telling them that the thing they are worrying about is a normal part of sexuality will help them feel a whole lot better. It can be really comforting to the worrier, and reassurance is very valuable, especially to someone experiencing disapproval – even revulsion and hatred. Forced marriages for both gay and disabled people are common.

Disabled people's reactions to realizing they are sexually diverse may lead them to happily use it to their advantage, perhaps using niche websites to find a partner. Alternatively, it may lead them to feel as if they are doubly or trebly stigmatized. Those worst affected seem to be disabled gay men, especially if they live with conventional and perhaps religious parents, or in a strictly-run residential establishment. They may not dare to 'come out', for fear of finding themselves unbearably unpopular. Some feel they cannot burden parents or staff with more problems and worries. A computer, smartphone or tablet (if they can use one unsupported) can be a godsend, providing a secret indulgence. Letting your clients know you are open and accepting when it comes to sex could help such clients confide in you, discuss their situation and move forward.

It is difficult for young people to learn about sexual diversity unless it is taught properly, because they probably mix with people who show no signs of being sexually diverse. In fact, they may hear words like 'poof' or 'fag' used as derogatory terms of abuse about gay men or 'weirdo' for those who enjoy unconventional lifestyles. This is especially awful for a young disabled sexually diverse person who has already suffered name-calling, and is another reason why they fear coming out. Young people who are sexually diverse are more likely to start using drugs, to self-harm or to attempt suicide – or else to demonstrate uncontrollable bad behaviour.

Disabled people who have become disowned by their families because of their sexual tastes may very well find themselves isolated, without the support that others may enjoy when they become ill or impaired. Hiring PAs or support workers who accept them with their diversities becomes doubly important. As stated elsewhere in this book, the job description needs to include the sentiment 'support me with my life, not your version of my life' and can include specifics like 'LGBTQIA' or 'kinkster preferred'. This will attract the right sort of PA. Discussions on identity, tastes and needs must take place before the PA is hired. Having carers who share the client's identity and tastes, and who know the scene, goes a long way to preventing the disabled person from feeling, and being, isolated.

Some people with sexual diversities daren't tell their doctors about certain problems, often with tragic consequences. Many sexually diverse people even put off doctor and hospital visits for fear of disapproval. A really great book, *Health Care without Shame*,[4] written by American doctor Charles Moser, includes some sound advice for sexually diverse people who are planning to see their doctor or enter hospital. The book has a chapter for health professionals too, and an enlightening glossary of terms at the end. Do read it!

Sexually diverse people may also fail to tell other healthcare professionals about their identity – see Eliason and Schope (2001).[t] Not telling hospital staff about their orientation, and who should be admitted to visit and/or have access to information about their medical condition, can lead to the individual worrying, and staff getting things wrong. Thus, asking open questions about, for example, who can be classified as family or who can visit will be useful for those with an unconventional family structure, such as some BDSMers and people who are polyamorous. The Royal College of Nursing and Unison point out that the term 'next of kin' has no legal meaning in healthcare, and that professionals should ask about, and comply with, the patient's wishes. This needs to be made crystal clear to patients when they arrive.

There are a few other texts to support you. The academic book *Intersectionality, Sexuality and Psychological Therapies – Working with Lesbian, Gay and Bisexual Diversity*[6] has a chapter on disability. The New South Wales Department of Education and Communities has a website on teaching sexual health[7] which, in its Sexual Diversity section, suggests some learning opportunities for understanding more about LGBTQIA, fostering tolerance and offering advice on what can be done in schools. *Eyes of Desire 2: A Deaf GLBT Reader* is a unique volume providing insightful, moving testimonies.[8]

The LGBT Health Summit[9] is held annually, and information can be found on its website. It covers mental health but as yet there is no sign it of including sex and disability. Stonewall has produced a guide on setting up LGBT staff networks.[10]

Outward appearances

Some people with sexual diversities like to express their difference in the way they look and dress to let people know they are not 'straight' and perhaps project some pride in the way they are. The ear-ring worn by gay men is a well-known example. Others prefer to keep their proclivities private, perhaps out of need for acceptance in their workplace and/or for a personal sense of privacy.

I find it very exciting when I watch disabled people experimenting with sexual self-expression and demonstrating a step towards self-empowerment by expressing their difference with body jewellery such as piercings, tattoos, brightly coloured hair and alternative clothing. I have been told that having a tattoo and piercing can be a way of reclaiming your body from your impairments.

On the subject of piercings, admissions nurses many need to know about them, so they can tell the patient which ones may need to be removed, or find ways to safely provide care with them inserted.

Lesbian women

One would have imagined that the lesbian disabled woman would find herself welcomed in the lesbian community, but this is not necessarily so. One young lady complained, 'I don't fit into the lesbian groups because I am autistic, and I don't fit into the autism groups because I am lesbian.'

There are many different kinds of lesbians, sometimes categorized as feminine (known as femme, or 'lipstick' lesbians) and 'butch'. Being a butch lesbian is not necessarily quite the same as being masculine or being a domme, but can involve being proactive when it comes to sex, and sometimes adopting/assuming roles and responsibilities more conventionally associated with being male. In 2012, Janet Jones made a short film, *Butch Losses*,[11] about her life as a butch lesbian with MS. She made the film as part of her presentation at a Lesbian Lives conference, where she wanted to raise issues and awareness on things such as social inclusion for disabled people, and to open up dialogue on the subject. The film reaches a pinnacle where she tells of how difficult it is to guide a new lover (whilst not ruining the momentum of the seduction) on how her body now works, in enough detail to enable them to understand. She declares, 'No one taught me this.' I can see her point: in all of the published guides to experiencing and enjoying sex when you have MS, nowhere could she have found any guidance on how to retain her butch lesbian style with a new partner. *Butch Losses* has been used by a social work lecturer to help students realize their own personal emotions, feelings and prejudices around disability, sexuality and lesbianism, so that they can use this information about themselves when working with clients, and work with more awareness and care.

Lesbians may make love to each other in a variety of ways, some using sex toys, some not. A couple who joined Outsiders told me they are very adventurous in their play, using role play, dressing up, toys, water sports and playing adult babies.

Assumptions may be made by health professionals that a lesbian woman would not be interested in her fertility when, in fact, she and her partner may have discussed her giving birth to a child.

Gay men

There are also many different kinds of gay men. For example, 'straight-acting' gay men, older, hairy bears, the athletic jocks, muscular, waxed, preened, most usually with tribal tattoos – called 'circuit boys'; and performers who specialize in being a drag queen, perhaps on television, sometimes the most common link between the gay and straight worlds. Gay men seem to love a drag show.

Not all gay men have anal sex and they may experience many different kinds of intimacy. Openly gay activist and author Peter Tatchell, who wrote the excellent book called *Safer Sexy – The Guide to Gay Sex Safely*,[12] later went public with his sadness that there are still so many wonderful things which gay men could enjoy before HIV and AIDS came along but which have since been denied them for over twenty years. Some are taking risks such as 'barebacking', which means having sex without using a condom. HIV infections are on the rise throughout the gay (also lesbian, bi and heterosexual) communities. Some of this is out of ignorance, some because they don't care, and frequently it is because people see the advances in treatment turning HIV into a so-called 'manageable condition' instead of a 'terminal' one!

Most gay men are no more accepting of disability than other people, and those who go to gay bars and clubs to pull, get off their heads, dance, and enjoy anonymous sex can be harshly lookist, rejecting visibly impaired men. Clubbers often clone, following fashions and fitting a certain ideal, usually homing in on the fit, well-endowed, good dancers. These men may have sex without caring about the other person. One disabled gay man spoke of the asset of not having an anal sphincter, for ease of entry!

Some gay men meet each other online and there are special sites for finding relationships and others for quick one-offs, kinky sex, and every kind of speciality. They tend to seek other men who totally fit their bill when it comes to sex, and might not worry if the perfect fit is a man with a disability, so disabled men may be accepted this way. That is why it is important for gay disabled men to work out precisely what it is that they are looking for sexually, and not let lack of partners prevent them finding out. You could support them in this very personal research. Dating sites are listed and described at the end of this chapter.

Many of our disabled and socially isolated Outsiders members use a library computer rather than sit at home on their own, because the library has a social network of computer users. But many libraries consider gay social networking sites indecent, so block them!

Queer Crips,[13] which is mentioned in Chapter 5, is a book about gay disabled men, full of stories expressing anger, frustration and triumph. It ends with a deeply moving chapter by the book's co-editor and founder of the Bent[14] website, Bob Guter. The most striking message in his chapter is how he found it impossible to accept his impairments and so could not accept other people with impairments either. Then he realized he should reach out to the others, and started a movement of mutual acceptance and peer support on his website, Bent, a step which in fact shaped him to become a happy and fulfilled human being.

Bisexual people

One disabled girl in Outsiders described herself as someone who falls in love with the person, not their gender, and I thought this was a very beautiful way of describing her bisexuality. But this is not always the whole story, as some disabled people need different kinds of sexual relationships to fulfil their sexual needs, and gender may be irrelevant.

Bisexuals often report that they feel marginalized, and disabled bisexuals feel they are shunned by disabled people for being bisexual, shunned by lesbians and gays for being bisexual, and shunned by all three lifestyle groups (bisexual, lesbian and gay) for being disabled! So, it is very important that disabled clients who identify as bisexual have your support, and know how to offer each other peer support, to swap experiences, and thereby gain confidence. Outsiders provides a place for this to happen.

Bicon[15] has become a British institution, and always aims to be welcoming to disabled people. It is a weekend of workshops and social events and opportunities. Conventions are held in different cities, and run by different people, every year. Bicon guidelines encourage participants to be disability friendly, and workshops are held on many topics, revolving around sex, disability and neuro-diversity. The convention attracts hundreds of people and, together with the Bifests, helps create a vibrant community.

A disabled Outsiders member who has attended a number of Bicons and Bifests commented that, because the events are organized by different people with different levels of awareness, approaches to accessibility and attitudes to the inclusion of disabled people can vary from event to event. He went on to say that attitudes can sometimes be more important than physical accessibility – the right attitude will generally lead to appropriate adjustments if physical access isn't perfect, to better inclusion, and to more equal opportunities to participate. The attitude of the organizers often creates a model for the participants of an event. Equal respect is what a disabled person needs.

Queer people

There is no one definition of what it means to be 'queer'. Amanda Gay-love, who runs disability-friendly workshops under the title of Queer Hearted,[16] says 'queer' is a process, not an identity, and this may explain why the numerous academic books on queer theory have failed to define it. A large part of Amanda's workshops is about people stepping into their individual and unique sexuality, and allowing it to be a source of power. Her 'Queer Conscious' orgasms, which she teaches, are based on Barbara Carrellas's breath orgasms mentioned in Chapter 2. Disabled people at Amanda's workshops find a space to be sexual and queer, and to access new ways of feeling sexual pleasure.

The term 'queer' suggests gender-bending in some form, veering away from male–female polarity. This does not mean that male–female couplings cannot happen with queers, because queer is ultimately inclusive, but it is about stretching the boundaries, exploring anything that is not hetero-normative. There can be an intellectual quality to it which, in the USA, has resulted in some progressive porn being made, such as Indie Porn Revolution.[17]

Being liberal, experimental and accepting of difference, queer people may be extra accepting of disabled people as their friends, and maybe also accepting of them as partners.

Transgendered people

'Transgendered' is an umbrella term describing anyone whose gender identity or expression is not the same as their assigned sex. This includes transsexual people and can include non-gendered, bi-gendered, multi-gendered and two-spirit people, drag kings, drag queens, some cross-dressers, and those rejecting the gender binary choice and reinventing gender.

Transsexual people

Many transsexual people may have felt they needed to make the decision to change their body to bring it in line with their gender, for their own sanity, feeling like a 'woman trapped in a man's body', or vice versa. It is important that the changes they make are for these reasons, not because they are simply trying to conform to conventional images of gender and labels, which will only make them more miserable.

While many transsexual people experience no problems during and after transition, some find that their friends, family and even partners find it difficult to accept the change and may reject them, leaving them at risk of becoming socially isolated. If this happens, it impacts on their physical, mental and emotional health, as well as their sex and relationship lives. There are networks and organizations of and for transsexual people, offering both support and social opportunities – especially in larger cities.

Some transsexuals have surgery to change their body to be as like their chosen gender as possible, but others leave their genitals as they are, relying on hormones to change their public appearance. Testosterone can make the clitoral head grow larger, though not as big as a penis. Many manage to live happy lives, with great sex, and I encourage you to read the very engaging little book describing such lives called *There Is No Word For It* by Laura Bridgeman and Serge Nicholson.[18] The book explains how they find and enjoy sexual pleasure. It is important for you to know that the trans person may identify as gay, bisexual or straight, and may be disabled, just like any other person.

If you work in a hospital and a patient comes in whose gender seems ambiguous, ask them whether, and if so how, they identify with regard to gender. Ask also what pronouns they prefer, and make sure that this is understood by all colleagues who are going to be coming into contact with them, while at the same time respecting and ensuring their privacy, and that everyone observes the confidentiality of these details. You and your colleagues should make sure you are aware of the Gender Recognition Act, and your responsibilities within it. You need to work out the best way of meeting the person's care needs appropriately and sensitively in discussion with them. It may be that a single room would be a sensible suggestion, if they would prefer it.

Transvestites/cross-dressers

Some people (mostly men, such as the British artist Grayson Perry) feel the need to dress in the clothing of the opposite gender, now and then, maybe in private or in public. Cross-dressing can be a sexual urge leading to masturbation or other sexual activity or it may simply help them relax and feel less tense. With some men usually liking silk, just wearing soft silky underwear can be sufficient.

Some women like to have a partner who shares her enthusiasm for clothes and make-up, and finding one such woman is a dream of many heterosexual trannies. Those not so lucky may practise their cross-dressing in secret. They may visit specialist transvestite services to help them get dressed up, or they go to escorts or a dungeon which provide a tranny wardrobe. Some go to tranny nightclubs to let their hair down. Those who mix in public cross-dressed might be wise to get professional advice on looking convincing if they want to avoid being stared at (and to minimize the risk of possible violence against them).

If a transvestite is in your residential home or school, they may need to discuss their needs; and the first thing for you to do is to suggest a specialist support group such as the Beaumont Society,[19] Transliving International[20] or Transformation.[21] You could ask them if they wish to mix with the other residents dressed up, in which case you can ask them if they might like you to organize an awareness session. Transvestites would be wise to discuss their tastes with potential PAs who will need to support them with an acceptance and positivity.

Many trannies feel they are little understood and isolated, so they do need to be taken seriously by you and those around them. A lovely book on the subject is *Miss Vera's Finishing School for Boys Who Want to Be Girls*.[22]

Intersex people

When babies are born, there is great pressure to name them boy or girl, but some (one in 2000) are born with a reproductive or sexual anatomy that does not fit the typical definitions of female or male. This can include atypical genitalia, chromosomes or internal sex organs. These people are intersex. They may, at puberty, not develop as expected; they may not feel they are either gender; they may or may not want to be ambiguous; and they may or may not be certain that they fit their assigned gender. Children have been operated upon to 'normalize' their genitals or sexual anatomy but in 2013 the UN Special Rapporteur on Torture[23] condemned non-consensual surgery on children to 'fix their sex', saying it could cause 'permanent, irreversible infertility and severe mental suffering'. Clinicians say they have moved to a more 'multidisciplinary' approach.

I would like to mention here the condition called Klinefelter's syndrome. It occurs in roughly 1 in 1000 males, many of whom do not have symptoms and only get diagnosed when they seek help for infertility. Those who do not try to have children may never be diagnosed, although today some mothers have the diagnosis when the foetus is in the womb. The men may have learning and behavioural problems, lack physical strength, lack awareness of gender, perhaps have small testicles, and find it troublesome making friends. These things may affect their love lives. Hormone replacement therapy (HRT) helps increase sexual pleasure in their mind and body. Still, the man may feel both female and male.

More support for intersex people can be found from Intersex UK,[24] the Androgen Insensitivity Syndrome Support Group,[25] DSD Families[26] and Klinefelter Syndrome Information and Support.[27]

Asexual people

Asexual people do not feel sexual attraction or have a sexual orientation. However, they may have sexual activity even if they have no desire to do so. The Asexual Visibility and Education Network (AVEN)[28] is one of the communities supporting them. If your client is asexual they may not need your support with sexuality, but may need you to support them with pressure from parents and others to conform, or other difficulties.

Kinksters

Those with fetishes and into BDSM (bondage domination, sadism and masochism) often call themselves 'kinksters'. Some are even beginning to use the term 'pervert', much as some gay people chose the term 'queer' to demonstrate pride in their difference and to reclaim the word from previously negative connotations. Most kinksters are still wondering when it will ever become safe to 'come out'.

This is especially true for those who are disabled. I'll never forget a boyfriend coming back from the pub and telling me a photo was being circulated and making everybody laugh. When the photo reached him, he saw it was a picture of me dancing at a fetish club with a man in a wheelchair.

It is decades since Lou Reed and The Velvet Underground recorded their *Venus in Furs* album in 1966. So it's taking a mighty long time for kinky sex to become universally accepted. However, the *New York Times* of 27 February 2013 ran an article on the subject which said that students feel they can tell their peers about their BDSM activities.[29]

Outsiders attracts kinky people together with all our other members. A group of dommes in London some time ago put on regular special nights for them, asking for requests in advance.

With a little encouragement, disabled people can be coaxed out of their shells and realize their inclinations. This makes a huge difference to them because so often they have had their sexuality repressed through being over-protected, and shielded from the world of sex with sometimes few social opportunities.

Mostly, disabled people find great happiness in their kinky lives. This is partly because they are freed from the obligations of straight sex by entering a very different world which understands stigma only too well. Getting into BDSM/fetish scenes with a partner can feel empowering for a disabled person: it is beyond the world of the establishment, care staff, social services and those who daily cramp their style. When they share it with a partner, it's a dream world, a goody bag of mutual secrets.

Disabled people may be more likely to have fetishes or to be into BDSM than other people, for several reasons. Many kinksters say they can think of no reason how their taste originated, but some recall what sparked it off. The parts of the brain where you feel pleasure and pain are close to each other[30] and sometimes, it seems, they get intermingled and the person finds pain a sexual turn-on. Some people recall a tiny experience in childhood, something which occurred at the same time as a sexual feeling, which they believe initiated their fetish. For example, being turned on when a woman walks behind a piece of furniture may trigger an amputee fetish. Disabled people, who may have been feeling horny in hospital, may develop a fetish for people in nurses' uniforms, or enjoy sexual pleasure from experiencing pain. This is not to say that all disabled people are fetishistic, and there is no research to prove how many are.

Those with Atypical Pervasive Developmental Disorder (associated with autism) may have curious ways of becoming sexually excited; for example handling parts of other people's bodies or clothing or hearing a specific noise. You need to confirm to them that this is not generally socially acceptable behaviour, without trying to isolate them any more. I would suggest that, provided the person asks permission to interact in the way that turns them on, they may be accepted. They might be able to find suitable partners who also have their condition, and understand, by looking online.

Fetishists

The word 'fetish' was originally used for a thing, body part or special activity which was essential for the fetishist to have an orgasm. These days, the word has become diluted to mean a thing, body part or special activity which turns them on. There are literally thousands of fetishes, and types of fetishists from smoothies who like shaved or otherwise hairless bodies, to those who fancy amputees or those who get off on Wellington boots. If you are disabled and have an easily accessed fetish, such as a fetish for dolls, this may be easier than wishing to be encased in rubber, but I know of a severely disabled young man whose PAs would support him struggling into and out of such outfits.

Fetishists tell me that the most unacceptable fetishes are those which are common occurrences, such as women wearing spectacles, because the last thing they want to do is freak out all the spectacle-wearing ladies around them with feeling that they are all objects of desire. Some women have fetishes too. For example, the devotees, mentioned in Chapter 2. Many women have a fetish about shoes, enjoying their vast collections and perhaps wearing stilettos during sex.

Fetish clubs have opened up in most towns and cities in the West, and are also popular in Israel, Australia and New Zealand. They tend not to cater to many fetishes or tastes, but provide dungeon monitors and equipment for BDSM. Guests arrive dressed up, most commonly in leather and rubber. Fetish clubs provide women with the opportunity to strut around – or wheel themselves around – in high boots and corsets, looking powerfully sexy while at the same time intimidating potential male gropers. This can feel sexually empowering for the women.

Fetish clubs are more welcoming to disabled guests than most night clubs, and I feel sure this is because both disabled people and fetishists feel stigmatized. Mind you, this welcome may not apply to the type of fetish club which has evolved to be more about displaying expensive rubber outfits than having fun.

Some disabled people advise being open about their fetish or sexual proclivity early on in a relationship, saying it is always best to establish all the sexual compatibility points right from the start, before discovering they have other things in common. If the couple fall head over heels in love before sharing the sexual information, spilling the beans might feel too nerve-wracking, and more so if they have a disability.

Fetishists do conduct relationships without telling their partner about their fetishes and inclinations, and sometimes this works out. They may need the occasional visit to a fetish club, lover or professional to top-up their fantasies. Their partner may find evidence of their secret passions online or in a pile of specialist magazines under the bed. It is sensible to understand and accept that people often fantasize when having sex, but partners often feel jealous and hurt. I advise disabled people to encourage their partners to feel totally confident in themselves before opening up.

I received a call one day about an amputee wanting to have a horse lower leg prosthesis made so he could better indulge in his fetish for being a pony and pulling riders in a cart behind him. The caller wondered if it would be OK to ask at the specialist centre, Queen Mary's Hospital, Roehampton. The wonderful thing about the medical profession is that, in fact, they often relish getting such requests – it brightens up their lives.

Power play and BDSM – domination, submission and switches

People who are into sexual domination take pleasure in exerting power in sex-play, and submissives in submitting to it. The two of them do this through role-playing, bondage and/or the infliction of pain. The submissive is actually in charge, as the dom needs to press their sexual buttons for it to work.

Power-play can be more about the participants being ideally suited in their sex play than it is about each individual's gender or their physical or sensory abilities. Some people engage in BDSM as 'switches', enjoying both dominance and submission.

Bondage is a practice whereby a person is constrained by being tied up. It may be with rope, using intricate knots and strapping, and this sometimes includes suspension, when the bound body is raised up from the ground, hanging by a suspension rope. Rope bondage is a highly skilled art, and brings the bound person into an ecstasy, perhaps reminiscent of being held in their mother's arms as a baby. Bondage can also be done with chains, tape, cuffs, chastity belts, among others. Another kind of constraint uses a body bag, perhaps made of rubber. I have known disabled people to enjoy being both the bondage artist and the bound.

Psychologists have begun to recognize the psychological value of such behaviour[31] and it is important to understand that a huge number of people like this kind of thing. The best-selling fantasy series *Fifty Shades of Grey*, by female writer E.L. James, proved that curiosity about the world of BDSM is now mainstream in society. In fact, in real life it is not dangerous, sick or irresponsible. Participants play by a code of being 'safe, sane and consensual'. They take responsibility seriously, and apply thought and consideration to their actions during sexual activity. This is something often sadly lacking in the activities of some straight people, who may mindlessly engage in straightforward sex without the same care and consideration. BDSMers often refer to those outside the scene as 'vanilla'.

Having claimed that disabled people can be more accepted in this scene, I have to say that one of our wheelchair-using Outsiders members was happy to enjoy his turn on the whipping bench in the local fetish club, where I encouraged him to go. However, he told me just before he died that he was never introduced around to other guests like the rest of the guests were. He never found his ideal partner, and died in 2013, never having had a girlfriend, at the age of 52.

I had an idea for people who cannot move their limbs, including quadriplegics who may be unable to reach up to touch their own head. My idea was that they can use one bodily function they do have: their voice. They could use their voice to attract, seduce and conduct a sexual relationship, as a dominatrice or dom. People with no feeling for it probably cannot learn to do this, but it is worth suggesting, just in case they do. Books such as *Screw the Roses, Send Me the Thorns*[32] and *Daddy's Girl*[33] can offer good learning material. A submissive may be found on Fetlife.[34] The procedure is usually that the dominatrice or dom interviews the sub to ensure the two of them are suited, and then they discuss and experiment playing together, before taking each other on as sexual partners.

A disabled person can use their voice to bring them opportunities so they can, at last in their lives, enjoy being responsible for, and care for, another person, instead of always being the one who is cared for by somebody else. Taking control over another can feel sweet, and bring much emotional pleasure to both parties, and the disabled person does not need to use strength of body, just their voice.

If a single disabled person discovers the delights of power play and wants to proceed with it, they may have to negotiate with their PAs, who might not approve. PAs may not wish to leave their client alone with a stranger who is into BDSM, because they might perceive them to be too scary for their 'vulnerable client', whereas another kind of lover might have been fine. A PA with such views would need educating. Kinky people should not have to feel they have to hide things from PAs and staff, or be fearful of, for example, having to explain the hooks in the ceiling.

I once experienced a brain-injured man who was sexually disinhibited, suddenly becoming obsessed with spanking my bottom (in a public place!). There seems to be no documentation of such occurrences and I have been unable to determine how common BDSM practices are with either brain-injured or learning disabled people. I have only heard of one learning disabled person into BDSM.

A treasure of a book called *Playing with Disabilities*[35] describes how some BDSMers with physical and sensory impairments have incorporated their impairments into their BDSM play. For example, a sub with a hearing impairment had her hearing aid thrown in the bin before being manhandled, fingered and pushed down onto the floor. She had a safe word which would indicate the dom must stop, in case she needed to use it. She tells of how good it is to know the erotic nature of her deafness and use it like a sex toy.

Another contributor to the book points out that it is sometimes useful to look upon your impairment, especially if it includes something limiting like pain or fatigue, as being another dominant in your life, if you are sub. The pain is part of your sexual dynamic.

Co-editor of that book, Angela Stassinopoulos, recognized that this phenomenon is a great leap and she felt 'the shock of the new' when she personally played with some of the disabled individuals. She says that she needed to spend a little more time talking before playing (or 'scening' as she calls it). She described what I had already heard, that sometimes disabled people find lovers are afraid to touch them, and Angela found that an extreme sensation can feel doubly wonderful. She writes about how very much touch can convey emotion and acceptance, and found such experiences 'poetic'.

Bob Flanagan was an American performance artist with cystic fibrosis who used BDSM to ease the problems of dealing with his condition and to help him cope with the pain. Being a masochist gave him a way to enjoy his sexuality and orgasm, with the pain and pleasure becoming inextricably linked. Bob felt the way he had control over his body was by handing control over to his dom, his lover, and this became part of their daily routine. Bob died at the age of 43, making him one of the oldest people with cystic fibrosis. All these things bring BDSM onto a new dimension of significance.

One gay man said to me:

> Having a partner with limited mobility when we were both interested in bondage and BDSM play was pretty cool. I would do things like tie a feather duster to the wheelchair and he would wheel along beside me with the feather tickling my body. It really can be a wonderful thing to have differing abilities and to use those abilities in the bedroom. I am sure some people, including other disabled people, would take issue with this statement, but I really do think it can open up new experiences for the more adventurous of us! It can also be a way of enhancing the closeness you feel for one another. Knowing that one of you is maybe reliant upon the other more physically can give an added dimension of trust and intimacy, that feels really special.

Exhibitionism and voyeurism

Exhibitionism and voyeurism can be relevant to disabled people, as a person with a physical impairment may find both of them easy to enjoy, and thus to use to spice up their love lives. The exceptions may be perhaps blind and deafblind people, although they may be able to enjoy the experiences verbally. Exhibitionism can bring empowerment. Displaying your body to show off your best bits, be they breasts or whatever, and being admired, can be a real sexual turn-on and a sexual high for most people. Watching a partner masturbate, or perform a little show from the other side of the room, can provide fuel for lust. Using mirrors, remote photography, webcam and filming can add more kinky dimensions. As the book *Exhibitionism for the Shy*[36] tells us, people can develop an inner character that can flaunt and tease. Carol Queen, the authoress, suggests dressing up using whatever the person finds exciting: shoes, sexy bras, uniforms and stuffed jockstraps. Such activities can encourage discussion and mutual understanding. This book can be recommended to disabled people, explaining that only some of it will be relevant to them but they may find that it opens them up to a lifetime of sexual communication and pleasure.

Swinging and dogging

Couples have been swapping partners and enjoying orgies for centuries, although they have not normally talked about it in polite society. Today, most swinging couples secretly answer adverts on the swing websites, then spend an evening together in one of their homes, all on the same bed and playing with each other's partners. These swingers don't tend to be particularly open to swinging with disabled people, although I have heard of disabled swingers in 'the lifestyle', as they call it. Sometimes, particular people get together to share sexual circumstances, for example blind couples may share sexual conversations and perhaps activity, because sex for blind people is not to do with visual stimulation, which makes it different.

Swing clubs and sex parties may only allow admission to certain ages and types of people, usually aiming to attract younger, good-looking people. I am always amused when the organizers reach the upper age limit they've been putting on guests and, guess what? The age limit rises!

Guests at the Outsiders fundraising ball really appreciate being at an erotic party where there are disabled people joining in. A high point for me was seeing three couples on a bed, with three wheelchairs parked beside it. One non-disabled guest told me that seeing disabled people enjoying themselves inspired him to really go for it!

Dogging suits couples who don't want to socialize before enjoying anonymous sex with others, and/or being watched by voyeurs who enjoy a free show. Physicality and looks are not important, so all disabled people would be welcomed. Much bizarre fun, using periscopes and torches, may take place in car parks, woods and public spaces; and the scene can have a kind of anarchic, crazy feel to it. My one excursion to observe dogging was not so exciting. It involved a long wait in a car with my two guides, Big Bernie and Ponders End Mike. Suddenly, I found myself watching a man having sex with his female partner in a car which had parked beside us. I slowly realized I was not too keen on watching, but my guides said the husband would lose his erection if I looked away! I then worried that his female partner might have to get up and go out in the car every time they wanted sex, so he could get a hard-on! I just hope she was an exhibitionist too.

So, for disabled couples or voyeurs who use cars and want a free sex show, or otherwise share themselves and their partners, dogging is an option. The X-Locator Dogging App is an anonymous geo-locator to find other doggers out in an area, to avoid long night-time waits, getting chilly.

Gay men may go 'cruising', having anonymous sex in places such as parks, gay sauna complexes, and the back rooms of sex clubs. 'Hook-up' is the term used for meeting a stranger online for a quick sexual encounter in a place of their choice, the online equivalent of cruising. Such anonymous activities include the risk that the other partner turns out to not be as described online, perhaps of a different age. They also run the usual risk associated with meeting a new person. It's always advisable to arrange to meet firstly in a safe public location such as a café, before moving on to somewhere more private for some fun. It's also always a good idea for any person, gay or not, to tell a close friend (or you, if you are the person supporting them at the time) of their location and what time they will be expected back, before embarking on any anonymous meeting. Your client may need to be comfortable enough with you to inform you that they are going off for random sex; do ensure they are carrying condoms.

Polyamory

Polyamory describes having a sexual relationship with more than one partner. There may be a primary partner with other secondary partners, or different partners for different things. Sometimes, people live with more than one partner, mostly one man with several women, but some women do live with more than one man (or woman) as partners.

An advantage of being polyamorous, if one or both of a couple is impaired, is that one partner may be able to fulfil needs which the other partner cannot. For example, a person may feel they need visual feedback from their body, sexy clothing, or activities which their visually impaired partner is not be able to provide. Rough sex may not be possible for a person whose body is in pain, and so their partner may want to take another in order to enjoy this pleasure.

Some polyamorists may not feel comfortable just taking lovers, needing love to be present to fully enjoy sex.

The polyamory community has a long history and is well established in the USA and the UK. They tend to be a tolerant group, accepting of disability. They meet together at gatherings and parties.

Seeking support with sexual problems and worries

Pink Therapy is a group of qualified sex and relationship therapists who specialize in people with sexual diversities. They can be found online[1] and most of them enjoy sexual diversity themselves and will be very accepting.

The Kink Aware Professionals Network[37] is a huge American resource which has no information on British professionals, but Pink Therapy *is* listed on the Kink Friendly Therapy website.[38]

BDSM and fetish equipment

This specialist gear is best bought from fetish fairs, and specialist shops and websites, rather than high street sex shops. Kinksters Paradise[39] are experienced at kitting out dungeons, clubs and people's homes with disability friendly, accessible furniture.

Finding friends and partners

Apart from Outsiders, there don't seem to be any socio-sexual groups for disabled people with all the various sexual diversities. However, the learning pack produced by the Older Lesbian, Gay Bisexual and Transgendered People's Network and Salford University, *Moving Forward*,[40] does deal with problems and solutions for social exclusion.

Gemma[41] is a self-help national group of lesbians and bisexual women, disabled and non-disabled, of all ages. Their quarterly newsletter is available in large print, tape, braille, and via email. There is an email group for members, and a taping circle, Tape Connection. The aim of the group is to lessen isolation for disabled lesbians.

The Gaydargirls[42] website is where lesbians and bisexual women can find partners. Lesbian and female bisexual couples can also meet 'like-minded' women, but disabled lesbians in search of fun sometimes receive bizarre responses from right-on political lesbians, telling them that they shouldn't be doing this! More open-minded lesbian and bisexual women can be found on Adult Friendfinder.[43]

Grindr was the first 'geolocation based' gay dating/hook-up app and now there seem to be numerous rival apps. They can be great for those wanting a quickie or hook-up. It seems a shame that this technology cannot be used to link isolated people with similar diversities to be in touch with each other locally, especially as they may feel unsafe going out in their area, and in need of comradeship.

Gaydar[44] is the biggest gay dating site in the UK, catering to both men and women, and one of its many features is the chat rooms, including one for disabled guys, one for blind guys, rooms for different age ranges, plus many fetishes and other interest groups. There is also an HIV-positive cruising room.

Many of the major dating sites offer same-sex opportunities, as do the Facebook-based dating apps such as Zoosk.

Recon.com is one of the largest fetish gay dating/hook-up sites on the web. It is certainly hugely popular in the UK and caters to myriad fetishes such as rubber, leather, skinheads, punks, bears, muscle guys, masters and slaves, and more.

Clubcollared.com is a spin-off dating site and a new social network site belonging to Collared, the gay fetish/BDSM club in London. It caters to younger gays, but older guys are welcome too. The website has a community feel to it, with forums and a large amount of cross-over with their club events. I am reliably informed that the club attracts a friendly crowd without the oppressive gay scene attitude.

Regard is the national organization of disabled lesbians, gay men, bisexuals and transgendered people. It is more of a disability rights campaigning group than a social club.

GLAMS[45] is a support group for LGBT people with MS which also has social events.

There are special dating websites for people wanting to meet transgendered people, but these may also be catering to men seeking 'chicks with dicks' for money.

'Munches' is the name given to local gatherings of hetero fetish and BDSM enthusiasts. Munches are purely for socializing and planning future events. The enthusiasts do not dress up in fetish clothing and usually meet in pubs, welcome newcomers, and would select an accessible venue, if asked. Your client could find the local munch online. Most fetish markets can also be good places for hanging out and socializing.

The website Fetlife[34] is the biggest hetero social networking website for those interested in BDSM and fetishes, as well as vanilla sex. It features individuals, clubs and parties, and has several disability groups.

Gearfetish[46] is an international fetish site, also welcoming to LGB and LGB-friendly straight people, with a huge range of fetishes catered for.

A polyamorous private dating Facebook page is called UK Poly Dating Classifieds.

I trust I have helped you better understand the vast range of pleasures your LGBTQIA, kinky and otherwise sexually diverse service users may well enjoy, and gone some way to encouraging you to be totally accepting and positive.

Resources

1. Pink Therapy: www.pinktherapy.com.
2. Royal College of Nursing (2003) *The Nursing Care of Lesbian and Gay Male Patients or Clients – Guidance for Nursing Staff*. London, UK: RCN.
3. Abbott, D., Howarth, J. and Gyde, K. (2005) *Secret Loves, Hidden Lives? A Summary of what People with Learning Difficulties said about being Gay, Lesbian or Bisexual*. Bristol: Norah Fry Research Centre, University of Bristol. Available at www.bristol.ac.uk/norahfry/research/completed-projects/secretloveseasyread.pdf, accessed on 8 July 2014.
4. Moser, C. (1999) *Health Care without Shame – A Handbook for the Sexually Diverse and their Caregivers*. San Francisco, CA: Greenery Press.
5. Eliason, M.J. and Schope, R. (2001) 'Does "Don't ask, don't tell" apply to health care? Lesbian, gay and bisexual people's disclosure to health care providers.' *Journal of the Gay and Lesbian Medical Association 5*, 4, 125–134.
6. das Nair, R. and Butler, C. (eds) (2012) *Intersectionality, Sexuality and Psychological Therapies – Working with Lesbian, Gay and Bisexual Diversity*. Oxford, UK: Wiley/BPS-Blackwell.
7. NSW Department of Education and Communities website for Teaching Sexual Health – Sexual Diversity: www.curriculumsupport.education.nsw.gov.au/sexual_health/inclusive/diversity.htm.
8. Luczac, R. (2007) *Eyes of Desire 2: A Deaf GLBT Reader*. Minneapolis, MN: Handtype Press, LLC.
9. LGBT Health Summit: www.lgbthealth.co.uk.
10. Stonewall Staff Networks: www.stonewall.org.uk/documents/network_groups_final_pdf.pdf.
11. Jones, J. (2012) *Butch Losses*. available at www.youtube.com/watch?v=8A67ZS_Sgwg, accessed on 8 July 2014.

12. Tatchell, P. (1994) *Safer Sexy: The Guide to Gay Sex Safely*. London, UK: Freedom Editions (Cassell).
13. Guter, R. and Killacky, J.R. (eds) (2003) *Queer Crips: Disabled Gay Men and their Stories*. London, UK: Routledge.
14. Bent – A Journal of Crip Gay Voices: www.bentvoices.org.
15. Bicon: www.bicon.org.uk.
16. Queer Hearted: www.queerhearted.com.
17. Indie Porn Revolution: www.indiepornrevolution.com/indie-porn.
18. Bridgeman, L. and Nicholson, S. (2012) *There is No Word for It*. London, UK: Hot Pencil Press.
19. Beaumont Society: www.beaumontsociety.org.uk, 01582 412220.
20. Transliving International: www.transliving.co.uk, 01268 583761.
21. Transformation (shops and dressing services): www.transformation.co.uk.
22. Vera, V. (1997) *Miss Vera's Finishing School for Boys Who Want to Be Girls*. New York, NY: Doubleday.
23. OHCHR (2013) *Report of the Special Rapporteur on Torture and Other Cruel, Inhuman or Degrading Treatment or Punishment*. Available at www.ohchr.org/Documents/HRBodies/HRCouncil/RegularSession/Session22/A.HRC.22.53_English.pdf, accessed on 8 July 2014.
24. Intersex UK – promoting the understanding of intersex people: intersexuk.org.
25. The Androgen Insensitivity Syndrome Support Group: www.aissg.org.
26. DSD Families – supporting families experiencing intersex: www.dsdfamilies.org.
27. Klinefelter Syndrome Information and Support: www.klinefeltersyndrome.org.
28. The Asexual Visibility and Education Network: www.asexuality.org.
29. Haber, M. (2013, 27 February) 'A Hush-Hush Topic No More.' Article in the *New York Times*.
30. Apostilodes, M. (1999) *The Pleasure of Pain*. Available at www.psychologytoday.com/articles/199909/the-pleasure-pain, accessed on 8 July 2014.
31. Richters, J., de Visser, R.O., Rissel, C.E., Grulich, A.E. and Smith, A.M. (2008) 'Demographic and psychosocial features of participants in bondage and discipline, "sadomasochism" or dominance and submission (BDSM): data from a national survey.' *Journal of Sexual Medicine 5*, 7, 1660–1668.
32. Miller, P. and Devon, M. (1988) *Screw the Roses, Send Me the Thorns – The Romance and Sexual Sorcery of Sadomasochism*. Fairfield, CT: Mystic Rose Books.
33. Black, S. (2007) *Daddy's Girl*. London, UK: Virgin Books
34. Fetlife: www.fetlife.com.
35. Stassinopoulos, A. and Rubel, R. (eds) (2008) *Playing with Disabilities*. Power Exchange Books. Available at http://rubelpresents.com/power-exchange-books/power-exchange-books-resource-series, accessed on 18 July 2014.
36. Queen, C. (2009) *Exhibitionism for the Shy*. San Francisco, CA: Down There Press.
37. The Kink Aware Professionals Network: ncsfreedom.org/key-programs/kink-aware-professionals/kap-program-page.html.
38. Kink Friendly Therapy: www.kinkfriendlytherapy.com/resources.
39. Kinksters Paradise: www.kinkstersparadise.co.uk.

40. Salford University Learning Pack (2010) *Moving Forward*. Salford: Older Lesbian, Gay, Bisexual and Transgendered People's Network and University of Salford.
41. Gemma: BM Box 5700, London WC1N 3XX; gemmagroup@hotmail.com.
42. Gaydar girls: www.gaydargirls.com.
43. Adult Friendfinder: www.adultfriendfinder.com.
44. Gaydar: www.gaydar.net.
45. GLAMS: glams@googlemail.com.
46. Gearfetish: www.gearfetish.com.

SUMMARY

Finally, here is a reminder of some of my most important suggestions in this book:

1. Support your clients to enjoy the sexual lives they want to live (and not your version of their life).

2. Make no assumptions and, if you are working closely with a client, dispel any assumptions they may have about you which might be inhibiting communication and trust.

3. Remember: ask, listen, take seriously, discuss and offer support, however unadventurous, strange or shocking things a disabled person says may seem to you.

4. Practice discussing sex with clients to gain confidence.

5. Ensure that you and your colleagues understand the laws regarding sex and disability. Laws are kept updated on the Sexual Respect Tool Kit.[1]

6. Discuss the need for better sex and disability education, including sexual diversity, with parents and in schools, and campaign for improvements.

7. Campaign for your governing bodies to include sex and disability training, policies and guidelines.

8. Meet your local sex therapist, pink therapist and male and female sex workers.

9. Take loneliness seriously, and support your clients in socializing, making friends, finding partners, communicating well sexually and using sexual services.

10. Call the Sex and Disability Helpline[2] and make the most of SHADA[3] for support, so you can enjoy your work without worrying.

Resources

1. The Sexual Respect Tool Kit: www.SexualRespect.com.
2. The Sex and Disability Helpline: 07074 993 527, 11am to 7pm weekdays.
3. The Sexual Health and Disability Alliance, SHADA: www.shada.org.uk.

POSTSCRIPT

Just in case you are feeling that this book is full of Outsiders members'
moans about the shortcomings of their care, I would like to end
with this poem. It was written by one of our long-standing Outsiders
members who was able to strike a beautiful balance in expressing his
appreciation of the care that he received, without being too forward.
Jonathan has cerebral palsy and a stammer and was, at the time of
writing the poem, aged 75.

A Valentine – of Sorts

The way
You help me
Bathe and dress
Makes me
Feel good
About myself

You touch me
With such
Respect, gentleness,
And lack of fear
That I feel whole
And unashamed.
Thank you

Jonathan Griffiths

INDEX